D1265349

THE FORUM FILES

THE STORIES BEHIND THE RICHMOND FORUM

DICK CLARK
KEN BURNS
RUDY GIULIANI
Condoleezza Rice April 10 2010
PHOTO
ANDERSON COOPER
CAL RIPKEN JR.
DINNER
CANDICE BERGEN
OMNI
LAURA BUSH Jan. 15 2011
SPIELBERG, KUSHNER GOODWIN Jan. 5 2013
GEN. COLIN POWELL Feb. 11. 2006
DINNER
PRESIDENT GEORGE W. BUSH Feb 22, 2014
THOMAS FRIEDMAN
TUTU
General Tommy Franks
BILL CLINTON FEB 8, 2013
TONY BLAIR Nov. 1. 2008
TIM RUSSERT Feb. 19, 2005
HOST
DINNER
TOM WOLFE March 11.

To James —
Writer to Writer

THE FORUM FILES

THE STORIES BEHIND THE RICHMOND FORUM

RAY McALLISTER

PUBLISHED BY THE RICHMOND FORUM
Richmond, Virginia

Published in 2015 by The Richmond Forum.

ISBN: 978-0-692-52546-3

Dust jacket and title design: Kevin Flores
Page design: Bill Chapman and Kevin Flores

Additional credits appear on page 148, which constitutes a continuation of this copyright page.

The text of this book was composed in Proxima Nova Condensed.

Printed in Richmond, Virginia, U.S.A. by B&B Printing.

FIRST EDITION

The Richmond Forum
6968 Forest Hill Avenue
Richmond, Virginia 23225
www.richmondforum.org

In Memory of Ralph F. Krueger, Jr.

— and —

Dedicated to
The Patrons of The Richmond Forum
and
The Staff at The Richmond Forum.
They never throw anything away.

TABLE OF CONTENTS

FOREWORD

The Richmond Forum stage is hallowed ground.

For the last thirty years—or for forty-seven years, depending on how you count it (I'll let the author explain that)—the biggest names in the world have traveled to Richmond, Virginia . . . to speak. And to do so on a stage so large that it can easily swallow the person who doesn't bring his or her "A game."

Before each speaker, unseen to them in the lights of the theater, but sensed deeply, is the largest and most respected lecture series audience in America. This stage and this audience are why names like Clinton, Bush, Blair, Thatcher, Gorbachev, Kissinger, Reagan, Rice, Bernanke, Tutu, Netanyahu, Bhutto, Cronkite, Brokaw, Spielberg, Redford, Winfrey, Goodall, Buchwald, Asimov, and hundreds more, have made the trip to Richmond over the years.

This season, 4,500 subscribers and sponsors from the Richmond Region (as well as Williamsburg, the Northern Neck, Fredericksburg, Northern Virginia, and points west) will attend each of five Forum evenings. Most of these folks have been with us for many seasons and in that time have spent a few enriching hours in the same room with some of the most fascinating, accomplished, and connected individuals in the world. And, most rare in 21st Century America, there is no separation between a Forum attendee seated in the theater and a Forum speaker: No glass of a television screen, no ink on paper, no sound bite, no reporting bias, and most importantly, no pundit telling anybody in our audience what they should think about what they have just seen and heard.

We ask each of our speakers to come to the theater in the afternoon for a sound check before the evening's presentation. The sound engineers fit them with their headset microphones and we ask them to rattle off something of their choosing so audio levels can be set—some use the opportunity to walk through a portion of their intended remarks, others recite some poem learned long ago in school, and others carry on a conversation with me, sometimes lasting well after the point that the sound man is happy—we finally see him standing quietly to the side, waiting patiently to remove our mics.

Aside from the all-important technical preparations, I really want our speakers to see the theater. To step out onto that massive stage before the house is full and the lights are in their face. To see the giant backdrops—created especially for their presentation—that will frame their every word. To see where the very top row of the upper balcony is.

Nearly to the person, every speaker asks me the same incredulous question: "And all of these seats are going to be full tonight? That's amazing." In recent years, since the addition of our very successful Simulcast Room in the theater's ballroom, I've been able to say, "Plus, 800 subscribers in the ballroom, and 100 students in our Student Room." Heads shake in amazement.

The longstanding and hard-earned reputation of The Richmond Forum precedes it and makes it possible for us to fulfill the first part of our mission statement: "To bring the leaders from the world stage to our stage in Richmond." The second half of our mission talks about why we do this: "To expand horizons, stimulate conversation, and inspire our community."

Although those particular words were crafted in 2009 by our board of directors, the mission has been there for a long, long time, as you will learn in these pages.

This book started as something nice to do in honor of our thirtieth season. My pitch to author and Forum subscriber Ray McAllister was simple: We want to tell the story of The Richmond Forum (including the behind the scenes stories) and also show how The Forum fits into a long tradition of lecture circuit speaking in America.

Honestly, we didn't realize what we were taking on in such a short period of time. The book had to be ready for our opening program in November. "The thirtieth season runs through April, doesn't it?", Ray kept asking as the project grew. And grew.

What started out as something "nice to do" quickly turned into something "important to do." Ray has successfully uncovered the mostly-forgotten history of this organization and given us the gift of perspective that can only come from a long view, as well as a fuller understanding of who we are and how such an impressive public forum was born here in Richmond, and grew to be the largest in America. Ray's ability to transform a thousand data points gathered from old files, notes, clippings, correspondence, and interviews into a beautifully written narrative is without compare.

I often note an interesting physiological phenomenon at our programs: When a Forum speaker has transfixed our audience, nobody is coughing. Nobody. If the speaker hasn't captured the audience's attention, you can hear coughing coming from every corner of the theater. Perhaps, I should have suggested that I do one of those testimonial quotes for the back of this book's dust jacket: *"I didn't cough once while reading this! – Bill Chapman."*

On behalf of everybody in the Forum family, I thank Ray McAllister for his good work and dedication to this project.

Before turning you over to his book, however, a parting word from another.

In his 2008 book, *The Open Road: The Global Journey of the Fourteenth Dalai Lama,* Pico Iyer wrote a wonderful passage about the obligation facing three high-profile speakers waiting to go on stage before a large audience:

"[Their] job now was to give this audience a human, living sense of contact that no audience could get from a screen (the crowd, after all, had been waiting for this day for months); and yet they had to leave behind them something that would outlast them, and maybe help people return to the clatter and commotion a little differently, in part by seeing how they could change the world by changing the way they looked at the world."

Perfect.

Bill Chapman
Executive Director
The Richmond Forum

PREFACE

It is a Saturday evening in late March 1991, and we are in a small room for last-minute preparation. Art Buchwald walks in and says hello. He sits by himself at the far end of the conference table. Soon, he pulls out a cassette player and pops in *Frère Jacques*—but with "Art Buchwald" substituted as the key lyric.

He has said nothing. He is grinning, however. This is his favorite song, it will turn out. Or the original is. The parody was the work of Ralph Krueger the last time Buchwald spoke at The Richmond Forum.

The author (right), reporter's pen and pad in hand, appears to be badgering Art Buchwald for cab fare in this March 1991 meeting, though no incident report was filed. In the background is Andy Rooney, Buchwald's co-presenter at The Richmond Forum.

Buchwald was a syndicated humor columnist back then, a print guy whose face and voice were rarely witnessed by audiences. Turns out he was one heck of a speaker, though, and a prince of a guy. We exchanged a couple notes later, and I would write a column on him when he died. I was a columnist for the *Richmond Times-Dispatch,* which is how I ended up on the panel of four asking audience questions that night for Buchwald and the other speaker, Andy Rooney, commentator on CBS's *60 Minutes.* I guess that's how. I'm just glad I was asked.

Anyway, Krueger, the Forum president, who is also in the room, is planning to have the whole audience sing the "Art Buchwald" parody to Buchwald this night. And he's got an *East Side, West Side* takeoff for Rooney.

Rooney shows up and sits down. Krueger is going over the format for us question askers. "I would assume I'm going to speak first," Rooney interjects.

"He speaks first," Krueger counters, nodding toward Buchwald.

"That's wrong," Rooney says.

It's no joke. Rooney thinks he goes first because Buchwald is funnier. Buchwald says Rooney goes first because he, Buchwald, is straying from the topic of "Humor and the Press."

Krueger, used to getting his way as president of the Forum, doesn't like it. "It wouldn't make sense playing your song first," he says to Rooney.

Ultimately, Krueger would give in. But there was this awkward moment when you had two of the funniest men in America in the same room.

And nobody was laughing.

So this was my introduction, not only the first time I was involved with The Forum, but the first time I had seen it, period.

What an introduction.

MOVE AHEAD TWO DECADES. Though I don't think I had misbehaved, I was not invited back to The Forum professionally until February 2012. Bill Chapman, by then holding the duties Krueger had, gave me complete access as editor of *Boomer* magazine. The speaker that evening was Quincy Jones.

Turns out it was hardly just an evening speech.

The day begins at seven in the morning, with equipment being moved into the theater. It will not end until well after midnight, when the post-program reception at a local hotel breaks up. In-between are

The author, still with notepad, is invited back in 2012 for a behind the scenes look at the Quincy Jones program.

myriad events, rehearsals, adjustments, flubs, moments of confusion, laughs, and cheers. (You can read about this day later in the book . . . when I necessarily refer to myself, awkwardly, in the third person.)

At the night-ending reception, Jones sits for pictures and snippets of conversation, a usual bonus for invited guests and corporate sponsors.

Three photos are taken of us. In two, Quincy Jones and I are holding wine glasses, and seem unclear as to what each other is saying. . . . Make of that what you will. In the third, a posed shot of my wife and us, "Q" has one hand on Vicki's shoulder and is using the other to point his thumb backward at me. I assume it was his usual thumbs-up gesture. But as I had been following the poor man around all day, it's entirely possible Q was dispensing of me with a derisive "*this* guy" gesture. Who knows. I prefer not to think too much about it.

A great evening, either way.

ALMOST EVERYONE WHO ATTENDS a program becomes a fan of The Richmond Forum and many, Vicki and I among them, become subscribers. Richmond is a middle-sized city, yet The Forum has gotten just about every major speaker over the years: presidents, world leaders, newsmakers, news reporters, entertainers, just plain interesting folks. And it has taken on every major issue: war, the economy, terrorism, cyber-terrorism, life, politics, race, music, space, science, diplomacy, football . . . Football?

How all this happened—and why it took, in essence, three tries over a half-century before a forum finally and completely succeeded—is as interesting a story as you might hope. This book, I need not tell you, was fascinating to work on. Not that it was easy. The Forum files themselves—from which this book takes its name in part—were a godsend because these people *throw out nothing.* Overall, there were thousands of pages of records (old ones in disarray, the 1960s freely intermingled with the 1980s) and seventy years of newspaper clippings here and elsewhere to go through, dozens of interviews to conduct, and the usual writing-rewriting-layout headaches of any big project. One issue, however, was more challenging still:

What to put in and what to leave out.

The Richmond Forum is, as Bill Chapman once said of just the blockbuster 2012–13 season alone, an embarrassment of riches. And The Richmond Forum is, as Ralph Krueger once said more off-handedly of the blockbuster 1990–91 season alone, not too shabby. (Historical footnote: Krueger added "but expensive as hell.") Great stories and photographs abound. In the end, we selected what we thought were the best—the most important, the most interesting, the most telling, the most unlikely, the funniest—realizing other selectors might have made other choices with just as much validity.

Not only will you learn who came (and who didn't) and what they said onstage, but what had been going on at the Forum offices and the board meetings, what was going on backstage, even what was going on at the dinners and in the limousines and at the airports (Forum staff almost always picked up their famous speakers at the airport . . . almost). It was not always pretty, but what has emerged is nothing short of remarkable.

So welcome to the world in five nights a year.

Welcome, ladies and gentlemen, to The Richmond Forum.

95
NEXT

CHAPTER 1

"BOSTON HAS A MARATHON, RICHMOND HAS A FORUM"

THE VALUE OF A PUBLIC FORUM IN THE 21ST CENTURY

"A city can point to a number of things it can be proud of, that it does better than other cities," a Richmond investment firm executive, Michael S. Beall, said in a 1995 magazine article. "Boston has a marathon, Richmond has a Forum."

Richmond has long known what it has in its forum—or rather, in its three forums. Two now little-known predecessors ultimately closed their doors. But they had laid the groundwork for what is now three decades—and counting—of The Richmond Forum.

In 1936, while the original forum was in its infancy, a local newspaper urged full support so that "our democratic institutions will be promoted and strengthened through public forums of this sort."

In 1967, just three years after the start of the second forum, *The New York Times* noted it was already "the largest lecture forum in the nation." In 1978, a national agency for speakers called it then the nation's best "in terms of audience turnout and the caliber of speakers."

In 1987, The Richmond Forum, the third incarnation, was begun, quickly reaching and often exceeding the standards of the previous two. Richmond had the gold standard—the Boston Marathon of the nation's forums.

It has not gone unnoticed. Through the years, its events have been reported by the national media, accolades and awards have been bestowed, and even imitators have sprung up, gladly acknowledging their inspiration.

THE RICHMOND PUBLIC FORUM
1934–1955
Richmond Council on Adult Education
and the University of Virginia Extension Department

THE RICHMOND PUBLIC FORUM
1964–1980
First Unitarian Church

THE RICHMOND FORUM
1987–
An independent non-profit educational organization

In early 1992, a few years after moving from Richmond to Hartford, Connecticut, Richard and Doris Sugarman were looking to make an impact in their new community. "It really is a fractured town," Richard explains. Indeed, in the tradition of New England independence, Hartford is not one town but thirty-two separate towns, each with its own identity. How could they ever be brought together?

A community forum might help. "I remembered my mother having been to The Richmond Forum and saying how much she enjoyed it," Richard Sugarman says. He contacted its founder, Ralph F. Krueger, Jr., and brought him to Hartford. "We wanted Ralph to come up here and spend a day with us, and talk about The Richmond Forum, and what advice he would give us."

It must have been worthwhile. Soon, the Connecticut Forum would join the list of public forums springing up in the footsteps of Richmond's.

Meanwhile, Richmond's thrived. In 2014, Virginia Commonwealth University's L. Douglas Wilder School of Government and Public Affairs honored The Forum and Executive Director Bill Chapman with an Excellence in Virginia Government Award. "Through the shared experience of five intense evenings of civil discourse held seasonally," the university said, "The Richmond Forum creates opportunities for Virginians to push beyond their mental boundaries while raising their collective understanding of the global challenges facing our communities."

In 2015, readers of *Style Weekly* voted The Forum "Richmond's Best Mind-Stimulating Event."

Harry Rhoads, CEO of one of the nation's most significant speakers' bureaus and thus perhaps best positioned to evaluate, puts it more simply. "Richmond's my favorite forum," he says without hesitation.

But . . . a forum? . . . in Richmond? . . . and why so good, anyway?

IT MAY SEEM IRRELEVANT IN THE 21ST CENTURY that ancient Greeks and Romans found both the exchange of ideas and public speaking important to the development of a citizenry. The public enrichment they discovered, however, would be deemed even more important as millennia passed and democracies grew: Only an informed electorate, after all, could make informed decisions.

The lyceum movement, so named for Aristotle's school in ancient Athens, was begun in 1826 and flourished through the rest of the 19th century, except during the Civil War, offering Americans opportunities to attend local lectures, plays and other adult educational programs. Abraham Lincoln spoke at least once to a lyceum gathering and Mark Twain spoke to a number. So many lyceums appeared, along with so many presenters, that a "lyceum circuit" sprung up. The movement, embraced by the middle class as a way to move up the economic ladder, was largely a Northern phenomenon, however. "The South simply did not have a large enough middle class to support regular lectures; New Orleans, Richmond, and Charleston were exceptions that proved the rule," wrote Susan Jacoby in her 2008 book, *The Age of American Unreason.*

The lyceum movement in Richmond was significant enough that a literary magazine, *The Virginia Lyceum,* briefly appeared, in 1838 and 1839, printing speeches from Richmond events, among other offerings. Jonathan Daniel Wells, in his 2005 book, *The Origins of the Southern Middle Class, 1800–1861,* found one educator's speech that touched on the raison d'être of the movement, even if somewhat haltingly: "In a lecture on education before the Richmond Lyceum that was reprinted in the *Virginia Lyceum,* James M. Garnett, a teacher of some renown in antebellum Virginia,

The speakers of the 1897 Richmond Lyceum lecture series, as profiled in the* Richmond Dispatch, *included an Arctic explorer, several noted authors, an art critic, and others.

emphasized the importance of continuing to read and learn after formal schooling ceased: 'Self-education, which Lyceums, if well conducted, are peculiarly well suited to advance, is a pursuit, not only every way worthy of the noblest attributes of man, but it is that which affords, under God, the only possible remedy for the previous neglect, or willful abuse of those attributes.'"

The Richmond Lyceum, conducted at several locations (including the rooftop garden at the then-new Jefferson Hotel in 1900), was active both before and after the Civil War. Its speaker lists included such notables as British novelist-playwright Anthony Hope Hawkins ("Anthony Hope," author of *The Prisoner of Zenda*) and, on a couple of occasions, Lieutenant (later to be Admiral) Robert E. Peary, the North Pole explorer. By World War I, however, the lyceum seemed to have moved from a mix of lectures and plays toward mostly concerts and balls. It disappeared not long afterward.

In less than a generation, however, a public forum movement would begin, carrying a more serious purpose.

During America's Great Depression, more than two-and-a-half million adults gathered in forums across the United States to learn and to deliberate about troubling public issues, according to a 2005 *American Journal of Education* article, *Educational Forums of the 1930s: An Experiment in Adult Civic Education,* by Robert Kunzman and David Tyack.

It's worth noting that Richmonders were right there among them; the first of its three public forums began in 1934.

The purpose of such forums, said President Franklin D. Roosevelt, was to engage people "in a continuous, fearless, and free discussion and study of public affairs. This should be the natural postgraduate program of all citizens."

Forum advocates claimed schools had not done enough to give citizens the tools for such crises as were arising. "At a time when some activists on the right and on the left wanted to indoctrinate youth, and demagogues promised simple solutions to obdurate problems," Kunzman and Tyack wrote, "the leaders of the forum movement wanted citizens to learn to analyze complex problems, to tolerate diversity of opinions, and to deliberate about disputed economic and political issues."

John W. Studebaker, U.S. Commissioner of Education, explained the need in an influential 1935 book, *The American Way: Democracy at Work in the Des Moines Forums,* which looked at a five-year adult education program being financed by the Carnegie Corporation.

Young high school and college graduates, struggling with their own Depression-era woes, he wrote, were indifferent to the nation's larger problems. But a forum of ideas, Studebaker contended, "helps to break down youths' indifference to the problems of government." Even an older adult "has begun to realize that a knowledge of his occupation or profession will not in itself equip him to understand what is going on in the world or even show him how his own economic life is affected by larger social and economic forces."

The discussion of ideas was the thing, Studebaker said. "No educational experience is more salutary than to trot one's pet ideas out on a track where the field is fast and the public is looking on."

BUT THAT WAS THE BETTER PART of a century ago when newspapers, books and radio were the only means of conveying ideas to the public at large—and those were out of the reach of many Depression-era Americans, figuratively, anyway, if not literally.

Today, information abounds. Sunday talk shows debate issues in segments, Internet TED Talks share experts' stories, and a Google search turns up anything in less than a second.

Thirty years after the start of The Richmond Forum, the question has to be asked: Are forums, even top-flight forums, relevant anymore?

"George Clooney said something very interesting," says Platon, the internationally known photographer who appeared at The Richmond Forum in late 2012. "'We have an opportunity to have more and more information—but we're rapidly losing the ability to connect.'"

Even when we seek news or information, Platon adds, chances are we go to a source tailored to our existing views. "The Richmond Forum is that shared experience, the collective spirit of many types of people." Platon, whose photograph-filled presentation at The Forum was strikingly powerful, adds, "It's more important than ever that we come together to feel each other's experiences. . . . We might just learn something."

Not for a moment, then, does Platon back off its importance. "Forums are relevant more than ever . . . and The Richmond Forum is probably the most well respected forum in the country."

Rhoads, the CEO of the Washington Speakers Bureau that has helped bring dozens of speakers of international renown over the years, says The Richmond Forum "gives a richer feeling to what's going on." He notes a former president's 2014 appearance. "George W. Bush's best applause line was: 'I'm not here to criticize my successor.' But what he does do is talk about what it's like to be president. That's something you don't hear anywhere else."

There is richness and there is excitement.

Krueger, the primary force behind starting both Richmond's second forum in 1964 and the current one in 1987, laid out some of his thinking in a newspaper interview shortly after the start of the earlier one:

"My dream for The Forum is that I would like very much to have the largest one in the country—I don't know why—but I really would. I keep thinking, Wouldn't it have been fun to be there when Winston Churchill did his 'blood, sweat and tears' thing, or to have been there for Mark Antony's 'Friends, Romans . . .'? Wouldn't it have been fun to have that happen here? Wouldn't it be something to have a public official break a national news thing on the stage of the Mosque at The Forum?"

The Mosque is the Altria Theater now—having also been the Landmark Theater along the way—but The Forum is indeed the largest of its type in the nation. And it is always "something," as Krueger put it.

Richmond businessman Richard T. Wilson III talked in 1995 about what might now be called "the wow factor" in having newsmakers appear in person: "It feels like

> "We have the capacity not only to change things but to change the times in which we live. More people, more communities should be doing what Richmond is doing."
>
> **GERALD L. BALILES**
> **Governor of Virginia, 1986 - 1990**

they're sitting in your living room. There's an exuberance and excitement that you can't get opening the newspaper or pushing the power button for your television." University of Richmond Vice President John A. Roush added that a forum can elevate the level of discussion throughout an entire community. "Even for people who don't go to The Forum, I think it has a ripple effect." Edward W. Rucker, Forum president at that time, having succeeded Krueger, said that reflected credit on the larger community. "The Forum strengthens our image as a city interested in current events, economic and political issues, and education."

KRUEGER, THE VISIONARY BEHIND THE FORUM, sometimes referred to it as "the world in four nights"—an appellation that should be updated to "the world in five nights," given the Forum's expanded schedule and, of course, a more complex world. Krueger often referred to The Forum as a "gift to the people of Richmond," as well. It is a gift that has been delivered in myriad ways, some not entirely expected.

Maajid Nawaz, a former Islamic extremist who now works to promote democracy in the Muslim world, was one of three panelists on a groundbreaking 2013 Forum program, "Islam: A Religion of Violence or Peace?" Each had significantly different views. Nawaz had appeared with one of the other two panelists in a different forum, forced to debate their differences in an emotional stand-off.

Richmond's was a more worthwhile setting, Nawaz says. "It wasn't really a debate. It was a conversation."

The evening was enhanced by The Forum's having educated its audience in advance, even suggesting the members read a particular book by each of the three. "I was particularly struck by how well-organized the event was," Nawaz says. "I was delighted that the audience was so aware. They had come prepared. Some had read our books. I was very, very happy." The program, discussing nuances of a difficult subject, with speakers few had known, drew high marks.

Gerald L. Baliles was governor of Virginia when The Richmond Forum opened its doors in 1987. He agreed to be its honorary chairman and eventually would moderate a panel with former U.S. Trade Representative Carla Hills and former Canadian Prime Minister Brian Mulroney, then moderate again when former British Prime Minister Tony Blair appeared. Baliles, long a supporter of educational opportunities and among the more thoughtful of politicians, later served as director of The Miller Center, an affiliate of the University of Virginia that specializes in presidential scholarship and public policy—and civil discourse.

The Forum would have gotten his attention even had he not been governor, Baliles says. "I've always been impressed with the fact that a city of this size could continually attract major speakers to discuss the major issues of the time."

Baliles considers The Forum "a continuing education class for the community," a near-necessity in a democracy because it gives perspective and thus an affirmation that all is not as dire as it may seem at the moment.

"As is so often the case, when you pull the lens back, you see things in context, in perspective," he says. The country has always been in transition, whether pioneering the wilderness, winning the Revolutionary War, fighting a bitter Civil War to end slavery and to expand opportunities, fighting two world wars or fighting a great depression, or living in today's world, he says.

"What you realize is change is constant. It's part of this country's history. It also makes you realize democracy is hard work. But the process we have, which we sometimes forget, is to look at these things critically and discuss them and try to reach understanding on them at least, if not consensus. It's our alternative to fighting in the streets."

For Baliles, the value of The Forum is that its range of speakers, collectively, provides understanding and context for the change and challenges ahead. "For those people who invest in Forum tickets," he says, "they're investing in their own future because they have the opportunity to see prominent people talk about these issues."

Baliles notes that the quote from Greek philosopher Heraclitus—"the only thing that is constant is change"—amounts to a charge to society. "We have the capacity not only to change things but to change the times in which we live." That requires action, which requires knowledge. Most people, he says, when they walk away from a Forum event, are more aware of the complexity of challenges and today's issues.

"More people, more communities should be doing what Richmond is doing."

Public Forum: A Richmond Institution

Again Richmonders to Have Chance to 'Trot Out Pet Ideas on a Fast Track With The Public Looking On'

BY ROBERT W. EHRMAN

NEXT January 7th the doors of the John Marshall High School swing open for the second year of Richmond's smartest, liveliest educational event.

On that day, and on every Tuesday night for ten or twelve weeks thereafter, Richmonders will have an opportunity to show the world that "no educational experience is more salutary than to trot one's pet ideas out on a track where the field is fast and the public is looking on."

That's what John W. Studebaker, U. S. Commissioner of Education, thinks of public forums, and it's just another way of saying that Richmonders will find in the free discussion of local forums an opportunity to ask questions, to clarify thinking, to exchange points of view, to understand vital issues of the day, to subject every statement to the test of truth and impartiality—in short, to practice that form of democratic government which can exist only with the active, intelligent consent of the governed. These are some of the considerations which last year prompted the Richmond Council on Adult Education to sponsor a series of city-wide forums known as the Richmond Public Forum.

A few individuals, to be sure, were skeptical of the outcome, but the council subsequently reported an attendance of nearly 5,000 people at a total of thirteen programs (ten had been promised). Forum leaders included the Abbe Dimnet, on Mussolini and Hitler; Mordecai Ezekiel, on Farm Relief, and Gerald P. Nye, on the Senate munitions investigations. So gratifying was the response of the general public that the committee was enabled to refund one-half of the amount contributed by the original guarantors, including such public-spirited citizens as Miss Cornelia Adair, Dr. Osborne O. Ashworth, Wheeler Beckett, John Stewart Bryan, Robert W. Daniel, George Dillon, Dr. J. Shelton Horsley, Misses May and Julia Moore, Forbes H. Norris, Mrs. Stuart Reynolds, Richard H. Smith, Dr. Lee E. Sutton Jr., William B. Thalhimer, J. Binford Walford and Bradford H. Walker.

Much of this widespread interest resulted from the efforts of last year's Forum committee, composed of Dr. John J. Corson 3d, chairman; Miss Adele Clark, Dr. Douglas S. Freeman, Miss Katharine Hawes, Dr. S. C. Mitchell and Dr. W. T. Sanger.

Breaks Down Youth's Indifference to Government

BEHIND this willing co-operation of patrons and public, however, there may lie a deeper and more fundamental reason. Many of the Richmonders who came to the Forum to trot out their "pet ideas" were adults who believe in extending their educational interests beyond youth into the adult years themselves. If, as in the excellent work of other forums throughout the city, they saw in the Richmond Public Forum an opportunity to bring their minds into contact with the thoughts and opinions of others, they did so, perhaps, with the conviction that education is a continuous, life-long process which must be ever adjusted to the swift changes and growing complexities of a modern industrial age.

The writer has a young friend who grad-

John J. Corson 3d, chairman.

J. W. Studebaker, United States commissioner of education.

> President Roosevelt says:
> "We need to have meeting places for the discussion of public questions, in the cities, hamlets, and on the farms throughout the length and breadth of the land."
> John W. Studebaker, United States commissioner of education, says:
> "We cling to our democratic ideals. We desire to find some method of preserving them . . . If we are to do so, we must hold education to a course in keeping with the independent spirit of the founders of our great republic . . . we must create . . . a complete program of public education in which the never-ending flow of governmental and social issues will be dispassionately discussed and scientifically scrutinized . . . Public forums . . . constitute . . . an effective means of insuring the essential growth in civic enlightenment among adults without which democracy cannot survive."

of thousands of other ill-fated ventures during the depression. Somehow, the golden egg of prosperity had hatched into a very ugly duckling.

"The men and women who have just left school and college," writes Dr. Studebaker in his book, *"The American Way,"* "are facing the problem of earning a living and finding their place in society. The duties and responsibilities of citizenship may have been impressed upon them by their teachers. Nevertheless, they tend to become absorbed in their own pursuits and in consequence to regard . . . larger questions with indifference . . . But the public forum provides an opportunity to discuss issues . . . By such means it helps to break down youth's indifference to the problems of government . . ."

"Just as surely," continues Dr. Studebaker, "does the older adult need this agency for enlightenment. In some fashion of forming intelligent opinions, but needs ready access to the materials from which such opinions can be formulated. He lacks time to read widely, but he is stimulated by the clash of opinion which arises from public discussion of significant and controversial issues. He sees . . . in the public forums an indispensable avenue to the more abundant life."

Fills Need of Impartial Clearing House

THE need for an impartial clearing-house of public opinion is even more apparent when we contemplate the countless special interests within a community—each constantly pressing its claims for special consideration, each appealing to a narrow constituency, each representing a particular point of view. Splendid and praiseworthy as many of such interests may be, they are frequently unable—by the very nature of their aims—to act in harmony with the

them stand or fall in the arena of sincere, intelligent public discussion.

As with political groups, so with other agencies through which public opinion is formulated: business associations, voters' leagues, church groups, philanthropic agencies, "social" or "welfare" organizations—all of these could find opportunities for reaching a wider audience by submitting their specialized appeals to the free discussion of the public forum.

But, the reader may say, will not public forums themselves become agencies of propaganda? It has happened in a few instances; can it happen in Richmond?

The answer to that question lies in the successful public forums of Des Moines, Ia., as described in *The American Way*. There they are publicly supported, and controlled by local education authorities. Their purpose and procedure have been and remain purely and simply educative. Under such conditions any attempt to sperad propaganda in a public forum must ultimately be recognized as such under an objective public scrutiny.

The Richmond Public Forum is publicly supported. Its programs and policies are controlled by the Richmond Council on Adult Education through its Forum committee, composed of Dr. John J. Corson 3d, chairman; Wilson Brown, Tennant Bryan, Miss Sarah Hartman, Dr J. Shelton Horsley, Mrs. John L. Ingram and Dr. Aubrey Straus. The president of the entire council is Forbes H. Norris, assistant superintendent of public schools, and the excutive director is Mrs. Ralph R. Chappell.

As a non-partisan, non-political, strictly educative organization, the council offers the Richmond Public Forum this season in the belief that its forum leaders will try to represent the opinions of people from every walk of life, and that Richmonders will help to make and keep them representative by writing to the council offices their suggestions for the conduct of the meetings and the topics of the speakers.

Forum Leaders Already Booked to Appear

AMONG the forum leaders who have already accepted invitations to address the Richmond Public Forum opening January 7 are: Nikolai Sokoloff, director of Federal Music Projects for the Unemployed, who will speak on January 21; February 4 brings Dr. C. C. Little, widely known cancer research specialist; on February 18, Stringfellow Barr and Scott Buchanan, of the University of Virginia, will debate the question, "Is History An Art or a Science?"; and on March 11, Father John A. Ryan of Washington, D. C., will discuss "The Church and Social Justice."

With the generous co-operation of the press, the radio stations, the public library, the school board, the college extension divisions, and other organizations and individuals too numerous to mention, the continuation of the Richmond Public Forum on a more permanent working basis is now an established fact. That many Richmonders have expressed a desire for its continuation augurs well for the growing leadership of Richmond in pointing the way to good citizenship.

Contemporary Americans prominent in the affairs of the nation mince no words when they speak of the crying need for popular understanding of the complexities of

CHAPTER 2

THE BIRTH OF A RICHMOND TRADITION

THE RICHMOND PUBLIC FORUM, 1934–1955

Richmond's first of three national-level forums would sprout during the Great Depression, seemingly the unlikeliest of times. The citizenry could scarcely afford food and shelter, let alone tickets to hear people talk.

Richmond, however, would prove to be near the forefront of a fledgling movement that came into being partly because there was a depression. President Franklin D. Roosevelt himself had urged such forums, saying "We need to have meeting places for the discussion of public questions, in the cities, hamlets, and on the farms throughout the length and breadth of the land."

In the spring of 1934, Richmond civic and education leaders formed a committee. The first public notice of its work came in a small story, buried on Page Ten of the September 26, 1934, *Richmond Times-Dispatch* under the single-column headline, "Public Forum for City is Plan of Educators." The afternoon before, the paper said, a not-yet-official group of 51 representatives called the Richmond Council on Adult Education had met in the public library. "Definite plans were made for establishing a Richmond Public Forum . . . to bring to the city prominent authorities on various topics for the purpose of conducting a series of approximately twelve public discussions."

After one season, the new public forum was hailed as a "Richmond Institution" by the Richmond Times-Dispatch, *1935.*

"We need to have meeting places for the discussion of public questions, in the cities, hamlets, and on the farms throughout the length and breadth of the land."

PRESIDENT FRANKLIN D. ROOSEVELT

The council president making the announcement was Forbes H. Norris, assistant superintendent of the city's public schools. The committee consisted of a number of leading lights, including historian and newspaper editor Douglas Southall Freeman and Medical College of Virginia President William T. Sanger. Others included Chairman John J. Corson, 3rd; Adele Clark, Katherine Hawes, and Dr. S.C. Mitchell. The Forum's executive director would be Mrs. Ralph R. Chappell.

THE FORUM SOON WOULD have an audacious plan. It would offer first-class intellectual fare for just twenty-five cents an evening. Tickets to the entire season would cost just one dollar. Civic clubs would help support the programs. So would individual, public-spirited guarantors. This was democracy in action.

The Richmond Public Forum opened its doors—the auditorium doors of Richmond's large John Marshall High School, to be specific—on Tuesday evening, November 6, 1934. Frederick J. Libby, executive secretary of the National Council for the Prevention of War, was the opening night speaker. Libby called for a "sane" approach to Asia: "There are no millions of young Americans that I know of who are willing to ruin their country and throw away their lives on the soil of Asia for the sake of our economic interests in China," he said. He urged that world armaments be reduced enough to police the seas so that the U.S. and Japan would not go to war. Military leaders believed Japan, and not China, was the most likely source for trouble, he said.

John Marshall High School, (Marshall and 8th Streets), Richmond, Va.

Libby's appearance had been sponsored by the Richmond Peace Council, but it was just one organization supporting The Forum. Others included the Southern Women's Educational Alliance Club, the American Association of University Women, the Council of Jewish Women, the Richmond League of Teachers, the Richmond League of Women Voters, the Richmond Academy of Science, and the Ginter Park, Highland Park, Forest Hill, Barton Heights, and Catholic woman's clubs, among others.

Next to appear on The Forum stage was perhaps the best known of the first season's speakers, The Abbé Dimnet, a French priest and author of *The Art of Thinking*. Dimnet's appearance, moderated by University of Richmond President F. W. Boatright, was held just one week after Libby's—at the home of the event's better-known co-sponsor, the Woman's Club. Indeed, a newspaper article on the speech made no mention of The Forum.

That article, using a nickname of the age for Italian dictator Benito Mussolini, carried the provocative headline: "Abbe Dimnet Praises Duce, Berates Hitler." Five-and-a-half years later, Mussolini would join with Hitler in World War II. But Abbé Dimnet, speaking on "Mussolini and Hitler: A Study of Dictators," praised him: "He is not an internationalist. He is a nationalist. He is a man of great mentality." Hitler, by contrast, owed his power to understanding mob psychology; even within Germany, there was strong opposition to him. The abbé said his travels in Italy convinced him Italians were not discontented with Mussolini's "benevolent dictatorship." The paper reported: "The abbe, white-haired, tall, slender and garbed in the dress of an Episcopal clergyman, held the attention of his audience through a discourse of nearly two hours."

THE FRONT PAGE of the *Times-Dispatch* on Wednesday, February 27, 1935, greeted readers with two unusual photographs atop Page One. One was a photo of legendary New York Yankees baseball star Babe Ruth, above the headline: "Ruth Signs Up With Boston Braves' Team"; after fifteen years as a Yankee, Ruth had been traded to another team for what would prove his final season.

Nearby was a two-column photograph of Senator Gerald P. Nye, being met at the train station for his appearance at The Forum, possibly the first Forum-related photograph in the paper.

Nye, chairman of the Senate Munitions Investigation Committee, had excoriated munitions makers at The Forum the night before, for "betraying" humanity in their manipulations to perpetuate war. "The most powerful lobby in this world is that of the munitions makers," the North Dakota senator said. He added: "I can tell you tonight, and the records of our investigation will substantiate what I say, that they have wrecked every disarmament conference which has been held since the World War. Why? Because they were powerful enough, influential enough, to see that delegates who went to those conferences owed allegiance to the munitions trust and not the peoples whom they were supposed to represent."

Profits of some firms during the World War had grown by one million percent, Nye said. "The DuPonts alone built up wartime profits of 400 percent," he added, "and yet Felix Dupont was complacent enough to [suggest] that had it not been for them, America today would be a German colony."

Most speakers of The Forum's first season were not necessarily as renowned as the first three. But they were all expert. And The Forum, which had begun the season by promising but ten programs, ended up offering thirteen. They drew total attendance of nearly five thousand to the John Marshall High School auditorium for the season, made up mostly of the 582 people who bought season tickets. "So gratifying was the response of the general public, that the committee was enabled to refund one-half of the amount contributed by the original guarantors," wrote Robert W. Ehrman in a full-page piece in the *Times-Dispatch's* Sunday Magazine Section as the second season approached. The Forum, Ehrman wrote, was "a non-partisan, non-political, strictly educative organization . . . [trying] to represent the opinions of people from every walk of life." Richmonders, The Forum hoped, would help keep them representative by making suggestions as to speakers and content.

In an editorial, the *Times-Dispatch* enthusiastically urged even more support for the second year. "Believing, as we do, that our democratic institutions will be promoted and strengthened through public forums of this sort, where prominent speakers deliver addresses and their audiences then ask them questions, we hope the people of Richmond support

The Weather
Cloudy, Colder
Winds: Strong N. W.
Max. Temp. 61; Min. 34
(Complete Report on Page 2)

Richmond Times-Dispatch

All-State Cagers—
Virginia basketball men pick star team; Spiders are given three places
(Turn to Sports Page)

85th Year — Richmond, Virginia, Wednesday, February 27, 1935 — Dial 3-3431 Calls The Times-Dispatch — Three Cents

Repeal Holds Lead of 7,000 In Alabama; End in Doubt

Wets Step to Fore After Early Lag; Heavy Dry Ballot Surprises, Upsets Survey Results

Official Count May Be Needed

Hard Liquor Majority Is Less Than Beer, Wine as Weather Proves Aid to Northern Drys

Shifts Allegiance

—Associated Press Photo.
George Herman Ruth

Ruth Signs Up With Boston Braves' Team

Gets 3-Year Contract as Player, Manager's Aide and Club Vice-President

By Alan Gould

Jeter Relates 'Torture' By Kidnap Trio

Trial of Richie Brothers Begins in Powhatan; Slashed With Knife by 2, Says Plaintiff

Denies Knowledge Of 'Stolen' Liquor

Jury May Get Case Today, Is Belief; Ambler Defense Counsel

Arms Makers 'Betrayal' Of Nations Scored by Nye

—Staff Photo.
Senator Gerald P. Nye (right) is shown being welcomed to Richmond by Judge J. Hoge Ricks as he arrived yesterday afternoon at Broad Street Station.

Senator Cites DuPonts' Profits and Claim as Savior of U. S. in Address to Forum

Continued on Page 3, Column 3.

State's Income Up 13 Million; Rum Sales Aid

MacCracken Enters Jail for Ten-Day Term

F.D. to Yield On Pay Plan, Labor View

Council of War Plans Long Siege to Force Prevailing Wage for Passage of Job Bill

Robinson Rejects Compromise Move

Glass Ready to Call for Study of Measure; Waits Chief's Orders

Compromise Move Made

Confers With Labor

—Associated Press Photo.
Senator McCarran

Duce Warns Of Mobilizing 8 Million Men

Tells World in General and Ethiopia in Particular of Italy's Man-Power

British Ship Flashes SOS, Feared Lost; Plane Missing

Freighter, Disabled, Has 26 Aboard; Europa Fails to Find Trace in Answering Call

Wintry Blasts Hit Richmond

Mercury Here Drops 35 Degrees in Day; Airliner Is Forced Down Near Orange

the Richmond Public Forum generously."

For that second season, national speakers discussed federal music projects for the unemployed, cancer research, the church and social justice, and even the wonderfully esoteric "Is History an Art or a Science?" Explorer Donald B. MacMillan talked of his expeditions to the North Pole. Dr. R. R. Moton, president-emeritus of Tuskegee Institute, took on "The Future of the Negro." John W. Studebaker himself, author the previous year of *The American Way: Democracy at Work in the Des Moines Forums,* appeared to discuss "Education in a Democracy."

THE FORUM WAS FOCUSING firmly on national or international events. But occasional programs came closer to home—literally—and could be rewarded with large crowds.

Dr. Paul Popenoe, director of the Institute of Family Relations, a large marriage counseling facility in Los Angeles, appeared for a memorable program Monday evening, October 25, 1938. Topic: "Can the Family Have Two Heads?" A record crowd of between 800 and 900 showed up to see Popenoe. They were not disappointed. "Pleasant in demeanor and employing a perfect speaker's stance, he literally held the poor husband and the mistreated wife up to be stared at by the audience and then, before his listeners knew what he was doing, he was speaking with that parrot-like rapidity of the wife angered by her tired husband's indifference to the family problems," the next morning's *Times-Dispatch* reported. "It was an all-around evening, made up of laughs, of serious thoughts, of questions. Once the speaker absent mindedly moved away from the microphone, and the audience, shut off from most of his words, fretted impatiently until Harris Hart, who had introduced him, directed him back to position."

Popenoe's position on the evening's topic: "The family not only can but ought to have two heads." He cited a survey showing that only thirty-five percent of marriages were on such a fifty-fifty basis—yet eighty-seven percent of those in them were happy. By contrast, only sixty-one percent were happy in husband-dominated marriages, and only forty-seven percent in wife-dominated marriages. During the audience-question Forum that followed his talk, one attendee asked if current marriages were happier than those of 2,000 years ago. Popenoe quipped: "I'm not as old as I look. But I believe we had many co-operative marriages then, and I doubt if there has been very great change."

Years later, it would become realized that Popenoe had led a successful campaign to sterilize the mentally ill, spawning a forced-sterilization law in California that inspired other states, and also had studied eugenics, the practice of selective breeding that would be proposed by the Nazis. Still, the so-called "father of marriage counseling" had been a huge hit with The Forum. Popenoe's program also resulted in an early example of Forum outreach: A follow-up program on the same topic was held the following week in co-operation with the Richmond Y.W.C.A.

AS THE WORLD CHANGED, so would The Richmond Public Forum.

In January 1940, American Civil Liberties Union lawyer Arthur Garfield Hayes met with Alabama Congressman Joe Starnes, chairman of the House Committee on Un-American Activities, to discuss a charged topic of the day, "What is Un-American?" The topic, or at least the participants, caused some concern. Forum chairman Aubrey H. Straus said the American Legion had been asked to send a participant but refused, writing: "We are in sympathy with the educational program of The Richmond Public Forum, but we do not care to be associated with this or other programs with the American Civil Liberties Union." Straus said he was sure many Richmond Legionnaires—he was one himself—disapproved of the stand.

Two months later, The Forum would turn the tables on the Legion, asking Governor James H. Price to veto the so-called Heller Bill endorsed by the Legion as a safeguard against anti-American doctrines. The legislature-approved bill would have required speakers urging forcible overthrow of the government to be kept out of public buildings. The Forum's steering committee, including such luminaries as historian and newspaper editor Virginius Dabney, urged the bill be

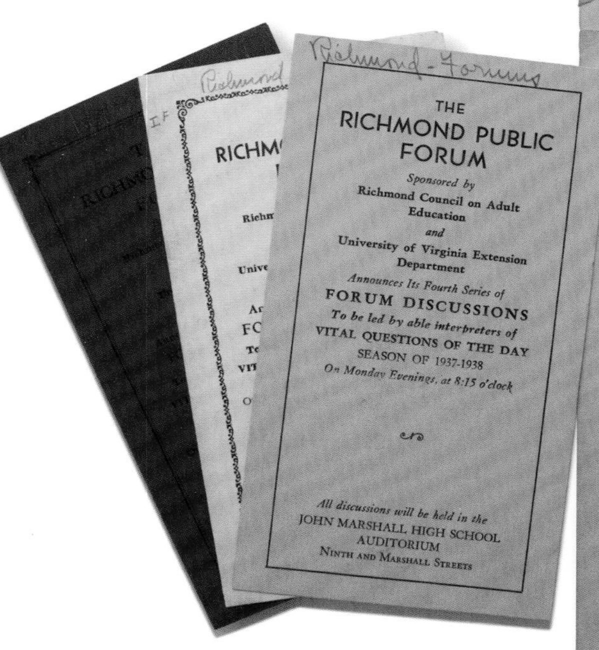

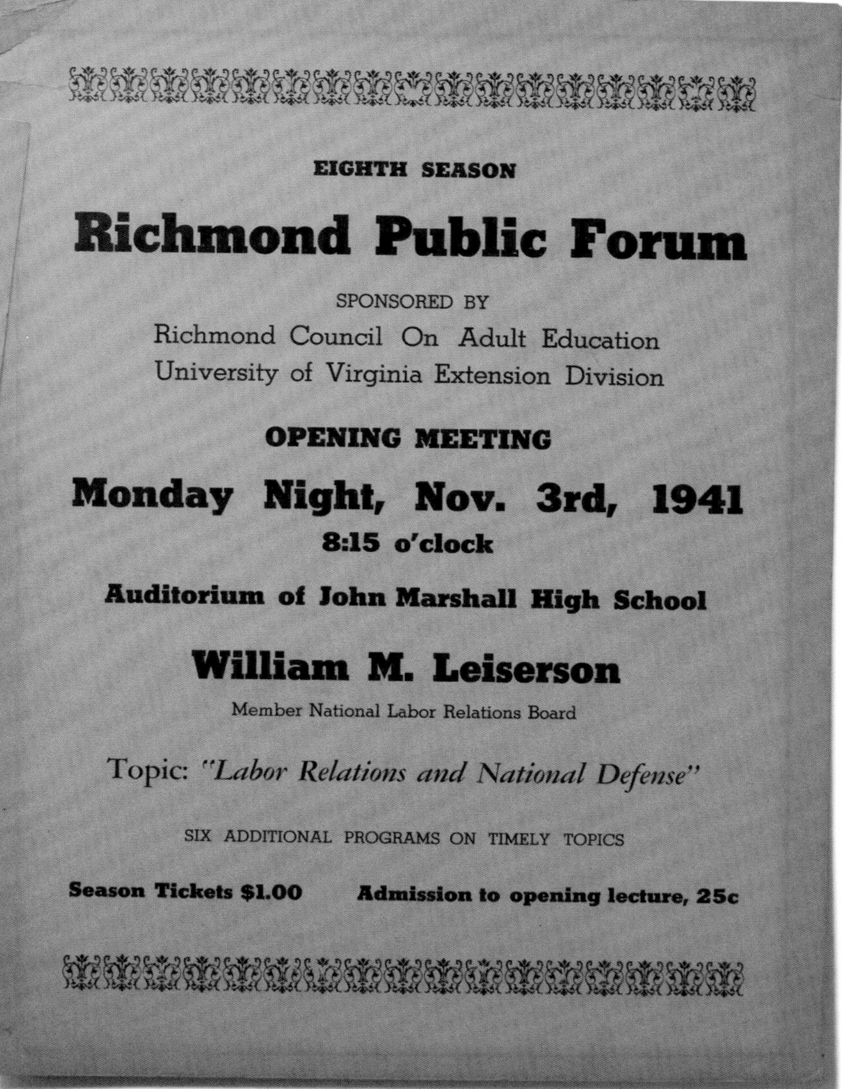

Richmond Public Forum program booklets from the 1930s alongside an advertising poster from 1941.

killed "as a menace to the cause of free speech, as setting a dangerous precedent and as utterly contrary to the principles upon which the State of Virginia and the United States of America are founded." Faced with a chorus of such objections, Price did veto the bill, calling it unnecessary and likely to prove "a continuing irritant."

As World War II approached, The Forum grew.

The December 2, 1940, appearance of Harvard University government professor William Y. Elliott brought its largest attendance ever, well over 1,000 people. Elliott said the United States, which would not enter World War II for another year, should "act" as if it were already in, "kick out" the German and Italian consuls, and give "all aid to England that is necessary to win the war." He was asked during the discussion period if he thought the U.S. should declare war immediately. He did not "shrink from that," Elliott said, but said it should send convoys to protect shipments from the U.S. "as far as Ireland, at least."

The 1,400-seat auditorium had been nearly filled for Elliott's appearance, thanks to an unprecedented sale of season tickets. Some single tickets were available at the door for fifty cents each.

World War II brought topics more tightly focused on overseas conditions, though it also resulted in a reduction of the number of programs. The 1941-42 season, for instance, began in late fall and offered but seven programs—still twenty-five cents apiece, all seven for one dollar.

Minnesota Congressman Walter H. Judd appeared November 12, 1943, giving the Forum audience a long-remembered talk peppered with such phrases as "the last war didn't fail—we threw it all away" and "When Japan went into Manchuria, the Japanese army marched down every main street in the United States" and "[the U.S. has] eaten up her cake of isolation with her own inventions." Judd, who had spent ten years as a medical missionary to China, said it was no longer possible for the U.S. to live in isolation. World War II was attributable to the failure to build an intelligent peace after World War I. "There'll be another and a more terrible war in a few years if we fail to build a durable peace this time."

Judd added: "Our own inventions have annihilated the two broad oceans which Providence placed on either side of us. . . . We invented the steamboat; Germany and Japan didn't do it. We invented the airplane; they didn't. We invented the submarine; they didn't. And these three inventions have made it impossible for us ever to be isolated from the rest of the world again."

Keeping an international focus even as the war wound down, The Richmond Public Forum's seven-program, 1945-46 season offered separate programs on Argentina, Greece, Germany, and education for international understanding, as well as a lecture by Archduke Felix of Austria on "Problems of the Peace Table." The series did include two more home-directed looks: "What is the Future of Atomic Power?" and, especially, "How Shall Our Cities Be Governed?" Ticket prices may have represented a coming post-war affluence: single programs had doubled to fifty cents. Season tickets now were $1.50.

The *Times-Dispatch,* in a November 1945 "Opening a Notable Series" editorial promoted that season opening "Atomic Power" presentation by a General Electric physicist. The physicist, Ralph P. Johnson, was a former University of Richmond professor who had been one of a team perfecting the atomic bomb. "A discussion of the future of atomic power by this brilliant young man should not only be of compelling interest to the people of Richmond, but it is typical of the authoritative addresses which The Richmond Public Forum has been providing for a good many years," the paper said. "Few organizations offer such rich fare at so reasonable a rate," adding "We commend the entire series . . . to the people of Richmond."

TROUBLE WAS ON THE horizon, however, even during the prosperous Fifties, even after attendance had grown, even after The Forum continued offering big-name speakers. The novelty was wearing off.

The 1950 season did not draw as many audience members as The Forum had been accustomed to. The following season brought some hope: In January 1951, Forum vice-president Herbert W. K. Fitzroy let it be known that the 1951 pre-season mail-order subscriptions had doubled those of 1950's. The season-opening discussion over President Truman's "Fair Deal"—*Raleigh News & Observer* editor Jonathan Daniels taking the "pro" position, and *Birmingham Age-Herald* columnist John Temple Graves taking the "con"—was expected to almost, but not quite, fill John Marshall High School's 1,400-seat auditorium.

There were fewer and fewer evenings like that, however, and fewer and fewer big names. The 1953 season, down to five programs, did feature journalist and author Cornelius Vanderbilt, Jr., on Europe; foreign correspondent Leland Stowe, also on Europe; Harvard University professor (and future adviser to President Kennedy) Arthur Schlesinger, Jr., on human freedom; teacher and columnist Max Lerner on the Middle East; and Democratic Senator Paul Douglas of Illinois on the American military and economy.

By 1955, the crowds were smaller still, though it was not always entirely The Forum's fault.

In The Forum's low-water mark, George D. Stoddard, chairman of New York University's committee for self-study and the former president of the University of Illinois, appeared to a much-smaller-than-usual audience Monday evening, March 7, 1955. He urged more people to go to college, but it wasn't his message that kept many away. The bigger villain was NBC's historic ninety-minute, live broadcast of *Peter Pan,* staring Mary Martin. The hit musical had only run four months on Broadway before appearing on television—and in color, making it a double rarity. "Forum President Herbert W. K. Fitzroy greeted the handful of persons present with a rueful reference to the *Peter Pan* competition," the *Times-Dispatch* editorial page would note days later. Across the country, other events were hurt. *Peter Pan,* so successful it would be rebroadcast live the following January, attracted a staggering audience of sixty-five million viewers. At the time, it was the largest television audience ever.

In 1955, Richmond Public Forum President Herbert W. K. Fitzroy (left), shown here two years earlier with fellow city leaders, would have to announce the bad news: The Forum was closing because there was "not sufficient demand for the type of big-name, national-issue program we have been presenting." Nine years later, The Forum would be resurrected. Richmond School Superintendent H. I. Willett, (second from left), would moderate the first program, with newsman Chet Huntley.

But televised musicals could not be blamed for most declining crowds at The Forum. In what would prove to be the final program, on April 25, 1955, "four prominent Southerners came to Richmond . . . and looked closely at racial relations in the South," as the next morning's paper put it. The more telling sentence, for the series' health, appeared at the end of the fourth paragraph: "A Richmond Public Forum audience of more than 250 persons heard the panel discussion." For a Forum that had drawn twice that many in its startup season two decades earlier, and frequently drawn more than 1,000, the new numbers would prove a death knell.

In an editorial some years later, *The Richmond News Leader* blamed lagging interest in the 1950s on a too-liberal slate of speakers. Though it always had a liberal bent, the paper contended, the early Forum had not eschewed other viewpoints: "From time to time, the Forum's directors would make an effort to be fair, or at least to be neutral: They would bring in an occasional conspicuous conservative, such as [Minnesota Congressman] Walter Judd, or they would arrange a debate between [Episcopalian seminarian, newspaperman and civil rights activist] Jonathan Daniels and [segregation-defending journalist] John Temple Graves. Many of their speakers were distinguished foreigners, correspondents, and authorities on oddly absorbing subjects." Most programs drew one thousand attendees or more, and the Forum board included city leaders.

But in the early 1950s, public interest waned, *The News Leader* continued, and programs drifted to the almost entirely politically liberal. "In April of 1955, considerable resentment was voiced when the Forum arranged a program of four white and Negro integrationists, led by [newspaper editor and civil rights advocate] Harry Ashmore, discussing the segregation issue. Plainly this was no true 'forum'—no opposing views were heard—and only 250 persons turned out."

WHATEVER THE CAUSE—liberals, competing forums, Peter Pan—by the fall of 1955, Forum President Herbert W. K. Fitzroy was telling some 2,000 former subscribers the plug was about to be pulled. Fewer than a hundred advance season tickets had been sold. The Forum seemed to have fulfilled its purpose, he wrote. "Today there are several specialized forums in Richmond. The last few series of our own forum have convinced us there is not sufficient demand for the type of big-name, national-issue program we have been presenting."

It had been a good idea but one that could not sustain. After twenty-one seasons, The Richmond Public Forum went dark.

Richmond Public Forum

Roger Johnson opened the workshop for organization of the Richmond Public Forum 8:00 in the Community Room of the First Unitarian Church.

Mrs. Alexander gave some background information on a former RPF which discontinued operating around 1950. Mrs. Alexander felt its most successful period was when controversial speakers were used and the audience participated through a question and answer period. When the programs became merely lectures, interest was lost. Season tickets were sold for five speakers to approximately 1500 pe for $1.00 which was gradually increased to Programs were held at the John Mar High School auditorium. Cash gifts w interested persons and comm series started. Mrs comm

CHAPTER 3

THE UNITARIANS RESURRECT THE FORUM

THE RICHMOND PUBLIC FORUM, 1964–1980

The city's second forum, again named The Richmond Public Forum, was the creation of the First Unitarian Church's adult education committee, having grown from church discussion groups. The new forum committee borrowed $500 in start-up funds from the church.

"It began one August afternoon in the basement of the Unitarian Church," Ralph F. Krueger Jr., chairman of the committee, would recall in a speech years later. "A group of us had gathered to create a gift we could give to the community. Someone suggested restarting the Richmond forum that had died some years ago. At that point, I swear I scratched my head—but I've been told that I raised my hand. And that's how I became the new Richmond Forum's first president. . . .

"I still remember my last question as the group broke up: 'What's a forum?' I had never been to one."

First, there would be a test run. On February 8, 1963, Krueger sent a letter to prospective donors. "We earnestly desire to bring to Richmond a series of nationally recognized speakers. To make this possible, we need your help on or before February 15th," he said. Dr. Arthur Larson, director of Duke University's World Rule of Law Center, would speak March 30—but only with their help.

Larson did appear on March 30, talking about legal dispute resolution as an alternative to war, at Mary Mumford School. By the next year, a new Richmond Public Forum would begin.

Handwritten minutes from a 1962 organization meeting of the new Richmond Public Forum. Note the misconception that the earlier forum had disbanded about 1950; actually, it was 1955. Note also the belief that successful programs resulted "when controversial speakers were used and the audience participated through a question and answer period. When the programs became mere lectures, interest was lost."

An informed citizenry for a working democracy

is the motivation for the rebirth of "The Richmond Public Forum". The Forum will bring to the citizens of this community personalities of national reputation to discuss issues that are current and significant. This year's program presents authorities in the fields of literature, news analysis and politics. You will find a spectrum of viewpoints as well as subjects.

This is an open forum at which ample time will be provided for questions from the audience.

CHET HUNTLEY
NBC-TV News Commentator
January 25
"Mr. President 1964?"

"No one is born with a 'nose for news'," says Chet Huntley. "It's something one develops the same as anything that must be learned". Chet Huntley has been developing his 'nose for news' since 1934 when he first began to broadcast on a Seattle radio station. Today, Huntley is one of the outstanding news commentators of our time, appearing regularly on the Huntley-Brinkley report on NBC-TV. Other assignments also include the "NBC White Papers", regular contributions to NBC Radio's "Emphasis" and such hour long TV specials as "The Land" and "The Many Faces of Spain".

A graduate of Washington State University, Huntley has covered many top news stories in the Far West as well as stories in Asia and the Middle East. Joining with Brinkley in 1955, the team blossomed with wide praise from the nation's TV critics and the ratings have continued to reflect the nation-wide popularity of the men.

GORDON D. HALL
Writer-Lecturer
March 14
"From Left to Right: an analysis of the mainstream vs. extremism"

Gordon Hall was described in a 1962 Saturday Evening Post article as a "fearless one-man task force . . . who flails the 'hate boys' with their worst scourge—exposure." The description couldn't have been more accurate because, for nearly 20 years, Hall has been a one-man FBI devoting his time to the investigation of and attack on hate groups. Although he frequently works with the FBI and is considered one of the nation's foremost authorities on hate organizations, Hall, who battles both far right and far left groups, has no official backing or tie-ups, no sponsors, no paid staff, no funds except what he earns as a lecturer.

Concerned with the dangers of extremism, and both appalled and fascinated by hate groups, Hall began pursuit of his career shortly after getting out of the service in World War II. Times were lean in those first few years but, Hall's persistant study and his growing recognition as an authority on such groups soon caused the picture to brighten. Today, Hall's lecture dates average about 125 a year, and his collection of data, statistics, and factual information relating to hate groups is the most extensive and complete in the country.

VICTOR LASKY
Author
April 4
"Follies of the New Frontier"

Victor Lasky, controversial author of one of the year's top best-sellers, "JFK: The Man and the Myth", has long been known as a hard-hitting, fast-digging reporter and journalist. In a journalistic career ranging over two decades, Lasky has interviewed and written about presidents, would-be presidents and statesmen (including a few dictators). He has visited and written about many of the hot spots of the world—Kashmir, Castro's Cuba, South Vietnam and Algeria.

Formerly a Washington correspondent, Lasky has worked for such newspapers as the New York World-Telegram and Sun, the Chicago Sun (now Sun-Times) and the defunct Paris (France) Post. In 1950 he co-authored the best-selling book on the Alger Hiss Case, "Seeds of Treason", and later wrote a full-length documentary on the Communist problem, "The Hoaxters", which was produced by Dore Schary for MGM. Lasky, who has lately been specializing in analyses of world and domestic affairs, now writes a syndicated column which appears in over 100 newspapers.

NORMAN COUSINS
Editor, Saturday Review
May 1
"World Report"

A distinguished editor, who stands as a symbol of America's creative, crusading and sensitive mind, Norman Cousins is a man of extraordinary talent and stature. Cousins, whose travels have taken him around the world six times, has lectured widely throughout Asia and has been an observer or correspondent at such events as the Asian-African Conference in Bandung in 1955, the Berlin Airlift in 1948 and Korean Crisis of 1951.

A recipient of many awards, including the Thomas Jefferson Award for Journalism in 1948 and the John Dewey Award for Public Service in 1958, Cousins is a member of the Board of Editors of the Encyclopedia Britannica and is a former Vice President of P. E. N., the world organization of writers, editors and publishers. He holds degrees from 15 universities and colleges. Among the outstanding books written by Cousins are "In Place of Folly", "Dr. Schweitzer of Lambarene" (a book-of-the-mouth selection in 1960), "In God We Trust", and "Talks with Nehru".

Go Out and Get Apoplexy

Once again, we should like to put in a good word for the Richmond Public Forum. This venerable Richmond institution, dead these past nine years, has been breathed back to life by a band of energetic local Liberals. Their first program brings Chet Huntley to the Mosque at 8:15 o'clock Saturday night.

Now, there are not but so many Liberals in Richmond, energetic or otherwise. In any given election, Richmond-Henrico will go nearly 2-1 for the conservative candidate. Mr. Nixon emerged from this district, if memory serves, with a walloping 25,000 votes to spare. The local power structure, in the popular phrase, stands just to the right of William McKinley. This includes us.

Yet it surely is a good and healthy thing for the Public Forum to be revived under this genial sponsorship. As we doubtless have remarked before, Conservative minds tend to get flabby when they talk only to themselves. It is a useful experience, like exercise and long walks, to hear Chet Huntley on politics or Norman Cousins on The Bomb. They set the adrenals pumping; blood rushes to the head; the old juices flow anew. Maybe next year the sponsors could consider Wayne Morse, Manny Celler, and Arthur M. Schlesinger, Jr. We can all get apoplexy together!

In all seriousness, the four speakers lined up for the Forum's spring season (three Liberals, one Conservative) are able and intelligent spokesmen. Their lectures will contribute significantly to the local scene. Season tickets for the four are only $5; student tickets are $3. These may be purchased at the usual ticket outlets, or by sending a check to the Forum at P.O. Box 531, Richmond.

At last report, about a thousand series tickets had been sold. Two thousand are needed to maintain a top-drawer level of speakers. It's a pity a more appropriate hall couldn't be found than the cavernous Mosque, but in time perhaps the Civic Center will provide. Meanwhile, Old Eyebrows will be here Saturday night. Go and make faces; or go and spur him on. You can still get home in time for Gunsmoke.

Above: An impressive lineup was booked for the first season of The Richmond Public Forum's 1964 "rebirth." Left: The Richmond News Leader *heralded the return of The Forum with an enthusiastic editorial. Opposite above: Program booklet from opening night, prepared, seemingly, at minimal expense. Opposite below: Typewritten remarks delivered by the new Forum's principal founder and president, Ralph F. Krueger, Jr., at the second program.*

There would be differences from the old one. The Forum would be held in a true auditorium, the city's fabled Mosque, and would be limited to four high-quality programs a year.

This new Forum sold season memberships for five dollars (three dollars to students) and single program tickets for two dollars ($1.25 for students). Some $11,000 would be brought in from ticket sales, with $10,500 being spent—$4,500 for speakers' fees, the rest on advertising, Mosque rental, printing, and so forth.

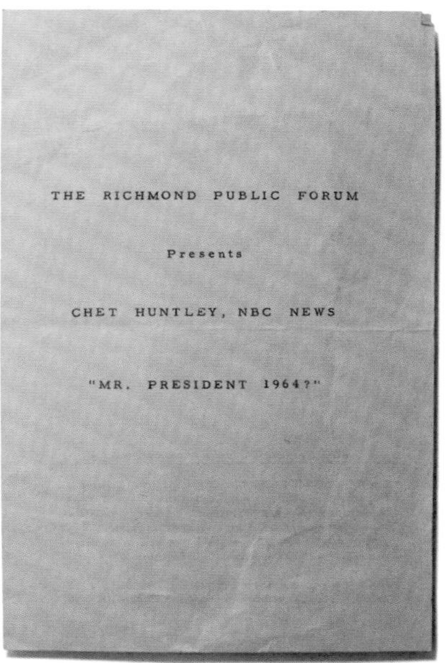

THE RICHMOND PUBLIC FORUM

Presents

CHET HUNTLEY, NBC NEWS

"MR. PRESIDENT 1964?"

Television news commentator Chet Huntley was the kickoff speaker, appearing January 25, 1964. Moderating was Dr. H. I. Willett, superintendent of Richmond Public Schools. Huntley took on racial discrimination and the big scourge of the day, Communism. Communism would have a few more victories, Huntley said, but the "big lie" would eventually be realized by the people of the world. Communism would fail.

Among those attending were students from John Marshall High School, along with history teacher Katharine Fontaine, reported the school's paper, *The Monocle*. Ann Lawrence, a senior, said, "The Forum was wonderful. I especially enjoyed the speaker's comments on Communism." The history teacher, however, believed a spark of disagreement would have made the evening more interesting. "Mr. Huntley did not evade controversial questions," Fontaine said, "but he gave his opinions with great tact."

Writer Gordon D. Hall, Kennedy biographer Victor Lasky, and *Saturday Review* editor Norman Cousins followed. They were big enough names that the first season was considered a success.

Good evening. My name is Ralph Krueger. It is my privledge to be president of your Richmond Public Forum. On behalf of the forum and the First Unitarian Church...welcome. And may I add it's nice to see all of you again. At our first meeting I told y

Welcome back. If you attended our first meeting you may miss the long flowing, somewhat wrinkled table clothes that covered our panel tables during the Huntley address. We too enjoyed the pleasant note of informality...however...we felt our current setting would make us look a little more professional. I sincerely hope you like our change of set.

It is my privledge now to introduce you to the panelists and moderator who will be conducting the balance of our program.

First, your questions were

Getting speakers was not easy, however. Repeated attempts to engage FBI Director J. Edgar Hoover failed. In October 1962, Hoover had written his regrets in declining to speak at the Unitarian Church itself. Now, less than two years later, in June 1964, he declined to speak at the new Forum. He would like to, Hoover assured The Forum, but "the pressure of official business and the many urgent matters confronting me on a day-to-day basis render my schedule extremely uncertain."

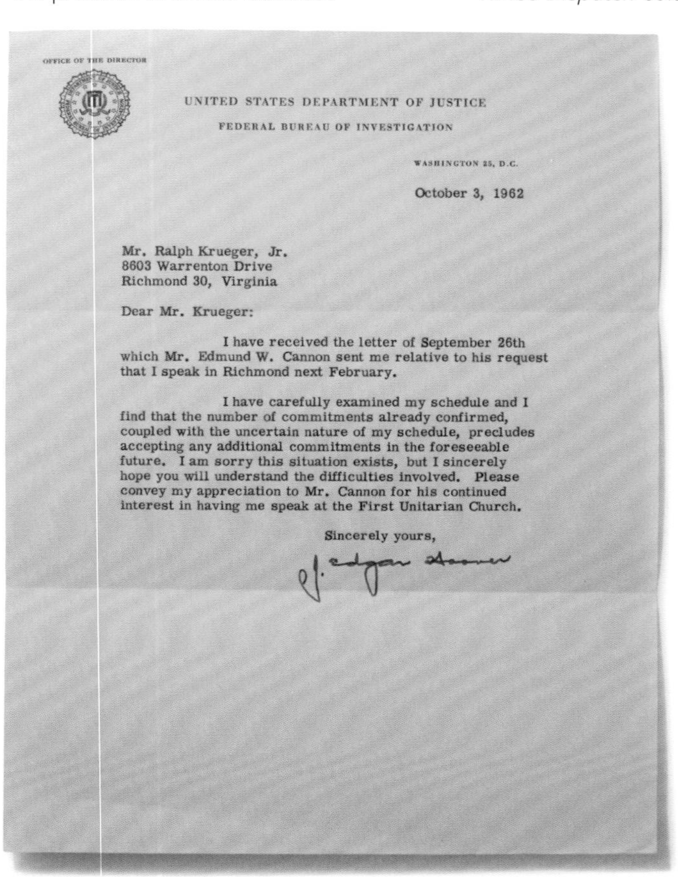

OFFICE OF THE DIRECTOR

UNITED STATES DEPARTMENT OF JUSTICE
FEDERAL BUREAU OF INVESTIGATION

WASHINGTON 25, D.C.

October 3, 1962

Mr. Ralph Krueger, Jr.
8603 Warrenton Drive
Richmond 30, Virginia

Dear Mr. Krueger:

I have received the letter of September 26th which Mr. Edmund W. Cannon sent me relative to his request that I speak in Richmond next February.

I have carefully examined my schedule and I find that the number of commitments already confirmed, coupled with the uncertain nature of my schedule, precludes accepting any additional commitments in the foreseeable future. I am sorry this situation exists, but I sincerely hope you will understand the difficulties involved. Please convey my appreciation to Mr. Cannon for his continued interest in having me speak at the First Unitarian Church.

Sincerely yours,

J. Edgar Hoover

FBI Director J. Edgar Hoover had his legendary files, and The Forum had a file on Hoover, containing mainly rejection letters going back to a first attempt by the Unitarians to invite him to speak in 1962.

The Forum's typical Saturday evening consisted of a reception and dinner, as well as a three-part program that may have made The Forum unique. Krueger described it in a January 1966 letter: "One of the most interesting aspects of The Richmond Public Forum and one of its big selling points is the question and discussion period that follows the talk each speaker gives. . . . Following the main talk by the speaker . . . a moderator and panel of five leading state and national figures question and discuss the issues with the speaker. Following this discussion, another panel, generally made up of local personalities, screens questions from the audience. The entire program ends by 10:45 p.m."

By year three, 1966, The Forum was attracting the big names Ralph Krueger had envisioned: Walter Cronkite, whose appearance nonetheless was The Forum's worst attended because of a vicious snowstorm; Supreme Court Justice William O. Douglas, who had retired from the court just months earlier, following a stroke; and General Maxwell D. Taylor, who continued to insist the Vietnam War was being won. Taylor's program was recorded and aired on WRVA radio two nights later.

Times-Dispatch columnist Charles McDowell, one of the panelists for Cronkite, typed a thank-you note afterward to Krueger, and noted The Forum's ascendancy:

"The snow was bad and the speech was maybe fair, but Mr. Cronkite turned out to be a pleasant fellow and I suspect that everyone enjoyed the evening. That isn't nearly as important, I guess, as your disappointment over the crowd, but the Forum is going so strong it can overcome a little bad luck."

By the next year, The Richmond Public Forum had its first sellout season. Even *The New York Times* was taking notice. The Sunday, February 5, 1967, *Times* profiled The Forum in a fifteen-paragraph story proclaiming the new series a "BOX-OFFICE SMASH."

Fortunately, perhaps, the *Times* had not had the inside story on the most recent speaker. Al Capp, the larger-than-life *Li'l Abner* cartoonist and conservative commentator may have been more of a whirlwind than any Richmond speaker before or since.

It started in typical Capp fashion. An Associated Press correspondent from Washington, Jay Sharbutt, wrote that Capp delayed going to a Forum reception. He told his hosts he wanted to sit down first with the press. Capp, he wrote, "looked and acted as if he would rather

THE NEW YORK TIMES, SUNDAY, FEBRUARY 5

RICHMOND FORUM BOX-OFFICE SMASH

Season Sold Out for Talks With Town Hall Motif

Special to The New York Times

RICHMOND, Feb. 4—A public forum with a town hall motif and big-name speakers does here what road versions of Broadway plays, rock 'n' roll bands and symphony orchestras frequently do not do: It fills up Richmond's civic auditorium.

All 4,564 auditorium seats are sold out for the season for the four combination lecture and question-and-answer sessions sponsored by the Richmond Public Forum.

It is a sell-out that makes the Keedick Lecture Bureau of New York City rate Richmond's as the largest lecture forum in the nation. And the forum, a product of the First Unitarian Church of Richmond, begun with a borrowed $500, has grown that big in four years.

A week ago it was Al Capp, creator of the "Li'l Abner" comic strip, who drew a capacity crowd. On Feb. 25, it will be former Senator Barry Goldwater.

Von Braun Scheduled

Dr. Mary S. Calderone, executive director of the Sex Information and Education Council of the United States, Inc., comes to town March 18. Dr. Wernher von Braun, director of the George C. Marshall Space Flight Center at Houston, is the April 18 attraction.

Those were the four names that stimulated this year's sell-out. This is the first year in the forum's four-year history that nobody could get in on a single admission ticket. All available seats had been sold at the $5-for-adults and $3-for-students season ticket prices.

Previous speakers have included Dr. Arnold Toynbee, William F. Buckley Jr., Walter Cronkite, Justice William O. Douglas, Gen. Maxwell D. Taylor, Dr. Walter Judd, Dr. Arthur Larson, Victor Lasky, Norman Cousins, Gordon Hall, Dr. William Vogt and Chet Huntley.

Besides the names, one of the big selling points of the forum is the question-and-answer session that follows the speakers' formal speeches. A moderator and panel of five leading state and national figures discuss issues with the speaker.

Questions Screened

After that discussion, another panel, generally composed of local news media representatives, screens written questions collected by ushers from the audience.

Forum directors believe that audience and local news representative participation help provide a feeling of belonging to the community and the audience.

The forum is run by volunteers from the membership of First Unitarian Church and is chartered as a nonprofit organization. It long ago paid back the $500 it borrowed from the church and now uses its income to attract better-known speakers. Their fees run as high as $2,500.

Further member participation comes in the selection of speakers. At the end of each season, season ticket buyers get a list of up to 40 potential speakers chosen by a ballot committee and listed in such categories as political, world events, cultural and miscellaneous.

Season ticket holders vote on their preferences. Efforts then are exerted to obtain the persons whose names a highest on the lists.

The forum idea is new one to Richmon 1934 to 1955, a similar less ambitious—progra ed under the sponso the Richmond Council Education. That for after 21 years and it First Unitarian Chur vive it four years ag

Another Richmonder Praises Local Forum

Recently the Richmond Public Forum closed another successful year in bringing to the Mosque four outstanding speakers.

We really owe a debt of gratitude to the First Unitarian Church of Richmond for its vision and marked success.

On each of these four Saturday evenings the Mosque has been well filled and at times almost filled to capacity. Men of all ages and walks of life have composed the enthusiastic and responsive audience.

It has certainly been heartwarming to hear discussions and the sharing of ideas by brilliant men and women, among them Dr. Wernher von Braun, our most recent and eminent guest speaker.

I'm sure that the First Unitarian Church has felt a warm glow of satisfaction in the knowledge that the Forum has again completed another great year. We, the public, also share in this joy and express a most sincere thank you.

MARJORIE B. OBER.
Richmond.

Above: The Richmond Public Forum becomes national news when covered by The New York Times *in 1967. Note the reference to 4,564 seats in the Mosque auditorium. This was the initial seat count in the majestic Richmond theater before successive renovations reduced the number of seats by nearly 1,000. Right: Praise was also rolling in at the local level, including this letter to the editor published in the* Richmond Times-Dispatch*, also in 1967.*

be hoisting an ale or two with the boys at Toots Shor's." He said no to an offer of sherry, ordered a coffee instead, and offered his opinions on Joan Baez, *Washington Post* cartoonist Herblock, and crime in New York City. After ten minutes, Capp was reminded he was late. "The interview was over," the correspondent wrote. "He stood up, wished me well, grinned again and plowed into a sea of outstretched hands. Some still held sherry glasses, and one couldn't shake the feeling Capp would have been much happier in a bar room that night."

AL CAPP
Cartoonist: "Li'l Abner"

He made do. Indeed, The Forum's pre-speech receptions, which included hard liquor, would be limited for years to only beer and wine among alcoholic beverages after that evening. Capp had proven hard liquor was too risky. Onstage, he would be his bombastic self, taking no prisoners. Afterward, a church member would question how softly Capp had been handled by panelists, and one of them, an editorial cartoonist from Kentucky, offered a written apology for being overmatched.

Krueger later would tell the *Times-Dispatch* there was never anyone like Capp:

"Al Capp's the only speaker we ever had who, one, asked for a woman while he was in town and, two, reversed the charges when he called us from Boston to ask for a tape of the show. He was cheap and he was horny. But in all fairness, Capp had the best control of that stage of anyone I'd seen up to that time. He was a dirty old man, but he was amazing." Capp did get his phone bill paid. He didn't get a woman.

Michigan Congressman Gerald Ford became the first president-to-be to speak at The Forum, appearing in March 1970, four-and-a-half years before becoming president with Richard Nixon's resignation. Ford talked about what he called "the New Federalism," but questioners wanted to know about the nation's postal strike (he would not use the military to deliver mail), the decision of Virginia Senator Harry F. Byrd Jr. and Congressman John R. Marsh not to run as Democrats (he would be pleased to have them in the Republican Party), and activities in Laos and Vietnam (no U.S. ground forces in Laos, continued peace talks and stability for Vietnam).

The Mosque • Saturday Evening • March 21, 1970
the
1970
Richmond
Public Forum
presents
Rep. Gerald Ford
A non-profit Virginia Corporation established as a community service by the First Unitarian Church of Richmond
TEXT

Returning to D.C., Ford jotted a note on the outside of the envelope carrying his Forum speech: "No

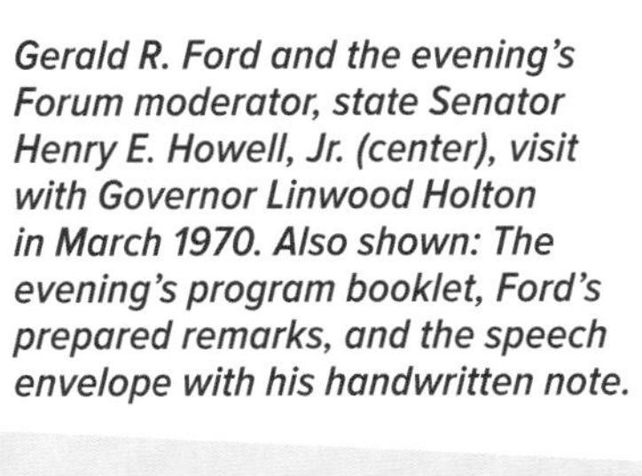

AN ADDRESS BY REP. GERALD R. FORD,
REPUBLICAN LEADER, U.S. HOUSE OF REPRE
BEFORE THE RICHMOND PUBLIC FOR
AT RICHMOND, VIRGINIA
8 P.M. SATURDAY, MARCH 21, 19
:30 P.M. SATURDAY
French nobleman said of Americans, "T
become its model."
time forth, Americans have been envied
admired, much maligned, and much misur
fficulty understanding ourselves.
enchman, De Toqueville, who saw
n America," De Toqueville talke
ns with their situation in lif
f Americans:
ly faith in the perfectibilit
ust necessarily be advantageo
consider society as a body i
in which nothing is, or oug
them today to be good, may
ger on the key character t
for something better, the
tomorrow.
ys been in this great and glorious
MAR. 21, 1970
RICHMOND, VA.
Gerald R. Ford
M.C.
SATURDAY
8:00 P.M.
RICHMOND PUBLIC FORUM
P/ No newsman saw me except photographer. Let's check Richmond papers to see if any coverage on Sunday or Monday.

Gerald R. Ford and the evening's Forum moderator, state Senator Henry E. Howell, Jr. (center), visit with Governor Linwood Holton in March 1970. Also shown: The evening's program booklet, Ford's prepared remarks, and the speech envelope with his handwritten note.

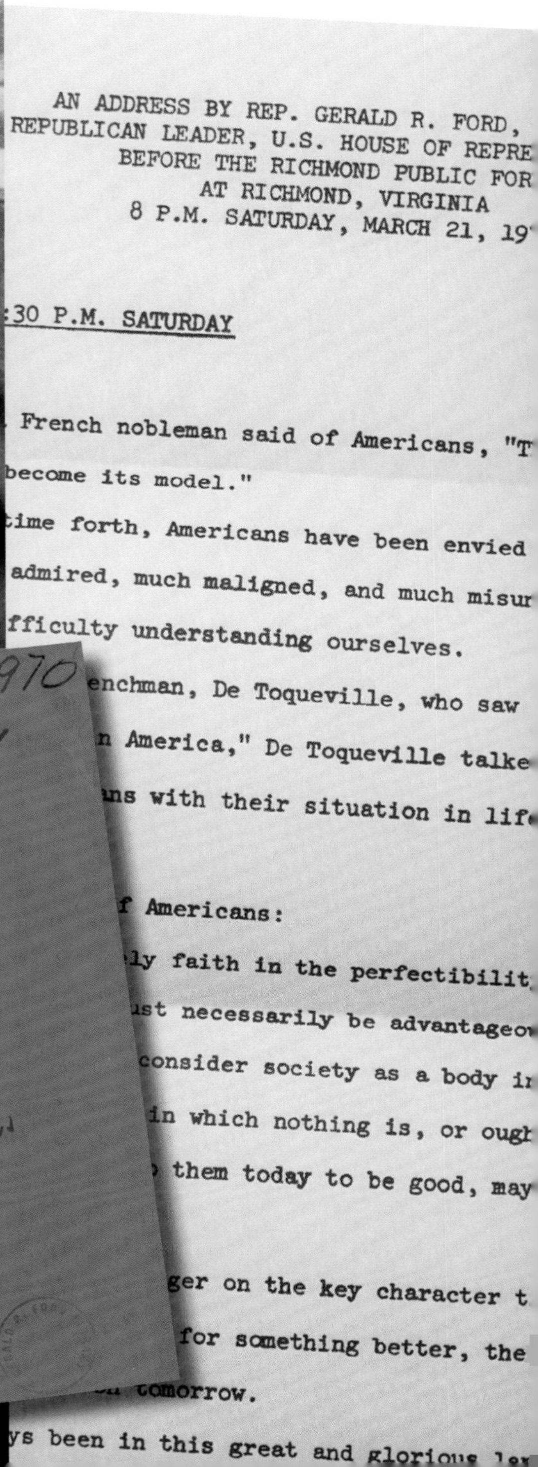

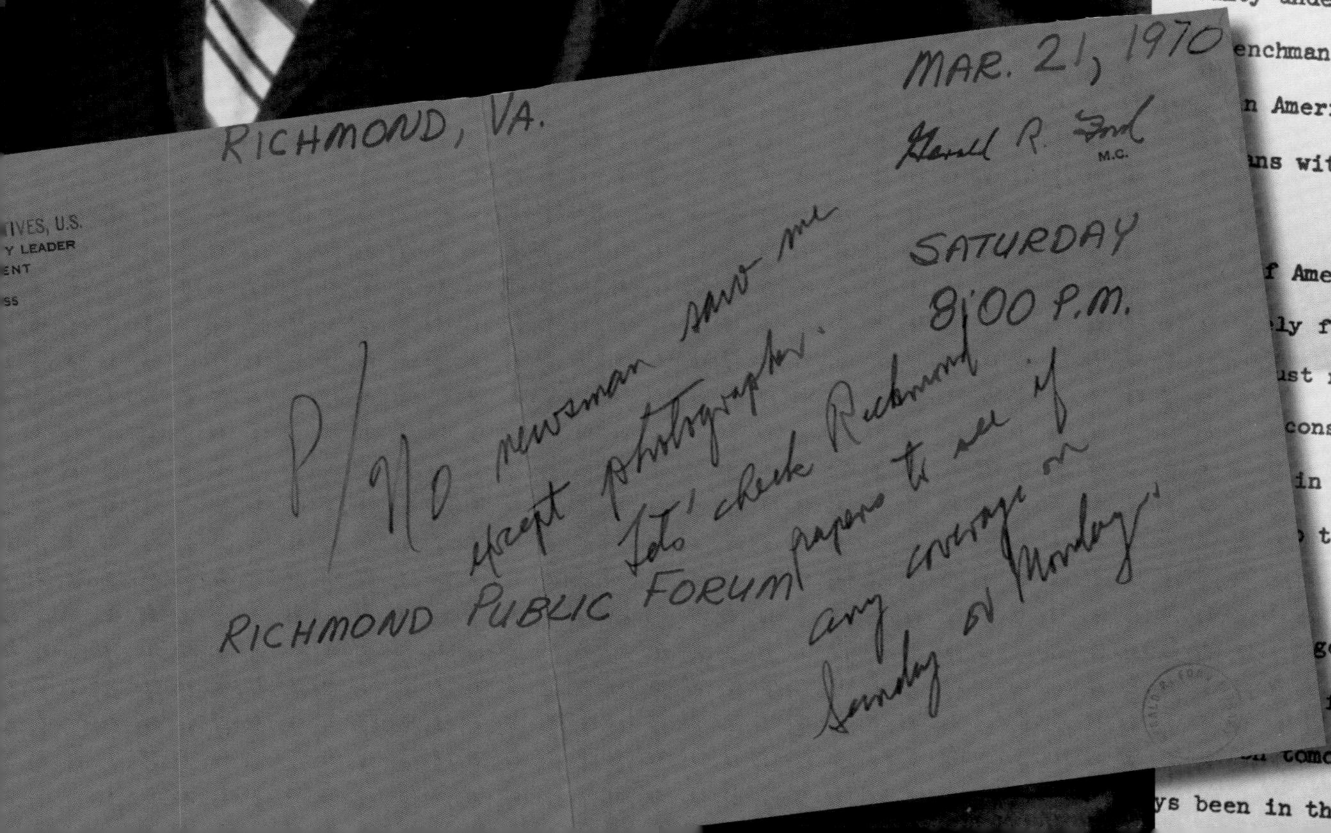

newsman saw me except photographer. Let's check Richmond papers to see if any coverage on Sunday or Monday." The answer: Shelley Rolfe's article on Page B8 in Sunday's *Times-Dispatch,* which reported in part: "The thrust of the formal speech was a presentation of Republican goals and was low-pitched. The tempo picked up when the question and answer period began partially because of remarks by State Senator Henry E. Howell, Jr., who served as moderator. The answer to every question produced applause from some segment of the audience. It was mixed applause which at times seemed to represent a standoff between conservative and moderate-liberal views."

DESPITE BIG-NAME SPEAKERS, The Forum sometimes seemed to be on a roller coaster ride.

"We had trouble selling tickets and would have 'boiler rooms'" to come up with solutions, remembers Elinor Kuhn, who had been with The Forum since 1967. Speaker fees went higher and higher. The money had to come from somewhere.

Financially, the 1973 season would be The Forum's weakest ever. Ticket sales were just over 2,000, most to season ticket holders who paid ten dollars. About 400 tickets a night were sold at four dollars apiece.

That meant more than a third of the Mosque's seats were empty.

Asa Whitt, one of the Forum leaders, blamed the choice of speakers for 1973. "The answer I would give is that one of the speakers was [Congresswoman] Shirley Chisholm. She was viewed in Richmond as an ultraliberal, so people didn't buy tickets," he said in a newspaper interview. After that, the Forum council decided the key would be to get "nobody too controversial, someone basically conservative," as Ruth McDonough, the speaker contact chairman, said. It was an unwritten policy that would hold sway for years.

By 1974, there was concern about The Forum's vaunted subscriber survey, from which attendees would vote for their favorites among about fifty potential speakers. One volunteer, Barbara Mabe, said the selection process suffered from being extended only to

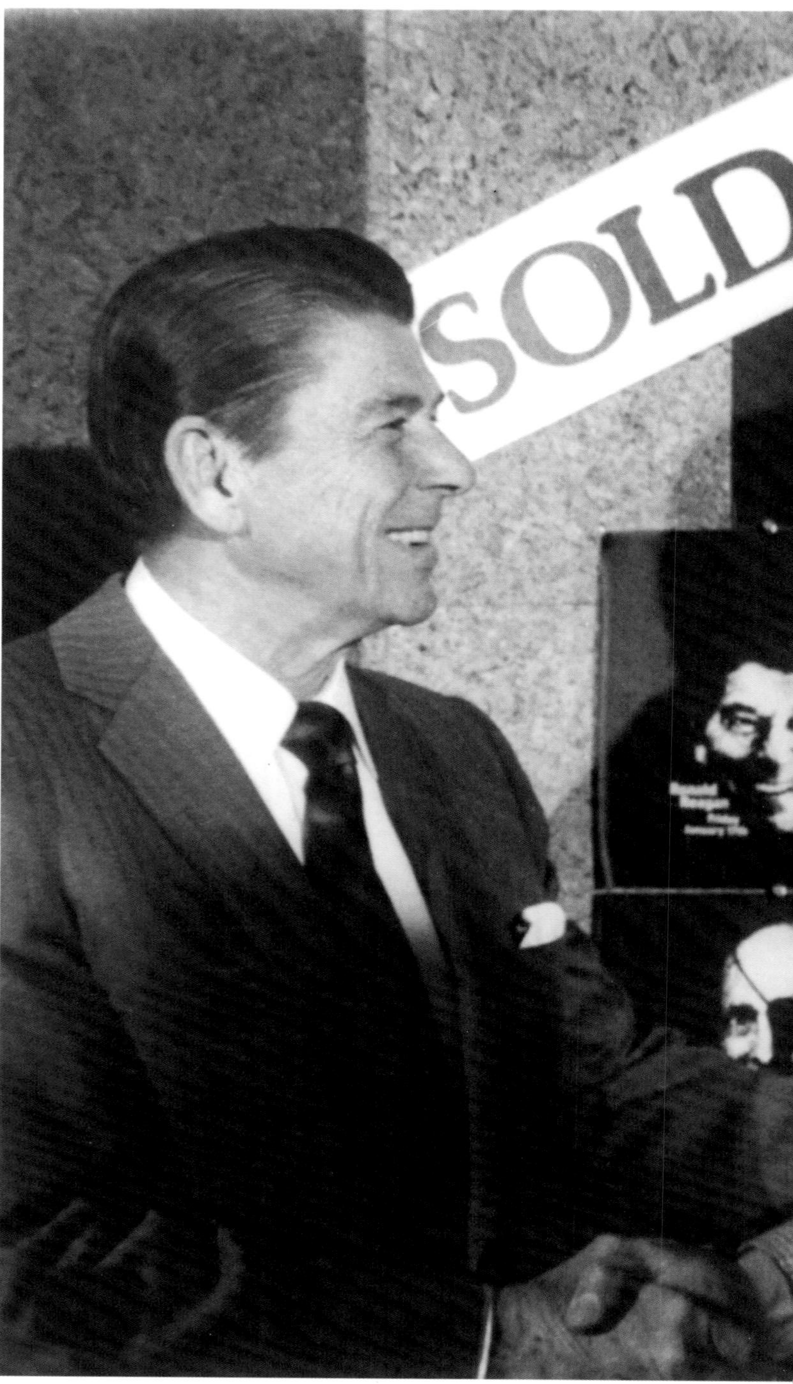

Ronald Reagan, who became the second president-to-be to appear at The Forum, talks with Ralph Krueger in front of a display trumpeting the blockbuster 1975 season, which became only the second sold-out season for the new Richmond Public Forum. The former governor of California would be elected president in 1980.

attendees. Thus it could "not come up with programs that would be vigorously received and supported by Richmonders of different orientations," she said.

Meanwhile, there could be friction between the grandiose plans advanced by Krueger and more modest ideas held by some leaders of the First Unitarian Church, which, after all, theoretically was in charge.

"Ralph was always thinking bigger, grander—what was good for The Forum," Kuhn says. "He wanted to go outside to corporations [for funding]. The church wouldn't allow it."

In May of 1974, The Forum's board met with the church's board of stewards in an unusual joint meeting prompted by criticism from within the church. Krueger and others put up a defense of The Forum, its finances, and speaker choices.

One church member suggested that a scaled-back speaker series, with lesser-known people, might be closer to Unitarian thinking and of greater interest to church members. Perhaps, but someone else noted the church had set up such in-house discussion programs the previous year—and drawn little interest. Forum President Candy Hecht (briefly holding a title usually owned by Krueger), noting the church had once staked The Forum to $500 in startup money, said The Forum would be glad to lend the church $500 if it wanted to start its own discussion series.

Despite the tension, the church board reaffirmed its support to The Forum and commended its volunteers. That bullet, at least, had been dodged.

The roller coaster went up again during the mid-1970s. The 1975 lineup had star power—Ronald Reagan, George Plimpton, Moshe Dyan and John Chancellor—and The Forum had its second sellout in twelve seasons. That was an expensive group, fees totaling $14,500.

Reagan would be the second future U.S. president to speak at The Forum, following Ford's appearance five years earlier. "To lick inflation," Reagan told the appreciative sold-out crowd, "we must undergo a recession . . . [and] a period of unemployment, though also alleviating the suffering of the less fortunate."

Three decades later, a woman who attended the Forum dinner remembered being so moved by meeting Reagan that she later worked on his presidential campaign.

"I had the opportunity to chat briefly with him," Lola Murray wrote to the editor of the *Times-Dispatch*. "As people have said, when someone was talking with Ronald Reagan, it was as if she were the only person in the world. I remember his warm smile as we talked about the Lane Sisters, football, and the movie *Brother Rat* set at VMI. I can recall his good nature and interest in our conversation. I thought, 'If this man ever runs for national office, I will vote for him.' That was how engaging he was; yet at the same time he exuded a sense of power to all those he encountered."

The next year, The Forum was able to bank money by paying only $12,000 for speakers. Of course, the lineup of Lowell Thomas, Sam Levenson, Louis Rukeyser, and a "Patriotism" panel of Jimmy Breslin, Lloyd Bucher, Victor Marchetti, and John Henry Faulk, was weaker than its predecessor. There was no sellout.

Even setting aside rising fees, however, merely scheduling speakers was becoming more difficult.

In February 1977, the executive committee was told the lineup it had been given just two months earlier for the coming season now was a no-go. Meeting notes share the reasoning: "Can't get Bishop Sheen, Mary Martin, Elliott Richardson, and Ruth refuses to deal with [the agent] on Moynihan, but will deal with Moynihan's lawyer. Still waiting for [former President] Ford, but may not get answer before Mar. 5th. Wanted to know if Ford turns us down, do we go to Moynihan now? Asa stated Andy Young might be possible."

The schedule would shift back and forth. Martin, at one time a near-certainty, would be out entirely. Sheen, a no-get, would be in. The turmoil of the season is reflected on the cover of a 1977 program booklet: One of the four programs is left blank, indicated as "still negotiating," and another promised speaker, Alex Haley—the author of the 1976 sensation, *Roots*—would abruptly cancel in what one

FORUM FILES

RALPH NADER'S TRANSPORTATION TRAVAILS

Consumer advocate Ralph Nader appeared twice at The Richmond Public Forum, in 1972 and 1980. For his first appearance, The Forum was not quite sure how to transport the speaker back to the airport. Not any car would do. Nader had famously written the best-selling book, *Unsafe at Any Speed: The Designed-In Dangers of the American Automobile,* which lambasted the American auto industry for neglecting safety.

Nader's speech was on "What Can the Consumer Do?" The Forum knew what it could do—put Nader in a solidly made foreign car. An in-house search came up with a 10-year-old Mercedes owned by Frank Kuhn, husband of Forum insider Elinor.

Solid, yes, and foreign-made, yes, but this particular Mercedes had a penchant for, sometimes, not going backwards. Tonight was such an occasion. Time after time, Frank Kuhn attempted to put the car in reverse. Time after time, with its famous passenger, the car refused the request. Finally, it obliged. Off the three headed for Byrd Field.

"Maybe," Nader suggested with more than a tad of irony,

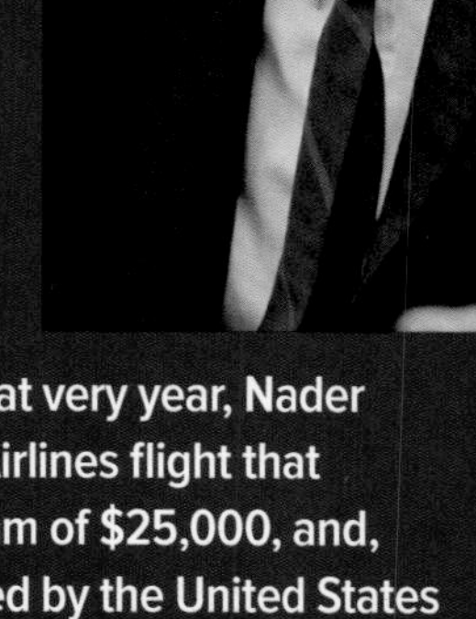

The problems were not over. The group did make it to Nader's flight with twenty minutes to spare. However, the airline captain, believing everyone was on board, had already closed the doors and prepared for an early takeoff, Elinor Kuhn recalls.

The alarm went up that a ticketed passenger named Ralph Nader—THE Ralph Nader—was attempting to get on board. The plane door was quickly opened, Nader boarded, and off the plane went.

It was, to be sure, a wise move. That very year, Nader would be "bumped" off an Allegheny Airlines flight that overbooked. He sued, won the huge sum of $25,000, and, four years later, had the ruling confirmed by the United States Supreme Court.

If there was one guy whose airline seat you didn't mess

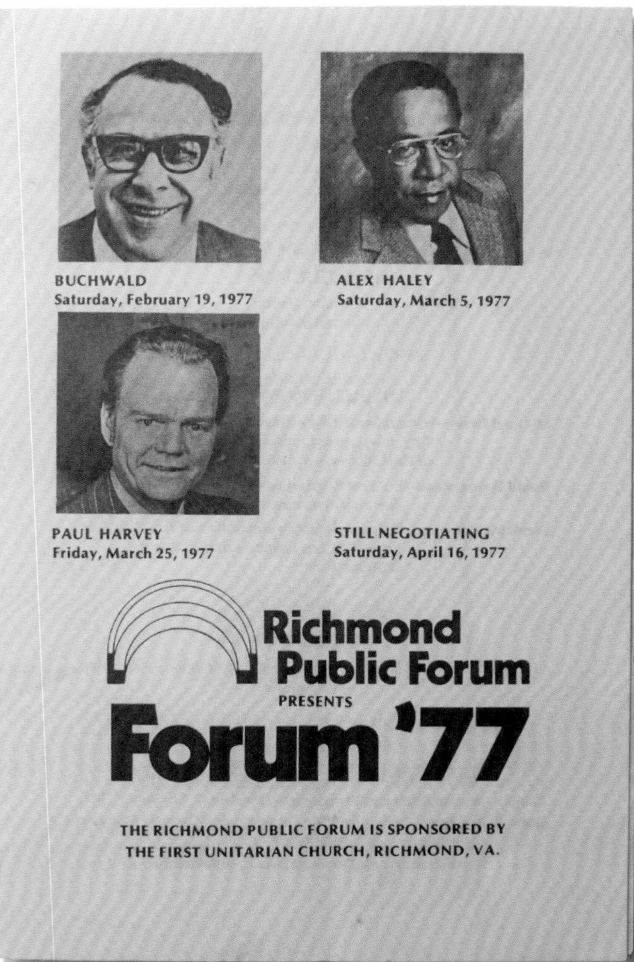

irate writer of a letter to the editor of the *Times-Dispatch* would call "a slap in the face to the directors of the Forum and to the people who purchased tickets to hear him speak."

BUCHWALD
Saturday, February 19, 1977
ALEX HALEY
Saturday, March 5, 1977
PAUL HARVEY
Friday, March 25, 1977
STILL NEGOTIATING
Saturday, April 16, 1977
Richmond Public Forum
PRESENTS
Forum '77
THE RICHMOND PUBLIC FORUM IS SPONSORED BY
THE FIRST UNITARIAN CHURCH, RICHMOND, VA.

In spite of it all, that season would prove to be The Forum's third sellout. The up-and-down Forum was riding high again.

Ed Larking of the American Program Bureau in Boston, which worked with several hundred public forums, even called Richmond's the nation's best "in terms of audience turnout and the caliber of speakers." Larkin credited the Forum leadership and public support. "You've got a great cultural resource," he told a newspaper reporter. "It's carrying on a great American tradition."

THE ROLLER COASTER WOULD DIP one last time.

For 1979, The Forum announced it would cut back on input. The promise to include only subscriber choices was tying hands. Beginning that year it would select no more than three people from the fifty-name ballots and then only if schedules allowed.

GETTING KISSINGER

The Forum has always found a few speakers impossible to "get." Sometimes they've wanted too much money. Sometimes their schedules would not allow. Sometimes they simply didn't want the gig, thank you very much.

Few were tougher to get than Henry Kissinger, the rock-star, globe-trotting diplomat. Time and time The Forum tried. Time and time the answer was no.

One prominent speaker they could get was Gerald R. Ford, the former congressman who had been appointed vice president following Spiro Agnew's resignation in 1973, then become president upon Richard Nixon's resignation in 1974. Ford spoke at The Forum in 1970, speaking passionately about "the New Federalism," returning federal money to the states, and turning welfare programs into "workfare." After leaving the White House, he accepted an invitation to return to The Forum in 1978.

What the public didn't know was that Ford's beloved wife, Betty, was having serious health problems. The Forum received a call the day before his scheduled appearance. "They said they were very sorry but Gerald Ford couldn't come," Elinor Kuhn recalls. "But in his place they had gotten Henry Kissinger."

Losing a former president was unfortunate but getting the "ungettable" Kissinger made it more than palatable. "It was a coup for us." It must not have been too bad for Kissinger, either. Eleven years later, he would return to The Forum.

Former congresswoman Barbara Jordan and baseball announcer funnyman Joe Garagiola topped those ballots. But Jordan was not tracked down and Garagiola wanted $5,000-6,000. Neither one, it would turn out, would be booked. Likewise, Watergate prosecutor Leon Jaworski and *All in the Family* star Carroll O'Connor were not available. Newsman Tom Brokaw was already committed to the Tuckahoe Woman's Club in town. Neil Simon was "sick and hard to obtain." Newscaster Hugh Downs wanted $7,000. And so on.

Ticket sales were low. At a February 22 board meeting, The Forum decided to discount tickets for seniors and students for the rest of the season. Maybe they could get someone in those seats.

The financial reckoning for 1979 was, in a word, dismal. Some $42,000 in ticket sales had been anticipated; only $21,000 came in. Revenues totaled but $26,000, while expenses, including $20,000 for speakers, totaled $37,000.

Programming was solid the next year but unspectacular. The 1980 lineup featured a return by Ralph Nader to debate nuclear power with Dr. Norman Rasmussen; advice columnist Ann Landers; *60 Minutes*' "Point-Counterpoint" speakers James J. Kilpatrick and Shana Alexander; and Watergate reporter Bob Woodward, who was to have opened the season but was shifted to the closing spot because of a snowstorm.

Ann Landers
In Person
at the
Richmond Public Forum
Sat. Apr. 12 at 8:15 p.m.
TICKETS ON SALE
AT
THE MOSQUE

Advice columnist Ann Landers knew how to grab an audience. She confessed she couldn't decide whether to discuss problems, the distinguished people of Richmond, or sex. "I decided to combine the three tonight," she said, "and talk about the sex problems of the distinguished people of Richmond."

But empty seats couldn't be ignored.

In 1980, The Forum averaged only 1,700 attendees, meaning now 2,000 seats were empty. Only $28,000 came in through ticket sales. Speakers fees alone totaled $30,000. The Forum went $17,000 deeper into the hole. There was only $3,000 left in the bank.

On September 12, 1980, Candy Hecht sent out a

Richmond Forum Short of Money

The Richmond Public Forum will collapse unless about $17,-000 is raised soon, its president said yesterday.

Candy Hecht said the forum has only about $3,000 in the bank, after covering last year's loss of about $16,000.

She said the average attendance last year was about 1,700 in the Mosque, which seats about 3,700. The crowds were relatively thin at a time when speaker fees were rising, and last year's fees for the six speakers at the four programs totaled about $30,000, she said.

amount is somewhere between $13,000 and $20,000, the forum's board "might feel secure enough to go ahead" with this season's program, but some board members were "pretty firm" about needing to have $20,000 in the bank before tickets are sold.

If programs are held, the season-ticket price is expected to be the same as last year's $15, she said.

She said the forum hasn't yet signed a contract with any speaker for this season.

The forum dates to 1934 and

The* Times-Dispatch *explained the woes after the 1980 season, which would be the last for The Richmond Public Forum.

letter to subscribers. "We repeatedly hear from those who attend The Forum that it plays a significant part in their lives. The question, perhaps, is how significant." A *Parade Magazine* story, she said, had recently noted that many speakers charge $10,000 to $15,000. "We are faced with an immediate question that only you can answer. Should we continue? It is up to you. By October 15, your Forum hopes to raise $20,000."

The answer, in a word, was no. The official announcement was made: There would be no 1981 season. The door was left open to a return in 1982 if the needed community support could be mustered.

In July 1981, however, Krueger told the *Times-Dispatch* that a return looked unlikely as "no strong sentiment had been registered when the cancellation of the 1981 [season] was announced."

Volunteers were dismayed, none more so than Krueger, but the series could not continue. The programs had been mostly first-rate, Krueger said, but the audience had not come in big enough numbers. He pulled out a theater term. "We lost 'the house,'" he said.

It had been a good idea but one that could not sustain. After seventeen seasons, the second Richmond Public Forum went dark.

FORUM FILES

BARBARA WALTERS' NO GOOD, VERY BAD DAY

Barbara Walters, the groundbreaking journalist who would become the first female co-host of *The Today Show* the next year, flew into Byrd Field for her 1973 appearance. She was to be picked up, presumably by Ralph Krueger, and driven downtown.

There were two acts of miscommunication: First, Walters' secretary forgot to inform Krueger the journalist would be flying on a private plane, meaning she would arrive at a different terminal than expected. Second, Krueger forgot to inform the secretary that he would not be the one picking up Walters.

So when Walters arrived at 4 o'clock, no one was waiting for her. When she had Krueger paged at the main terminal, no one responded.

If only this had happened in 1973: Richmond Forum volunteers greet Barbara Walters on the Richmond International Airport tarmac for her second Forum appearance, in 1991. Eighteen years earlier, no one met her.

Her trip would get no better. Walters took a cab to the John Marshall Hotel, which, as bad luck would have it, was hosting the annual Jefferson-Jackson Day Dinner. The Democratic Party's dinner doubled as a drinkfest. It was no surprise when, stepping onto an elevator, the visitor was greeted by an inebriated guest.

"You're Barbara Walters, aren't you?" he asked.

She smiled and said, "Yes."

His unsolicited observation: "You look a hell of a lot better at seven o'clock in the morning than you do right now."

Somehow, she was civil at that evening's program. "In fairness to Ms. Walters, onstage no one would have known she was having a very bad day," Krueger said later. "But backstage, every one of us felt her rage."

Nearly two decades later, in 1992, Walters would return to the new, successor Richmond Forum. "We never mentioned her first visit," Krueger said. "Neither did she."

ickets Available
Tickets Sold
Tickets Remaining
1563
1561
2
893
878
1211
624
594

CHAPTER 4

THIRD TIME THE CHARM?

RALPH KRUEGER AND THE SEEDS OF A NEW FORUM

For nearly six years, Ralph Krueger was without a professional raison d'être.

In time, friends and business acquaintances encouraged him to restart The Forum. Several would join him in throwing $50 apiece into a fund. But re-starting something that had failed financially, even while succeeding in other respects, could not be done overnight—if it could be done at all.

If anyone could lift a phoenix from the ashes, however, it was Ralph F. Krueger, Jr. His passion was not far from his talents and those were often considerable. Krueger was a jack of all trades, particularly if they related to the performing arts or simply to the art of persuasion. He was master of more than a few.

A native of Schenectady, New York, Krueger served in the Navy during World War II, graduated from Syracuse University with a degree in radio and television communications, and became a radio disc jockey early on. With his charm and deep, mellifluous voice, Krueger was a natural.

THE "DAY DREAMER SHOW"—1:00 - 4:00 P. M.
MONDAY THRU FRIDAY

Now in its fourth year, this is Niagara Falls' most listened-to afternoon radio program. The "Day Dreamer Show" is carefully planned for well-balanced good music. MC Ralph Krueger is a past master in ad libbing, poetry, passing on a thought for the day, interviewing people from every walk of life. Other features within the show include, "Pink & Blue"—"Meet the Bride" and of course news, weather and social notes. It all adds up to a very listenable and informal radio program, with the highest afternoon rating in the Niagara Falls area. Success stories, we have them daily.

Opposite: Ralph Krueger, shown here in 1990, had been a success in radio, on the stage, and especially in the advertising world. What he wanted most was a successful Forum. Above: Trumpeting Krueger's afternoon ratings, "the highest . . . in the Niagara Falls area."

In 1955, noted *The Radio Annual and Television Yearbook*, Krueger was hosting "The Day Dreamer Show" at WJJL-FM in Niagara Falls. There he played soft music from the likes of David Rose and Nat King Cole for local housewives in the afternoon. "I had three fan clubs of married women," he told the *Richmond Times-Dispatch* years later. "My first wife liked it a lot."

He moved in 1958 to Richmond and its 50,000-watt radio station, WRVA-AM. Krueger quickly took to the local stage as a part-time actor, and there he found success, too. In a 1958 production of George Bernard Shaw's *Major Barbara* at the Virginia Museum Theater, *Times-Dispatch* reviewer Edith Lindeman called the thirty-two-year-old Krueger "a comedy find."

Ralph Krueger (center) backstage in the 1963 Virginia Museum Theater production of Teahouse of the August Moon.

Meanwhile, at WRVA, he moved from on-air to the advertising side of the business. There, too, he was a natural. In time, he started Krueger Creative Services, winning local awards and a national Clio Award. He became known for company jingles, being sought out across the country for his expertise. He created Sears commercials, in which customers, live, tried to start a lawn mower, with the slogan "Starts first time, almost every time"—the "almost" apparently being a necessary caveat. He did voice work for local companies' commercials, as well, including Best Products, Two Wheel Travel, and the Great Big Greenhouse and Nursery—the last with a young copywriter and broadcast producer who would one day lead The Forum himself, Bill Chapman.

And, of course, in 1964, Krueger had begun The Richmond Public Forum with the help of other volunteers from the Unitarian Church. The Forum, everyone agreed, had been his true love. It still was.

But he had started it once—and lost it.

Could it be started again?

IN THE FALL OF 1985, Krueger and others held exploratory meetings, conducted a "feasibility study" and declared Richmond was ready for a new Forum.

The Forum had to be big, of course. And Krueger was not about to be hindered by the same funding limitations. Operating independently of the Unitarian Church would allow him to seek the corporate help he believed essential to bringing in big-name speakers.

In January 1986, the group incorporated as The Richmond Metropolitan Forum, though that name would be changed to The Richmond Forum, Inc., just ten months later. This version would no longer be The Richmond Public Forum, as the two previous enterprises had been. It would be simply The Richmond Forum.

The old Forum council, consisting of a number of members of the new Forum, met in April 1986 at the First Unitarian Church to vote to turn over assets—$9,300 in cash, plus two lecterns, six tables, backdrop props, and the Forum symbol. The new Forum would get the cash once it had received at least $25,000 in pledges, reserved an auditorium, and contracted with at least one speaker. It would get the furniture simply by hauling it away.

Krueger and others went to local companies, getting them to sign on as sponsors. The question he once could not answer—"what's a forum?"—was now his way into a sales pitch, thanks to his previous experience:

"What's a forum? . . . It's the news with Chet Huntley, Walter Cronkite, David Brinkley or Harry Reasoner. It's people who care about people with Harry Golden, Dr. Erich Fromm and Margaret Meade. It's history with Arnold Toynbee, the court with William Douglas, the war with General Maxwell Taylor, peace with Norman Cousins, politics with Barry Goldwater and Ronald Reagan, laughing with Henry Morgan, George Jessel, Dick Gregory, Roger Price and Dave Garroway, all on one

COMMONWEALTH of VIRGINIA

Office of the Governor
Richmond 23219

Gerald L. Baliles
Governor

May 30,1986

Mr. Lee Iacocca
Chief Executive Officer
Chrysler Corporation
P. O. Box 1919
Detroit, Michigan 48288

Dear Mr. Iacocca:

I understand that representatives of the Richmond Forum have contacted you concerning participation in the first Forum program of the season in January, 1987. As Honorary Chairman of the Richmond Forum, I join in their invitation to you to come to Richmond to participate as the featured speaker. It would be my privilege at that time to present you with the Forum's Golden Gavel Award.

For many years the Richmond Forum has been a vital part of a very vibrant community. Your presence at the season's premier would add greatly to the Forum, and give Virginia's capital the opportunity to acknowledge the many achievements of your professional life, and give you an opportunity to see one of America's truly outstanding cities.

I encourage you to accept the Forum's invitation.

With kindest regards, I am

Sincerely,

Gerald L. Baliles

GLB:rmf

"We never had the governor helping," Ralph Krueger said, in explaining one reason the new Forum would succeed. Virginia Governor Gerald L. Baliles (above) did help—but even he couldn't persuade automaker Lee Iacocca to be the first speaker.

program. It's science with Wernher von Braun, love with Dr. Joyce Brothers and Joe Namath, sex with Masters and Johnson and Mary Calderone, foreign affairs with Henry Kissinger and Arthur Schlessinger. It's religion with Archbishop Fulton J. Sheen. It's the world in four nights."

A typical fundraising letter, as it went out over the signature of the new Forum's sales vice president, Phillip G. Perkins, greeted local businesses:

"It is with tremendous pleasure that I announce the return of Richmond's very successful Forum. You may remember that for 17 years, The Richmond Public Forum was lauded as the premier program of its type in the United States. . . . Reborn as The Richmond Metropolitan Forum, the new organization is headed up by its founder and current President, Ralph Krueger. . . . As originally conceived, Ralph envisioned The Forum as 'a gift to Richmond' given in the truest spirit of community sharing."

Commitments began to come in, enough, at least, to consider a restart plausible.

Lorna Wyckoff, then publisher of the *Style Weekly* arts publication, remembers "I went on a whim to the Unitarian Church" and met with the group. "The big problem would be money," she remembers. "This was the most auspicious thing that ever happened to me." The timing was perfect: coincidentally, she had a meeting scheduled the following week with the head of the city's Retail Merchants Association. The association, a non-profit, had recently sold its for-profit credit bureau and had money on hand. "Jeff [Smith] wanted Richmond to have a forum for conversation about international affairs; I heard this from him and connected him with Ralph Krueger." The agency's board approved a $25,000 gift and the new Forum had a major sponsor.

Corporate support was important, but political support wouldn't hurt. On May 12, 1986, The Forum sent a letter to Virginia's governor, Gerald L. Baliles, asking him to be The Forum's honorary chairman—and, oh, by the way, could the governor contact Lee Iacocca and ask him to be the leadoff speaker in 1987?

The Forum had secured Diane Sawyer and Hodding Carter for later panels. But it wanted the legendary automaker Iacocca to make an opening night splash. When the Forum board met two days later, however, it recognized Iacocca was no sure thing. "Ruth McDonough suggested Ted Koppel as an alternative to Lee Iacocca, if he should turn us down," say minutes of the meeting.

The Forum wrote Iacocca on May 28, inviting him and promising him both the chance to present the first-place award for a statewide high school essay contest—and to receive the first "Golden Gavel Award," which, of course, did not yet exist. Two days later, Governor Baliles also wrote, promising to present Iacocca the Golden Gavel award himself.

Good enough. With money, a start on speakers and the governor himself, the new Forum was ready to announce its restart.

A corporate and individual fundraising drive officially kicked off June 5, 1986, and the next day's *Times-Dispatch* announced "Speakers' forum revived in Richmond."

The article recounted the two previous forums and their closings. Krueger attributed the 1980 closing to three years of losing money and a recession. "We weren't the only thing that went down: forums all over the country went down. We lasted longer than most," he said. But Krueger laid the financial losses on The Forum's choices, as well. "We were unable to get a lot of the people we wanted. . . . We went along conventional lines to get them." This time, other ways would be tried, including going directly to speakers, rather than through agencies. "We never had the governor helping us before," he added.

Ticket prices would necessarily be higher. Speakers who wanted $5,000 in 1980 now wanted $25,000, Krueger said. Corporations would be helping, though.

Despite the Governor's help, Iacocca would turn down the invitation. Thus in November, less than two months before the kickoff, there still was no commitment from anyone for the important leadoff spot. Internal memos said newsman Peter Jennings was the tentative speaker.

By December, the speaker for January had been confirmed—not Iacocca, not Jennings, but Koppel. The budget was set, too. Season memberships would cost thirty dollars, triple what the old ones had been. Selling 2,500 memberships would bring in $75,000. The all-important sponsors were adding $140,000. That would balance the budget at $226,000–even including whopping speakers' fees totaling $110,000.

The Richmond Forum was a go.

RICHMOND
FORUM
Post Office Box 14687
Richmond, Va. 23221

Unitarians, Oil Men, Neighbors, Friends and Members of our audience:

For some of you, tonight is first night. But for many of us, tonight is the continuation of a 17 year history.

We recall January of '64, the Mosque stage. The speaker Chet Huntley. That was our beginning. Known then as the Richmond Public Forum it was the Forum that presented Henry Kissinger, Shirley Chisholm, Ronald Reagan, Shana Alexander, Gerald Ford, Harry Golden and Moshe Dayan.

The New York Times declared it the largest Forum in the country. It often filled the Mosque.

And as we reopen tonight we thank those Unitarians who nurtured the dream and gave it life for 17 years. To Asa, Mort, Doug, Elinor and Ruth thank you for the past, thank you for the present and future as well.

...kfast group of friends who said "have you ever ...he Forum?" They were the Oil Men. For their ...

FORUM FILES

THE OILMEN'S ASSOCIATION

In the mid-1980s, small business networking clubs, sometimes called "tips clubs," often met to share ideas, information and even prospects. One Richmond group, which gathered at Aunt Sarah's restaurant on Midlothian Turnpike, took on the name "The Oilmen's Association" for fun. It even created a logo with a gushing oil well.

The "oilmen" included software consultant Phil Perkins, stockbroker Paul O'Donnell, corporate-chaplain-to-be Mark Cress, moving company founder Vaughn Dunnavant, realtor David Jefferson, architect Tom Gresham—and Ralph Krueger.

"Ralph's stories were long-winded and filled with references to notable people he knew and/or befriended in the past," Perkins says now. "He counted Benjamin Netanyahu as a close friend and regaled us with stories about public figures such as Art Buchwald and Diane Sawyer."

There was something about Krueger and those stories, however. "He waxed particularly poetic when talking about the glory days of The Richmond Public Forum," Perkins says. "We were all impressed with the lineup of politicians, people from the entertainment business and world leaders that Ralph and his team had convinced to become part of the program."

The thought began to take hold: Could The Forum be revived?

"It wasn't an easy sell to say the least. In fact, Ralph vigorously opposed the idea because of the long hours and dedication needed to make it all work," Perkins says. "Ralph finally agreed but on one very big condition: The Oilmen's Association had to become the first board of directors for the new Richmond Forum, or at least form the core. Most of us agreed, some less enthusiastically than others."

Perkins took on the lead role of soliciting corporate funding, meaning he contacted such local companies as Thalhimers Department Stores and S&K Famous Brands. "I particularly remember meeting with Stuart Siegel, chairman of S&K at the time, in his well-appointed office, and successfully convincing him to support our new endeavor," Perkins says. "I recall that he was extremely happy that the Forum would return, as were many of the business owners and executives."

CHAPTER 5

REINVENTING THE FORUM

THE KRUEGER YEARS OF THE RICHMOND FORUM: 1987–1993

A week before the opener, the *Richmond Times-Dispatch,* under the headline "Welcome Back," editorialized: "For those who mourned the demise of The Richmond Public Forum in 1980, the organization's resurrection is splendid news. During the 17 years of its previous existence, it enlivened, enlightened and, at times, enraged the city with provocative programs featuring distinguished political leaders, journalists, authors, entertainers, social commentators and speakers from many other fields. Now, as [The] Richmond Forum, it intends to follow the same format."

The next day's newspapers ran the first of a series of clever Forum advertisements, most prepared by Barbara Fitzgerald, who, like Krueger, had come from the advertising world: "Within 6 days, an event will occur in Richmond, Va., that will have the national news media descending upon this city." Beneath were pictured Ted Koppel, Paul Duke, Diane Sawyer, and Charles Kuralt—all speakers or questioners for the season's four programs.

On January 24, 1987, the stage was relit.

The Richmond Forum was underway.

Former U.S. Ambassador to the United Nations Jeane Kirkpatrick (closest), television newsman Marvin Kalb (center), and Soviet journalist Vladimir Pozner, seen from the theater wings, February 20, 1988.

Within 6 days an event will occur in Richmond, Va., that will have the national news media descending upon this city.

The event is the return of the Richmond Forum, bringing with it for the 1987 Season the people who make the news and the people who make it fascinating. They'll all be here to talk, to interview, to alert us, to entertain us. And to answer questions from you the audience.

On opening night, January 24, the Retail Merchants Association of Greater Richmond presents Ted Koppel, sharing stories and insights about the news and the newsmakers.

On February 21, Philip Morris presents Paul Duke, moderating a discussion on "Iran Yesterday, Iran Today." Panelists will be Robert C. McFarlane, former Assistant to the President for National Security Affairs, and Hodding Carter, a prominent member of the Carter Administration and a respected journalist himself.

On March 7, Colonial Savings and Loan will present Diane Sawyer in a "60 Minutes" format, interviewing Tip O'Neill, followed, of course, by a session in which the audience can interview them both.

And on March 27, Charles Kuralt offers views on the New South, as seen from the perspective of a man "On the Road."

It all adds up to four fascinating evenings unlike any other entertainment you'll find in the city. Season tickets for all four programs are $30 and are available at the Mosque. Or mail check to Richmond Forum, P.O. Box 14687, Richmond 23221. For further information call 254-3255.

There were opening-night kinks backstage. "Nobody knew what they were doing. There was a lot of running around," Lorna Wyckoff, the evening's moderator, remembers. "The stage manager sent me out on stage before I was introduced."

No matter. Onstage, Ralph Krueger welcomed the audience and let it be known that private and corporate donations had brought costs within reach. Season tickets would have cost more than $100. "Because of their gifts," he said, "your tickets were $75 cheaper."

Ted Koppel, award-winning anchor of ABC News' *Nightline*, had the audience howling with laughter, both the *Richmond Times-Dispatch* and *The Richmond News Leader* would report. His first words onstage, "I am delighted to be able to have this opportunity to be here tonight," were delivered in a dead-on impersonation of Henry Kissinger. He used his best Richard Nixon voice to relay the president's remarks when asked his opinion of the Great Wall of China: "One can only say, upon looking at this wall, that it is truly a great wall."

That led to Koppel's "It's a Grand Old Flag" parody regaling the Wall, which he and other correspondents had drafted in 1973 in China:

It's a grand old wall, it's a long-standing wall,
Wins the prize for its size and its age.
It gave just rewards to the Mongol hordes,
Drove the Kulaks away in the raid.
From Beijing to the seas, it has saved the Chinese,
Till the days of the Kuomintang.
From Ming to Han, and on and on
With the Great Wall, you can't go wrong.

The new incarnation of The Richmond Forum kicks off January 24, 1987, trumpeted by advertisements (above), and the Mosque theater marquee (next page), and welcoming remarks by Virginia Governor Gerald L. Baliles (program format, next page). Forum President Ralph F. Krueger, Jr., (above) introduces the evening's featured speaker, ABC anchorman Ted Koppel (right).

Format
Ted Koppel
The Richmond Re-Opening Night Forum
January 24th., 1987

The Forum featuring ABC Anchorman Ted Koppel makes use of one pa
and a moderator. Their interplay with the featured speaker and the
outline for part one is included with this format.

STAGE SETTING PART ONE

As the audience enters the Mosque the curtain is drawn. In fron
of the curtain are two podiums. One at stage right, a second at st
center.

OPENING REMARKS

At curtain time the President (Ralph Krueger) comes on stage and
to the podium at stage right. He greets the audience, informs them
the evening is made possible by a grant from the Retail Merchants
Association of Greater Richmond and C & P and introduces the Govern
the Forum's Honorary Chairman of the Board.

THE GOVERNOR

The Governor enters through the curtains at center and moves to
center podium.

Governor Baliles will extend a welcome to the audience on behalf
the state and welcome the Forum's return to Richmond. At the conclu
of his remarks he'll return the program to the President. And leave
stage.

INTRODUCTION OF MR. KOPPEL

Mr. Koppel will be introduced by the President of the Forum.

THE SPEAKER MR. KOPPEL

Upon introduction Mr. Koppel enters from center curtain and moves
to his podium at center stage and begins his 45 minute address.

At the conclusion of his remarks he returns the program to Mr. Kr
and leaves stage. NOTE: Historically the audience will call you ba
a curtain call.

CLOSING REMARKS, PART ONE

Before dismissing the audience the President reminds them to regis
to vote for next season's speakers, to write questions to Mr. Koppel,
to convert singles to seasons if they choose.

Audience dismissed for 15 minutes.

DIANE SAWYER AND THE SOUND MAN

"Acoustically perfect" was the description marketing people laid onto the Forum's home, the 1932 auditorium known as The Mosque. The Mosque was indeed a beautiful civic treasure. But even with expensive microphones and speakers, in truth, it often fell short of acoustic perfection.

Still those imperfections couldn't explain the weird squawkings that emanated from newswoman Diane Sawyer's microphone on March 7, 1987, the third night of The Richmond Forum's inaugural year. Sawyer, a correspondent on CBS News' *60 Minutes*—and later to become an anchor with ABC News—was to interview Brent Scowcroft on the Tower Commission's findings about the Iran-Contra scandal.

Instead, only these strange electronic noises were audible. Sawyer looked over at Ralph Krueger, standing backstage, with a "What can I do?" gesture. Krueger rushed to the sound booth at the back of the auditorium. He opened the door in time to hear the sound man say: "She's sitting on it!"

"On what?"

"The transmitter." Apparently it had slipped down behind Sawyer on the chair. "I'll solve it!"

And with that, the sound man dashed from the booth. He strode onto the stage, went right to Sawyer's chair and adjusted the transmitter at her rear.

Sawyer's microphone had also slipped, however—inside her sweater top.

The game audio man went after that, as well.

Sawyer, nonplussed, interjected. "I don't know who this man is," she said in what may have become the Forum's greatest ad-lib. "But I can assure you what he's doing, my mother wouldn't approve." ❞

Diane Sawyer interviewing Brent Scowcroft on March 7, 1987.

IN 13 YEARS "ON THE ROAD," CHARLES KURALT HAS TALKED TO SOME OF THE STRANGEST PEOPLE IN AMERICA.

NOW IT'S YOUR TURN.

The man who's heard it all will be telling it all on stage at the Mosque Friday, March 27. That is the evening Charles Kuralt will close out the Richmond Forum's 1987 Season with a lively look at "The New South."

Kuralt, whose encounters "On the Road" were a regular feature of "60 Minutes" for more than a decade, is now the host of "CBS News Sunday Morning." He has also authored a recent book, *Southerners: Portrait of a People.*

Tickets are $12 each at the Mosque and all Mosque outlets. Charge to MasterCard or VISA by calling 780-4213.

For further information call the Forum at 254-3255.

CBS On the Road *newsman Charles Kuralt wrapped up the first season in April 1987.*

The levity gave way to Koppel's stinging remarks about American "mediocrity." He criticized business, medicine and especially politics: "We've encouraged the displacement of thoughtfulness by the cult of the cliché." But he was toughest on his own profession: "overestimated, overexposed, overpaid." Koppel said he was among those partially responsible for America's "becoming a nation of electronic voyeurs [whose] capacity for dialogue is becoming a faded memory."

The night had gone well. Though drawing but 2,000 people again, the same attendance that had helped doom The Richmond Public Forum, the ballyhooed first program kicked off an inaugural season that would prove a success.

After the season concluded, Krueger assessed the start-up. His report to his board of directors was not falsely modest:

"We did it. We started with absolutely nothing but a talented group of committed people—people who said they'd make it happen. And they raised nearly $216,000, presented four noteworthy Forum programs with nationally prominent personalities, were mentioned by many of the country's leading newspapers, and tackled the major issues of Iran, freedom of the press, and the Tower Commission. The program attracted a house in excess of two thousand nightly, and to the best of my knowledge, the new Richmond Forum was universally welcomed.

"The doubters—we were told with today's speakers fees, the new forum would never make it. We were told there was no need. No one would come. We were told that corporations wouldn't care and that a five-hundred-dollar donation was all we could expect.

"Of course, the doubters were wrong. The community cared, the corporations cared. And we all cared together. And I thank all of you for caring."

Krueger said The Forum had reinvented its approach. Advertising costs were slashed through in-kind contributions—ad space or air time received in exchange for dinners and tickets. Speaker contacts were divided up: ad man Lee Mumford lined up Diane Sawyer; former newspaper man and political aide Andy McCutcheon connected with Paul Duke; and Krueger himself, Charles Kuralt. Going out and selling tickets

IF YOU'VE GOT TICKETS TO SEE OPRAH WINFREY THIS SATURDAY NIGHT, PLEASE PLAN TO ARRIVE A LITTLE LATE.
THE MOSQUE THEATRE
RICHMOND • VIRGINIA
RICHMOND FORUM PRESENTS
OPRAH WINFREY
SAT JAN 23 1988
LIKE ON SUNDAY.
Because of a change in her filming schedule, Oprah's appearance at the Richmond Forum has been delayed for 24 hours. She will now be here on Sunday, January 24, instead of Saturday, January 23. Everything else stays the same. The time is still 8 p.m., the place is still the Mosque, the sponsor is still the Retail Merchants Association, and Oprah is still the hottest ticket in town.
There's still time to call the Mosque Box Office (780-4213) to reserve your seat for Oprah and the rest of this exciting 1988 Forum Season. Saturday, February 20, is the date of the Great Debate between Jeane Kirkpatrick and Vladimir Posner, with Marvin Kalb as referee. On Friday, March 11, George Will comes to town; and Friday, April 29, will mark the triumphant return of Art Buchwald. Season tickets are $30, single shows $15. Call today – with this great a lineup, there's always the danger of being *too* late.
The Richmond FORUM

Oprah Winfrey's 1988 appearance, moved to a Sunday for her filming schedule, still stands as one of fewer than a handful of Richmond Forum programs held on a day other than Saturday. She was worth the wait, regaling the audience with personal stories, including how she faked a break-in when she was thirteen. Right: Winfrey with Forum President Ralph Krueger outside The Jefferson Hotel. Opposite: Winfrey waits backstage at the Mosque.

to attendees, rather than being the domain of Unitarians, was accomplished through advertising and strong programs. "We learned they'd come to us," Krueger said.

Some found Krueger's ego, while important for the growth of The Forum, off-putting. Even old friends like Elinor Kuhn were not always immune. On one occasion, she recalls, "I said, 'Ralph, you can't have everything your own way.' He said, 'Do you want to be on this committee or not?'"

The Oilmen's Association, a networking group of business friends who had persuaded him to restart The Forum, was re-thinking its involvement. Krueger's earlier co-workers "knew exactly what to expect in terms of the approach that would be taken as things ramped up," Phillip G. Perkins says. "The rest of us had no idea."

Their enthusiasm was high—initially. "I have to say that Ralph was a strict taskmaster and wouldn't hesitate to raise his voice and be accusatory during board meetings," Perkins says. "No one ever worked hard enough to suit him and he let us know it." Business professionals didn't like it. Several resigned. Perkins stayed longer but left when his company promoted him.

Give Krueger credit, however, Perkins says.

"I must admit I was excited and just a bit proud when The Richmond Forum took off and again became a success," he says. "For all his ranting and raving, Ralph had done it again. You might disagree with his approach, but you certainly had to appreciate the importance of the culture he brought to our city."

SEASON TWO BEGAN with one of America's biggest names: Oprah Winfrey. The program was delayed because of a change in her filming schedule. The Forum quickly advertised, showing an original ticket for Saturday, January 23, 1988, but suggesting: "If You've Got Tickets to See Oprah Winfrey This Saturday Night, Please Plan to Arrive a Little Late. . . . Like on Sunday."

Oprah—as everyone called her—had begun *The Oprah Winfrey Show* just two years earlier. The nationally

syndicated talk show would run for twenty-five years and become the highest rated of its kind in television history. She stood atop every public opinion poll.

Still, Barbara Fitzgerald remembers Oprah as being without pretension, before the show and during. "She said, 'I know I'm late, but please wait. I've got to pee.' I loved her show. She did lots of readings from other women."

For her introduction, Krueger called to Hawaii for help. Live, over the Mosque loudspeaker, came the famous voice of actress/comedienne Carol Burnett. Burnett was a fan, too. Oprah, she said, was smart, inquisitive, and funny.

Oprah talked about her beginnings in poverty, her spiritual beliefs, highs and lows, a TV station's efforts to change her looks, her weight battles—"I diet for a hobby," she said—and the price of fame.

The evening included an extended Q&A. One questioner wanted to know how Oprah could separate herself from the show. "I don't. The show is like a social service agency. I do carry it around. It's very hard not to."

To another questioner, she said she didn't study to be an actress. She simply believed she could be one. When she was thirteen, she wanted a new pair of glasses that her mother said they could not afford. So young Oprah staged a fake burglary, knocking things off her home's tables and breaking her glasses. She told police that not only had there been a break-in, but she now had

CAR TALK

After dinner, Forum speakers and a few others usually are driven to the auditorium in a limousine. The trip is a chance to share small talk. Some speakers get their thoughts together or steel themselves for the evening's appearance.

But the trips can be revealing in themselves.

When NBC News anchor John Chancellor and former Secretary of State Henry Kissinger rode together to The Richmond Forum in 1989, the newsman got in a little needle. Kissinger mentioned what he thought had been an unforgivable trick played on him by interviewer David Frost. "Tell me what it is," Chancellor said, "and I'll try it tonight to see if it works in Richmond."

Conservative columnist William F. Buckley Jr. and liberal congressman Charles Rangel appeared onstage on 1989, a month after Chancellor and Kissinger. Attendees might well have concluded that Buckley and Rangel hated each other. Certainly, they were worlds apart ideologically. But in the limo, Buckley revealed it was not an all-consuming hatred.

"Charlie, my wife sends her regards and affections," Buckley said, though adding, "Now that's the last nice thing I'm going to say to you tonight."

DUE TO THE VOLATILE PERSONALITIES APPEARING ON OUR STAGE THIS YEAR THE RICHMOND FORUM IS REQUESTING THAT THERE BE NO FINGER-POINTING, SABRE-RATTLING, PERSONAL ATTACKS, NAME-CALLING, SHOUTING, OR OTHER OVERT SIGNS OF HOSTILITY.

Sam Donaldson, February 3
Sponsored by the Retail Merchants Association of Greater Richmond

Dr. Henry Kissinger & John Chancellor, February 25
Sponsored by Philip Morris USA

William F. Buckley & Rep. Charles B. Rangel, March 25

Dr. Carl Sagan, April 22
Sponsored by C&P Telephone

IT IS ALSO REQUESTED THAT MEMBERS OF THE AUDIENCE ABIDE BY THESE SAME RULES.

Season tickets are now on sale at the Mosque Box Office, 780-4213.

THE RICHMOND FORUM

Forum advertising played up the potential combustibility of the 1989 speakers, with a wink to the audience. Top: Henry Kissinger responds to a question from newsman John Chancellor.

amnesia, too. It was an audacious performance. What followed was a pleasant afternoon at the hospital with concerned doctors and doting nurses. "This is great," she thought. "This is for me."

Oprah, a coup for The Forum, had not been on the original 1988 schedule. But scheduling, as always, was subject to availability and fees of popular speakers. Often enough, The Forum found itself scrambling to nail down contracts with speakers it thought would appear.

In July 1987, for instance, the Forum executive council was told the 1988 season was tentatively set: Alan Alda; Carl Sagan; Barbara Walters and Jimmy Carter; and George Will. It was an impressive lineup.

It also didn't materialize. Alda and Sagan both declined soon afterward. Indeed, only Will would actually appear in 1988, though Sagan would appear the next year. Walters took the Forum stage in 1991–92. Alda, however, would not be booked for another 27 years—for the 30th anniversary season of 2015–16. Carter never did appear at The Forum, though his immediate predecessor and four successors in the Oval Office all did, either before or after being president.

Still, The Forum was gaining strength. Some 3,299 people came to listen to newsman Sam Donaldson kick off the 1989 season. "He was the most nervous backstage guy I've ever seen," Krueger said of Donaldson.

Sagan's 1989 visit attracted attention. His was an early warning about what would come to be called climate change, as well as other man-made threats, the type of discussion The Forum prided itself on being able to share early. Sagan, astronomer and host of the popular *Cosmos* series, heralded technology. But advances can come with problems, he said, citing a handful, including the burning of fossil fuels that create a "greenhouse

ABC's assertive newsman Sam Donaldson (above) bragged onstage that he was "blessed with a voice that will pierce your ears." Backstage, he was surprisingly nervous. Astronomer and TV host Carl Sagan (above right) was entertaining while delivering early warnings.

effect" and could flood coastal areas and destroy farmland, as well as chlorofluorocarbons from aerosol cans that destroy the ozone level and threaten the food chain. They require worldwide action, Sagan said. It would be a decade or more before others would echo his warnings.

In March 1990, legendary *60 Minutes* newsman Mike Wallace defended his program's controversial journalistic practices of misrepresentation and hidden cameras. "Obviously, you can't just walk in and ask the man if he's a charlatan."

Wallace, who had a reputation as a tough interviewer, had the tables turned during the Q&A. One audience member asked if *60 Minutes* wouldn't be the first to go after a business that played by those rules. "It's a difficult position to take . . . in public," Wallace conceded. His defense: Such approaches are "always an effort to find out some information we can't otherwise."

AFTER THAT SEASON, The Forum was on strong enough footing to announce a fifth program would be added to the standard four each year. The Forum year would now start in November.

Thus the 1990–91 season began in November 1990 with German Chancellor Helmut Schmidt. The season also would include H. Ross Perot, Art Buchwald and Andy Rooney, and all-star panels on the military and space.

"Not too shabby," Krueger offered to *New Age* magazine shortly before the season, "but expensive as hell."

He seemed not to be bothered. "What we've attempted to do, and apparently are getting a reputation for doing, is going first class," Krueger told the magazine. "In every way that we can, we attempt to bring the best people that we can bring." He loved doing that. "I have the most exciting job in the world. I love it. It's a dream come true."

Volunteers felt that way, too. Margaret Pace joined The Richmond Forum in 1991 as assistant to the president,

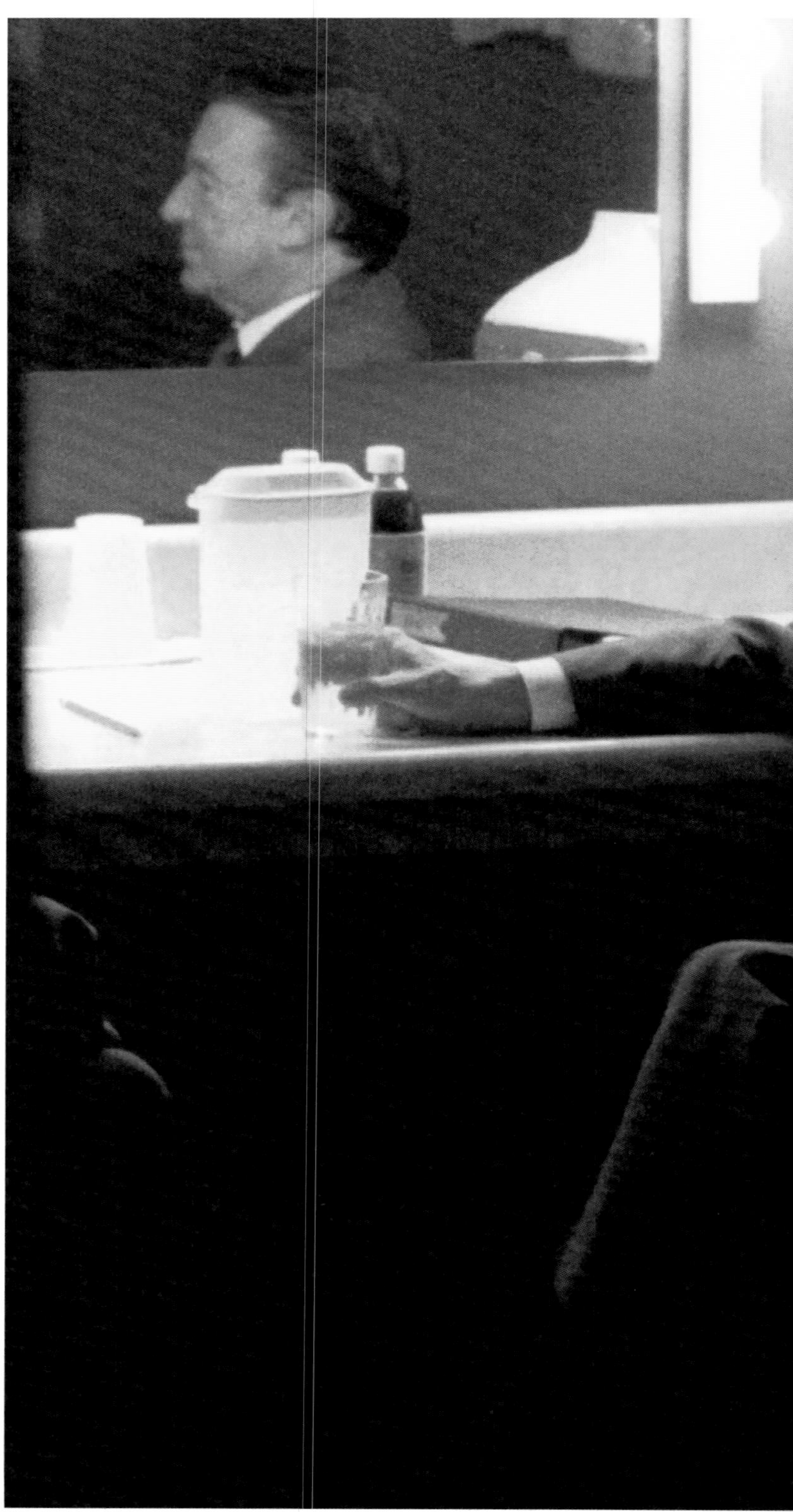

60 Minutes ***newsman Mike Wallace relaxes in the "green room" of the Mosque in March 1990. Wallace had been scheduled for January but became ill. The rescheduling, or date "reversal," resulted in what was probably the most confusing ad in Forum history—at least for anyone without a mirror.***

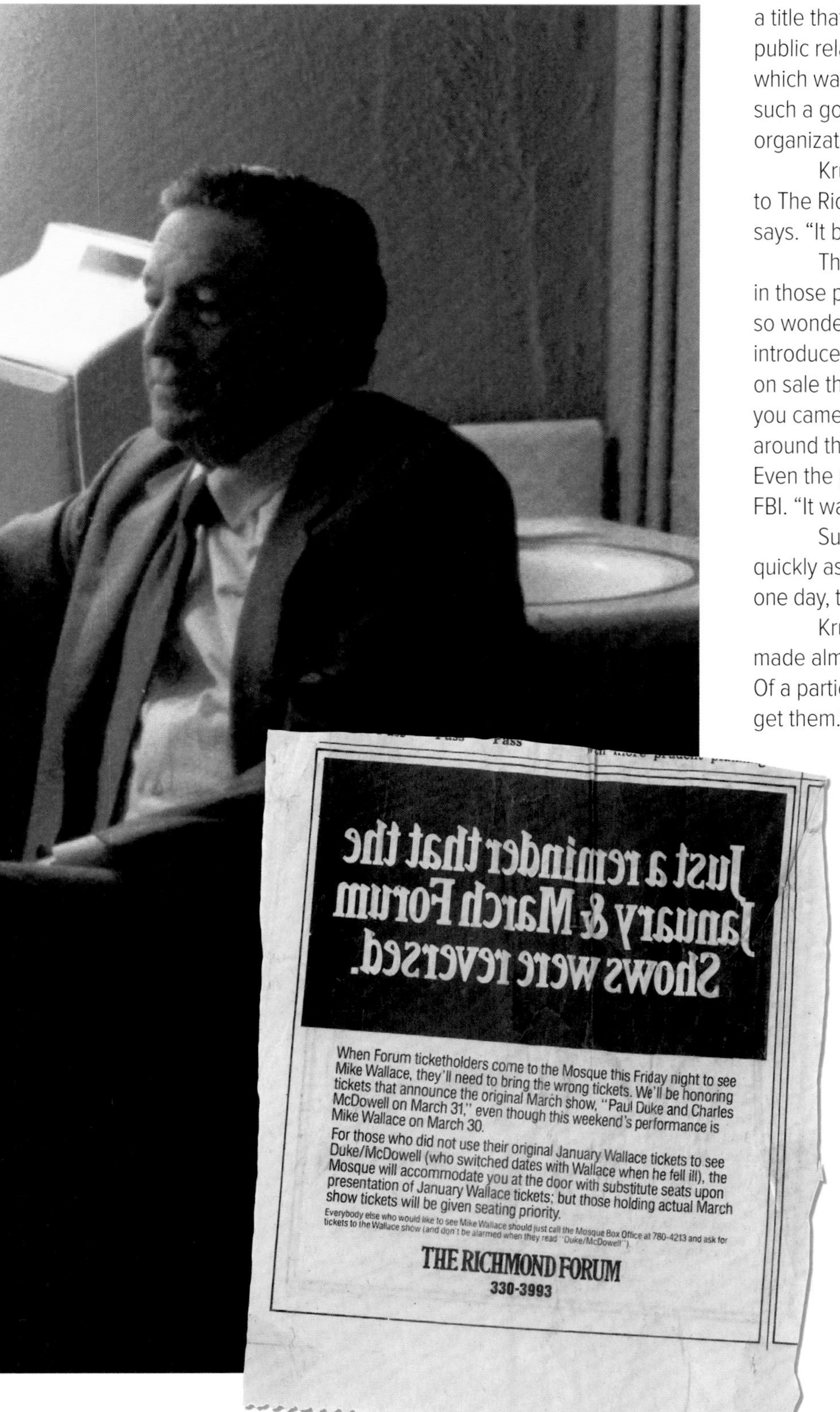

Just a reminder that the January & March Forum Shows were reversed.

When Forum ticketholders come to the Mosque this Friday night to see Mike Wallace, they'll need to bring the wrong tickets. We'll be honoring tickets that announce the original March show, "Paul Duke and Charles McDowell on March 31," even though this weekend's performance is Mike Wallace on March 30.

For those who did not use their original January Wallace tickets to see Duke/McDowell (who switched dates with Wallace when he fell ill), the Mosque will accommodate you at the door with substitute seats upon presentation of January Wallace tickets; but those holding actual March show tickets will be given seating priority.

Everybody else who would like to see Mike Wallace should just call the Mosque Box Office at 780-4213 and ask for tickets to the Wallace show (and don't be alarmed when they read "Duke/McDowell").

THE RICHMOND FORUM

330-3993

a title that shortly became director of development and public relations. "I was brought on to help raise funds, which was easy," Pace says. "Everyone loved it, it was such a good program. It was such a community volunteer organization."

Krueger had a name for it. "He would always refer to The Richmond Forum as YOUR Richmond Forum," Pace says. "It belonged to the city of Richmond."

That was especially so when tickets went on sale in those pre-Internet days. Everyone pitched in. "It was so wonderful when tickets would go on sale. Ralph would introduce a slate of speakers in April. Tickets would go on sale that [following] Monday. In the morning, when you came in, people were standing in a line that wrapped around the building." Volunteers were answering phones. Even the police were volunteers, Pace says, and even the FBI. "It was such a great thing to be involved with."

Susan Rekowski was another volunteer who quickly assumed other duties. "I was sorting ZIP codes one day, the next I'm in development meetings," she says.

Krueger, whom she calls "a fantastic mentor," made almost a game out of the duties, Rekowski says. Of a particular investment firm, "Ralph said, 'You'll never get them.'" Rekowski did, of course. Down the road, that would be invaluable. "Ralph got sick," she says. "I raised a lot to keep The Forum going."

Corporate and community support weren't always enough, however. A few Forum positions, including Krueger's, had become salaried over time. The bigger financial issue, however, was the continuing increase in fees for top-name speakers.

Several years, The Forum ran deficits. Some board members complained Krueger kept the financial books at home and his projections didn't always materialize: a speaker proposed at $50,000 might actually end up costing $60,000 or $70,000. There was never a whiff of impropriety. Instead it seemed the vision was to get the very best—and worry about what it cost later. On occasion, The Forum couldn't pay bills until ticket renewals came in.

(Continued on Page 49)

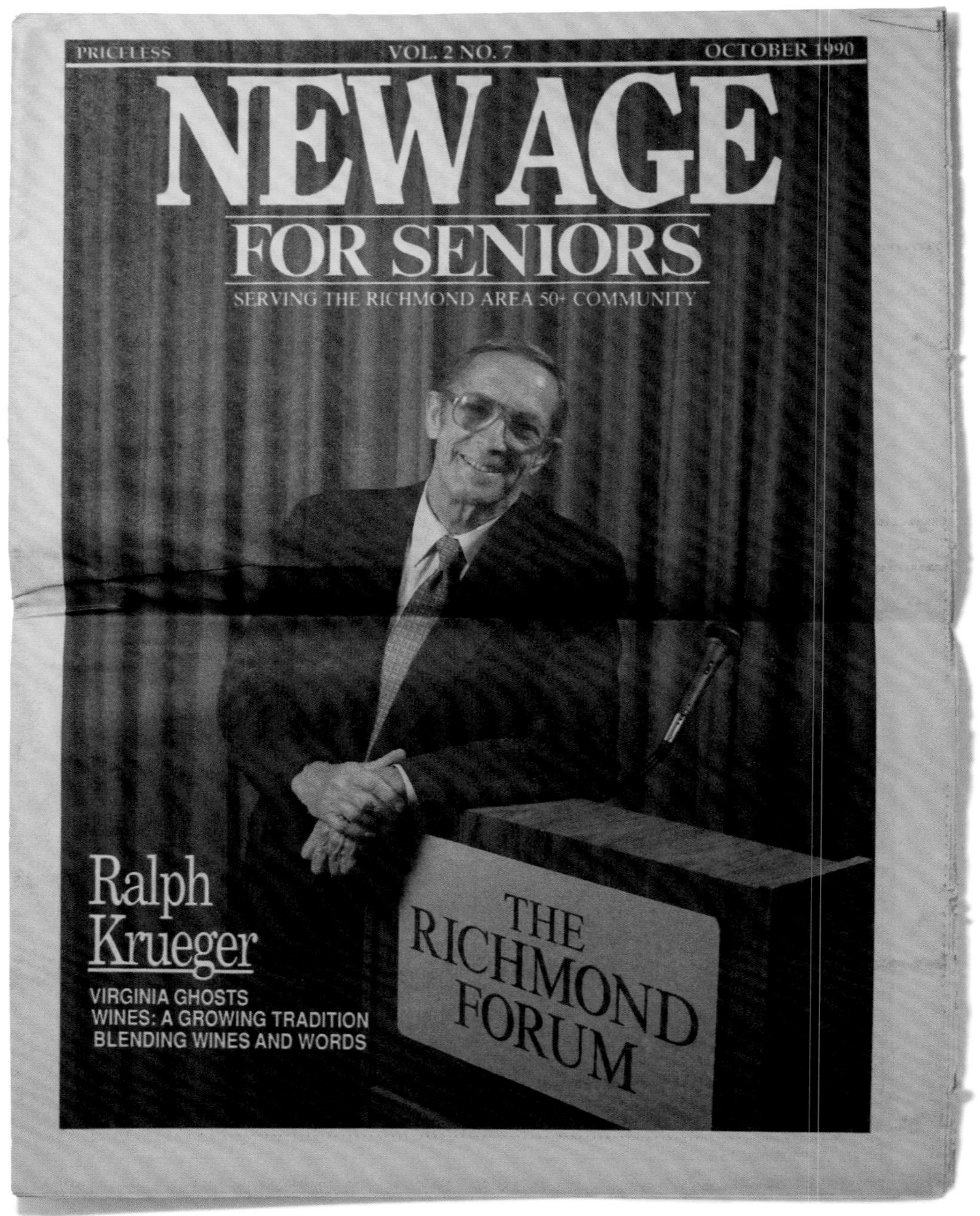

PRICELESS VOL. 2 NO. 7 OCTOBER 1990

NEW AGE
FOR SENIORS
SERVING THE RICHMOND AREA 50+ COMMUNITY

Ralph
Krueger

VIRGINIA GHOSTS
WINES: A GROWING TRADITION
BLENDING WINES AND WORDS

THE
RICHMOND
FORUM

Commenting on the big names landed by The Richmond Forum:

"Not too shabby. But expensive as hell."

RALPH F. KRUEGER, JR. // President, The Richmond Forum

THEY SAID IT AT THE FORUM

On three women applauding her as she left a bathroom stall: "That is fame, honey. Beats *People* magazine every day."
OPRAH WINFREY // January 1988

Asked if his Soviet journalists could publicly criticize their nation's leaders: "Not yet."
VLADIMIR POZNER // February 1988

"I have great difficulty seeing how the Soviet Union can make it economically on any hypothesis. I think [Gorbachev's] chance of survival is 50-50."
HENRY KISSINGER // February 1989

"Sometimes a reporter does have to dissemble . . . to break an important story. A worthwhile end sometimes justifies deceptive means."
MIKE WALLACE // March 1990

"We were in the Middle East because we don't have an energy policy. If they were selling bananas, do you think we'd be there? A brain-dead person in an institution would have realized after 1973 that we needed an energy policy."
H. ROSS PEROT // February 1991

"I am a TV news anchor, a role model for Miss America contestants."

TED KOPPEL // January 1987

On the American Revolution: "If there'd been a woman in 10 Downing Street at the time, it would never have happened."
MARGARET THATCHER // January 1992

"To say oil is not important is stupid. On the other hand, to say 'blood for oil' is stupidly simplistic."
NORMAN SCHWARZKOPF // February 1992

"Yes, sometimes we were too slow in making political decisions. And sometimes we paid a high price for it . . . [But for successor Boris Yeltsin], not one of their goals has been achieved. There is a real danger of Russia's disintegration."
MIKHAIL S. GORBACHEV // April 1993

DIVERSITY

Through its three decades, The Forum has strived for a diverse lineup, both in topics and speakers.

In its three opening years, The Forum had brought Diane Sawyer, Oprah Winfrey, Jeane Kirkpatrick and Charles Rangel to its stage. But the 1990–91 lineup of five programs showed eleven speakers taking part—and all were white men. A letter to the editor of the *Times-Dispatch* said the speakers were worthwhile, but added: "I also perceive a void—a variety of voices and opinions are being overlooked." The writer urged Forum President Ralph Krueger to "pursue a more varied roster of potential speakers."

Krueger wrote back: "Regrettably, the writer is right." Two factors are at play, he said: votes on potential speakers by those attending The Forum and speakers' willingness to attend. "We tried for a month to get astronaut Sally Ride to commit to The Forum and offered her thousands of dollars to do so. She felt she could not make the commitment in time for us to make the announcement by April 28."

Krueger urged Richmonders to support diversity with their Forum votes. "We would welcome both women and blacks—indeed, representatives of any culture or ethnic group—as our featured speakers, as has always been our policy."

Barbara Fitzgerald, one of The Forum's inner circle, says that was indeed the policy—and then some. "It always worried Ralph that he didn't have more African-Americans in the audience," Fitzgerald says. "He was constantly looking for African-American and women speakers." She adds that he "was trying really hard" to integrate both the audience and the speaker programs.

THE GENERAL AND THE LITTLE GIRL

The Forum's Q&A session took a different approach, for one question, at least, when General Norman Schwarzkopf appeared in February 1992. Read by news talk host Larry King, the one question had been submitted well in advance—by an eleven-year-old.

Lindsey Moran, sixth-grader at Stonewall Jackson Middle School in Hanover County, beat out more than 700 other pupils in a contest by country radio station K-95, WKHK-FM.

Onstage, King read her winning question: "If you could have a private meeting, what would you tell a child of an Iraqi soldier killed in Desert Storm?"

Schwarzkopf was impressed. "It's a beautiful question," he said.

He answered carefully: "War is a profanity. Man has got to figure out a better way to stop problems rather than to kill each other." Specifically, he would tell the Iraqi child: "When you have war, people get killed." He would say he hoped the father was fighting for what he believed, because it's a tragedy otherwise. And the child should remember the father to support the cause of peace in the future.

The general's answer received a round of applause.

Moran also liked it—and agreed. She was impressed with how thorough it was. "I couldn't actually believe he was doing it."

The program and the question were featured in Larry King's column two days later in *USA Today.* King wrote the general had "responded beautifully" to the question. The evening had gone well. "Officials of the Forum said it was the best in the event's 23-year history," King wrote, the count obviously including the previous Forum's run.

Lindsey Moran, today an attorney and an investigating officer for the Maryland Commission on Civil Rights, remembers the evening well.

She says her question was an outgrowth of family discussions on the news and Operation Desert Storm. She

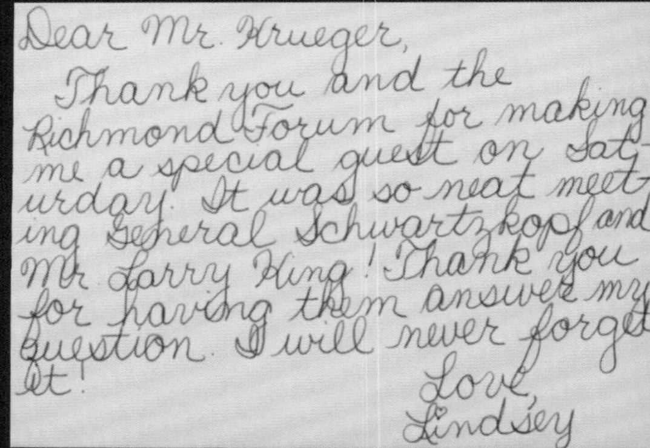
Dear Mr. Krueger,
Thank you and the Richmond Forum for making me a special guest on Saturday. It was so neat meeting General Schwartzkopf and Mr. Larry King! Thank you for having them answer my question. I will never forget it!
Love,
Lindsey

remembers the day of The Forum being exciting—she and her mother went shopping for a dress that day—and that she was panicked by slow traffic on the way to The Forum.

Meeting Schwarzkopf at a pre-program reception, "I was awestruck," Moran remembers. "The general was a living legend and I was just a random kid who won a contest. During the introduction, I was visibly shaking." Many, including Forum officials, photographers and Larry King watched as she walked up to him.

"He must have seen how overwhelmed I was. He smiled warmly and shook my hand. He then turned to face the media and put his arm around my shoulders and squeezed. The flashbulbs exploded! After a few seconds, he joked 'are we supposed to dance?' I giggled, which broke the tension and helped me to relax."

The rest of the evening is a blur. Moran does remember sitting in the Mosque listening to Schwarzkopf talk with King, sometimes kidding, sometimes serious. "I didn't think it was possible that one person could be so charming and engaging, even when answering some very difficult questions."

Moran went on to attend the Virginia Military Institute, as part of the second class of women to attend the formerly all-male school. She completed the infamous "ratline" but

…ed military life was not for her. She transferred … graduated from the College of William … ary, then graduated from the University of … ore School of Law.

…he never again saw the general, who died …2.

…It was not until I was older that I truly …rstood General Schwarzkopf's impact on the …," Lindsey Moran says. "He was a great leader …was forced to make life-altering—and life- …ng—decisions, which he did with aplomb."

…ral Norman Schwarzkopf and CNN interviewer Larry … (above) at The Forum's on-stage desks. Schwarzkopf … sixth-grader Lindsey Moran (upper left), whose question … e general beat out 700 other entries in a radio station … est. Afterward, Moran wrote to thank The Forum—and … wrote about the evening in his USA Today *column.*

Stormin' Norman, civilian

LARRY KING'S PEOPLE
News & Views

On a recent Saturday in Richmond, Va., yours truly and **Gen. H. Norman Schwarzkopf** shared the podium as speakers at the Richmond Forum. Four thousand attended, and I asked the general one hour of free-flowing questions. We then took queries from the audience, and I also asked questions that the schoolchildren of the city had written the prior week.

Officials of the Forum said it was the best in the event's 23-year history. The general was in great form (even wearing suspenders I had given him through **Gen. Tom Kelly** during the war). He's about halfway through his book, which Bantam will publish this fall. He's doing about five speeches a month. Schwarzkopf told me speaking for groups is like "white-collar crime." You get a lot of money and the speaker

to get involved in the education field. He misses the camaraderie of the military, but wouldn't want to go back. "I trained a lot of young men and women and now it's their turn to lead."

The winning question from a student: "What would you say to the daughter of a dead Iraqi soldier?" Calling it a "great question," Norman responded beautifully about "the stupidity of war" and that her father didn't die in vain if he was brave and was called to duty "by a leader he had no choice in choosing."

WHATEVER BALANCING ACT was going on behind the scenes, onstage, programming remained strong. Former British Prime Minister Margaret Thatcher's January 1992 appearance drew attention from near and far.

Not all was of the usual kind. An ad in *The Irish People* newspaper sought picketers for the event, *Times-Dispatch* reporter Mike Allen noted. "The British war criminal, Margaret Thatcher, is coming to Richmond, Va., on January 19th," read the ad. Meanwhile, in Richmond, Krueger received four letters threatening Thatcher, postmarked New York City. This was serious. He forwarded them to the FBI, which sent agents to supplement Thatcher's Scotland Yard contingent.

Thatcher flew across the Atlantic on the Concorde, reaching Kennedy Airport in New York the morning of the speech. An eight-passenger jet from Richmond's Universal Leaf Tobacco Company, made available as a donation to The Forum, was waiting on the runway to fly her to Richmond. From Richmond's airport, Thatcher rode in a pea-green, Rolls-Royce Silver Spur with diplomatic plates—armored, of course.

"This is the most security for anybody since Oprah Winfrey," Robert Dementi, The Forum's photographer, said that night. "John Chancellor and Henry Kissinger—they just came regular-ticket, first class, through the terminal."

Outside the Mosque, the temperature was twenty-two degrees. But some twenty protesters marched—carrying placards. A "pro-Maggie" group of counter protesters also marched.

Audience members were frisked as they went in, creating a slow-moving line that went around the Mosque onto Main Street. "Scotland Yard stopped me from going through the line," Susan Rekowski says.

Inside, Thatcher said "Ron Reagan" and his defense buildup could take much of the credit for the collapse of Communism. "The main message of this century has to be, to future generations, 'Look: Stand by and build on those great traditional values which built the U.S.,'" she said. "We might really and truly build a peaceful world for the next century."

The "Iron Lady" was also quick with a quip. On her aversion to deficits: "I was raised Methodist. That explains quite a lot." When a questioner wanted to know how Thatcher, who had twins, rated herself as a parent, she dead-panned: "Both stayed at home until they were well into

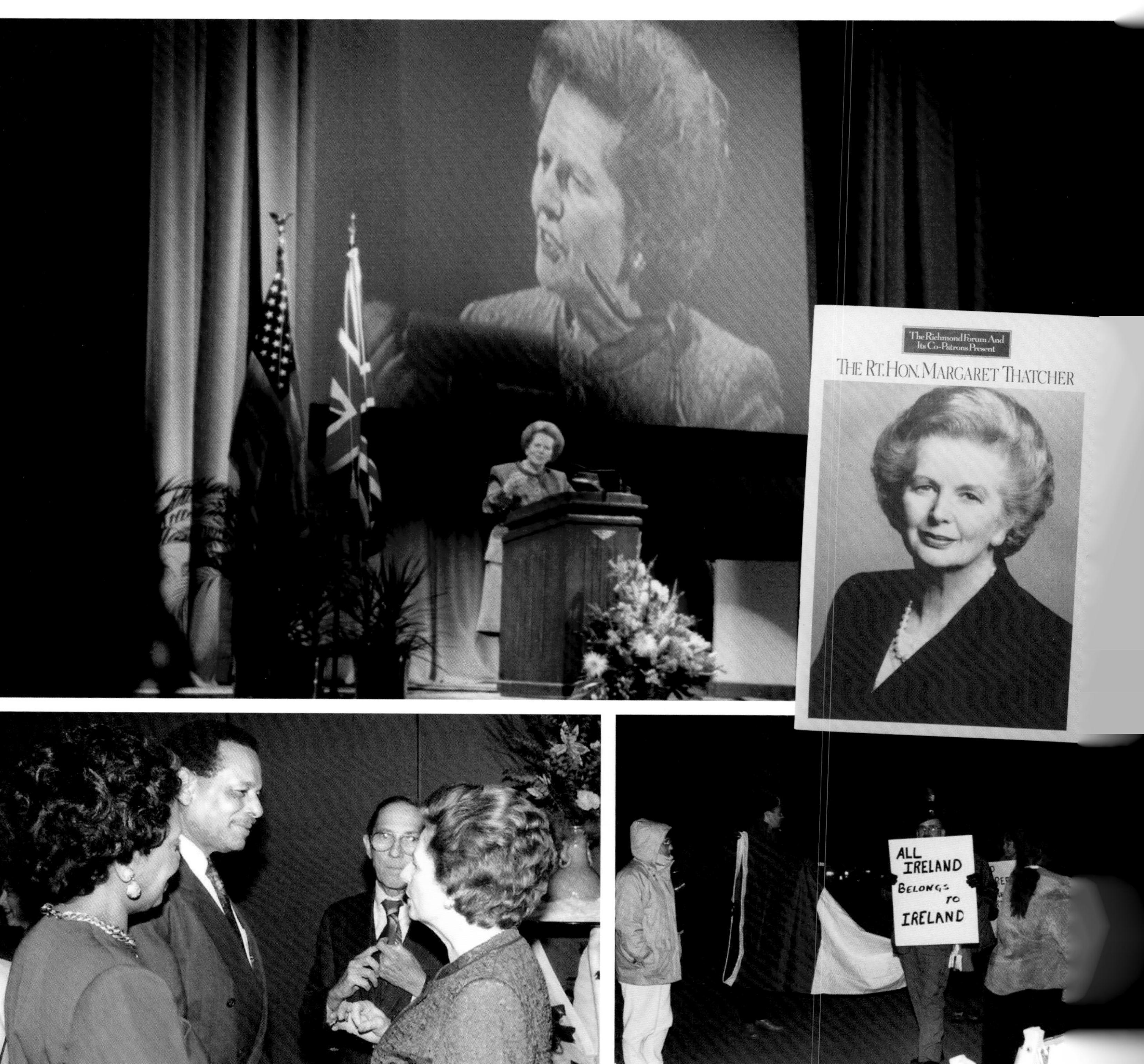

Top: Former British Prime Minister Margaret Thatcher; program book for her January 19, 1992, appearance. Lower left: Richmond Mayor Walter T. Kenney and his wife, Mamie, greet Thatcher as Ralph Krueger looks on. Lower right: Placard-carrying protesters outside the Mosque.

their twenties. That, I reckon, was a compliment to 'Mum.'"

There may never have been a more enthusiastically received night in The Forum's history than March 27, 1993, the night Bill Cosby came to town.

Cosby, just coming off the eight-year run starring as Cliff Huxtable on *The Cosby Show,* one of the top-rated shows of all time, was The Forum's first six-digit speaker; his fee far surpassing that of Margaret Thatcher and even exceeding the amount paid in total to Norman Schwarzkopf and talk show host Larry King.

The day didn't start off auspiciously. Future board member Mike Bland remembers he and two others went to the airport to pick up Cosby from his twenty-two-seat Gulfstream aircraft named *Camille* for his wife. A limo pulled up on the tarmac alongside the Forum car, however, briefly disappeared, then reappeared sporting the license plates of the governor. Cosby hopped in the limo. He would speak at The Forum but not take part in other events. Instead, he would spend time with Virginia's governor, L. Douglas Wilder.

Bill Cosby, who regaled the Forum audience, spent most of his offstage time with Virginia Governor L. Douglas Wilder.

"He did not show up for the dinner. I felt a little cheated," Bland says. "But he left a lot of people laughing. It was a fantastic standup routine, no swearing, that had everyone hurting from laughing."

"That was a great program," agrees Margaret Pace. "He loosened up by throwing a football backstage with Grahame Rees' son, who was eight to ten at the time. He was one of the best speakers we ever had."

Grahame Rees, then head of Rees Jewelers and a Forum board member, says he was able to bring one family member backstage for a photo op. "I chose my son, Jamie. Cosby and Jamie struck up a conversation." Just before Cosby went onstage, he asked the dad's permission to "pull a stunt with Jamie"—that is, have the boy go out when Cosby was announced. "Jamie 'chickened out' and it never took place. But it did make the Richmond newspaper the following day . . . It was awesome, at least to me. Jamie's mother didn't see it exactly as I did."

Barbara Fitzgerald's ten-year-old daughter, Sarah, also got to see Cosby backstage. "He called her over to see him and sat down and talked to her," Fitzgerald says. "Talked to her for a long time. She was laughing. It was very impressive. He was Dr. Huxtable that night."

Two decades later, Cosby would make headlines for accusations by dozens of women that he had drugged and raped them in the past. The similarity of their claims, coupled with Cosby's statements in court documents, changed his reputation from that of a beloved father figure to a societal monster.

Bland says Cosby is the worst example of a few Forum speakers who faced controversies later, including Greg Mortenson, accused of fabricating parts of a best-selling book about his humanitarian work, and even Rick Wagoner, forced to resign as head of General Motors after massive losses led to a temporary government bailout and takeover.

Bland judges their visits by their presentations that night. "They were controversial later, but that doesn't diminish what they brought to The Forum."

MIKHAIL GORBACHEV was the only speaker during her years at The Forum who was not represented by a lecture agent, Margaret Pace remembers. Getting the Soviet Union's last Communist leader, the reformist who had served from 1985 to 1991, before anyone else, was a feather in The Forum's cap.

It wasn't easy, but The Forum nailed it down in 1992, the year before the program. "I can hear Ralph hang up the phone and start yelling, 'We got Gorbachev! We got Gorbachev!'—jumping up and down," Pace says.

By early 1993, when he was to appear, however, Krueger was ill. He had had a litany of ailments: diabetes, lung cancer, a heart attack, a stroke, and kidney failure.

“(Gorbachev) would just jump out of the car and say ‘Hello’ to random passersby. ... literally like a kid in a candy store meeting everyday people.”

MARK POUNDERS

He was often hooked to an oxygen machine, and sometimes to a dialysis machine. By March, the sixty-seven-year-old Krueger was scarcely able to perform his duties. “When Cosby came, he wasn’t feeling too great,” said Mary Jo Krueger, his second wife, with whom he was about to celebrate his twenty-fourth anniversary. “So I said, ‘You know, I’ve never had a date for The Forum. Why don’t you sit with me?’ And he did.”

The back-to-back appearances of Bill Cosby and Mikhail Gorbachev were among The Forum’s most noteworthy—and, in some respects, unlikely—appearances.

Particularly Gorbachev’s.

Mark Pounders remembers the former Soviet leader wasn’t at all what he expected. Pounders’ company chauffeured speakers for The Forum and was a program sponsor, so he had the inside story on Gorbachev’s evening:

“He drove the Secret Service crazy because he would ask our driver to stop so that he could get out of the car and meet Americans. He would just jump out of

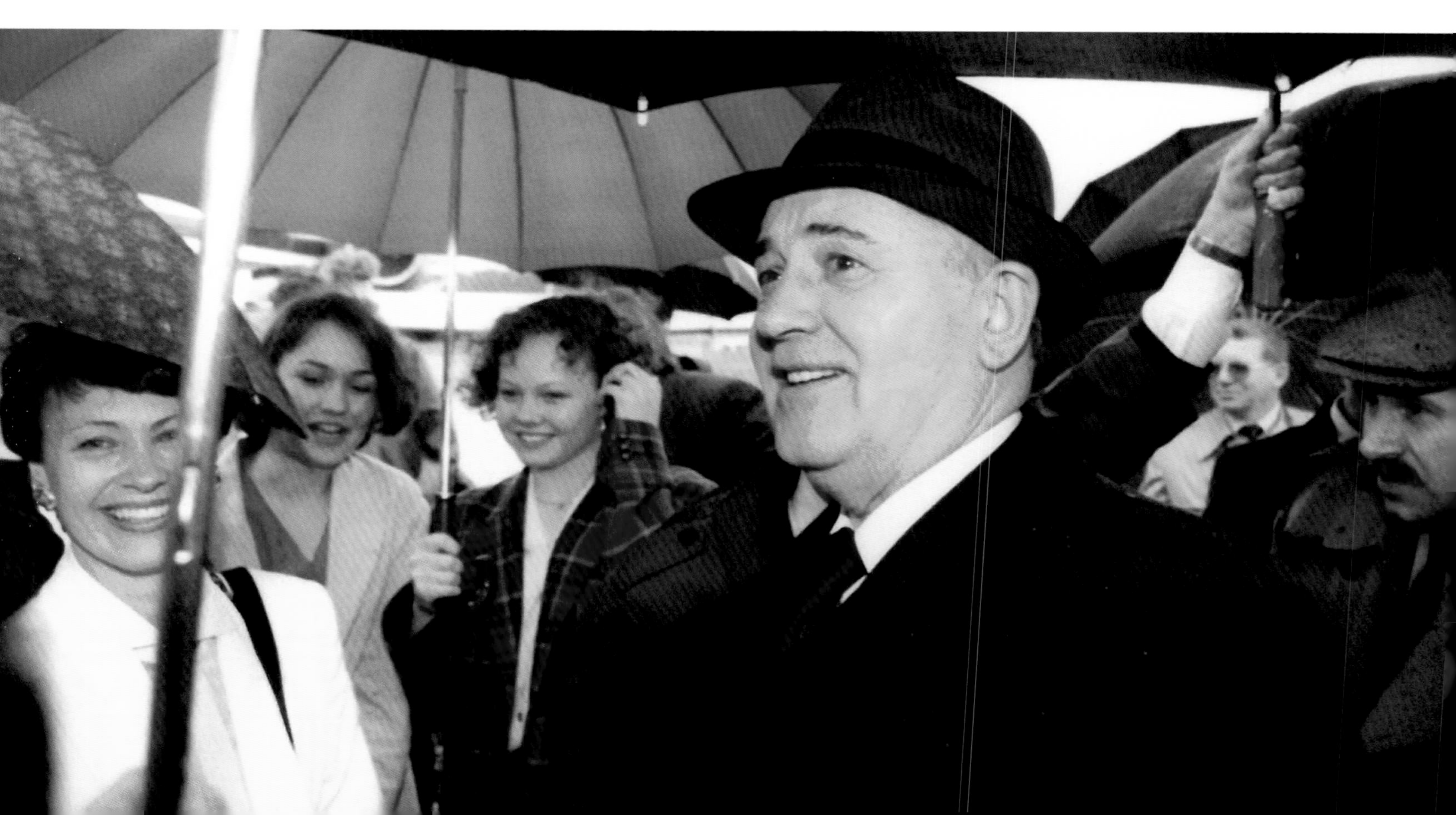

Former Soviet leader Mikhail Gorbachev drove the Secret Service crazy, jumping out of his car to greet Richmonders, then entering and exiting the theater through the front door. Backstage, Gorbachev spent time with the dying Ralph Krueger. For the Forum founder, his last program was perhaps his biggest. Below: Invitation to dinner with Gorbachev.

the car and say 'Hello' to random passersby.

"It was the most entertaining and heartwarming experience I can recall—a world leader who was literally like a kid in a candy store meeting everyday people, at odds with the very strict and aggravated Secret Service, and there was nothing they could do. I remember folks on the street being in complete disbelief at who was walking up to them. I'll never forget it, how approachable the man was. And I never looked at him in the same way from that day on."

After dinner, Gorbachev asked to go in through the front door of the Mosque, rather than through the usual speaker's entrance backstage. He didn't ask so much as demand. Forum officials said they didn't have security for that. He and his wife walked in, anyway, up the aisle past the seated guests.

Gorbachev was introduced that night by Krueger. It was a struggle. Immediately after finishing, the Forum president had to walk offstage and collapse onto a couch next to the oxygen machine.

Onstage, Gorbachev ridiculed the power struggle between his successor, Boris Yeltsin, and the Russian parliament. Immediate free elections, not a referendum, were needed. "For almost 100 days now, we have seen scenes of almost Shakespearian passion," Gorbachev said through an interpreter. "We cannot waste an hour." The next day's *Times-Dispatch* covered Gorbachev as the lead story, taking two-thirds of the top of Page A1. His remarks went out worldwide.

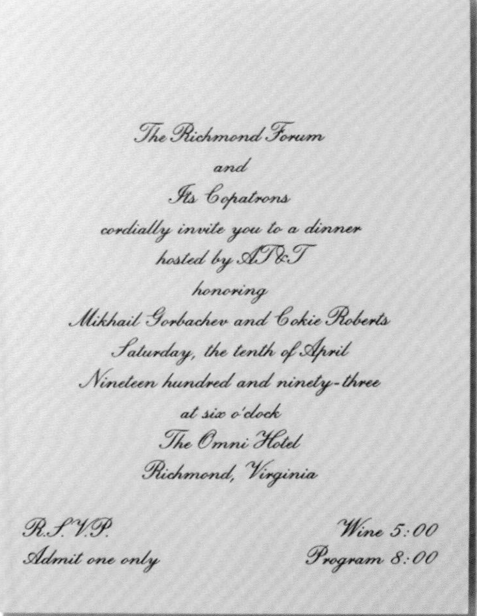

The Richmond Forum
and
Its Copatrons
cordially invite you to a dinner
hosted by AT&T
honoring
Mikhail Gorbachev and Cokie Roberts
Saturday, the tenth of April
Nineteen hundred and ninety-three
at six o'clock
The Omni Hotel
Richmond, Virginia

R.S.V.P. — Wine 5:00
Admit one only — Program 8:00

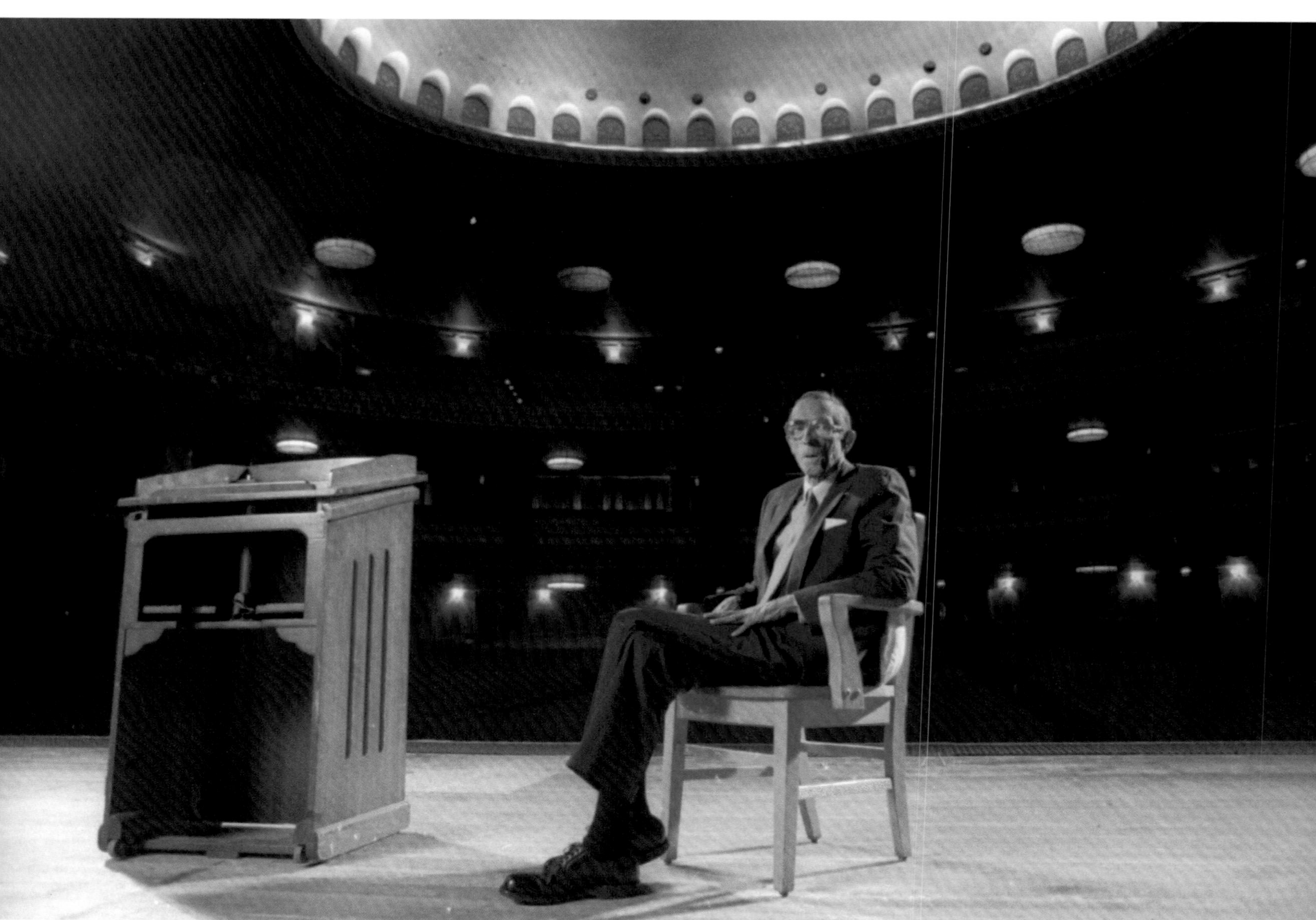

Above: The final portrait, taken by the Times-Dispatch. *Right: Portrait of Ralph Krueger by artist Bill Nelson* *(See pages 56–57)*.

FOR KRUEGER, IT WAS a success, as well. The Forum staff knew what it meant to him. "Ralph, his thing was to hang on so he could introduce Mikhail Gorbachev. He was so proud of that," Susan Rekowski says. "That program was what kept him alive," Margaret Pace says.

His wife, Mary Jo, had said the same thing shortly after. "He was really intent on being there," she said then. "He just loves it. What can I say?"

After the success of the Gorbachev program, there was only one thing left for Krueger to do:

An exit interview.

Krueger sat down with *Times-Dispatch* writer Bill Lohmann for a large feature story that was published Sunday, April 25, 1993. The headline: "Forum Father."

Full testament was given to Krueger's ego. He didn't think small, Krueger admitted—"That's one thing I don't think I can be accused of"—and he was satisfied that cities like Atlanta had used Richmond as a model for starting their own forums.

Krueger reiterated his passion: "This is the most exciting job I've ever had. For some reason, it seems to draw on everything I know how to do." That included organizing, selling, promoting, rubbing elbows with the rich and famous. "Kind of intuitively, I know what should be done next."

Krueger was near death. But he eagerly agreed to pose for a panoramic photograph, seated in a chair next to the lectern, the full expanse of the theater behind him. Krueger had to be pushed onstage in his wheelchair, needing his oxygen while the photograph was being set up. When the time came, the wheelchair and oxygen were removed from the frame.

Fittingly, the article concluded:

"I really feel we've given Richmond a gift," Krueger said. "Hopefully, it will sustain itself for a while."

Less than a month later, the Forum father, Ralph F. Krueger Jr., was dead.

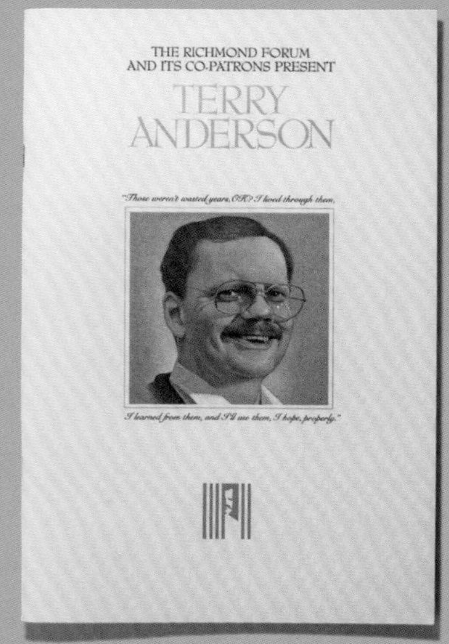

THE RICHMOND FORUM
AND ITS CO-PATRONS PRESENT
TERRY
ANDERSON

THE PORTRAITS

For several seasons during the 1990s, patrons received a little something extra on their copies of the printed programs: limited-edition artwork, in the form of speaker portraits.

"Ralph Krueger wanted the programs to be a keepsake from the evening that sponsors could display on their office coffee tables," Margaret Pace explains, "so that's why they were oversized with nice artwork."

Portraits first appeared for the 1990 season, commissioned by the Forum art director, Dale Moore, who had worked at Krueger's advertising agency. But in reprising the idea for the 1992–1993 season, new art director Doyle Robinson went all-out. "I was sharing office space downtown with Bill Nelson," Robinson says. "I talked him into doing them at sort of half price. And he got really into them. He did a real good job."

Nelson was a nationally renowned artist even then, his work frequently appearing on major magazine covers and in national ad campaigns.

"I was glad to be working with Doyle and, let's face it, all artists wanted to be accepted and to produce work locally," Nelson says. While most of his work was for national and international clients, working with Robinson as a designer made it an easy call. "Doyle made my work sing."

Nelson drew the portraits from photographs, using Prismacolor pencil on charcoal paper. No, he adds, he didn't meet the speakers. But in taking the job, "there's always the selfish factor, too: Maybe I'll get to meet one of these

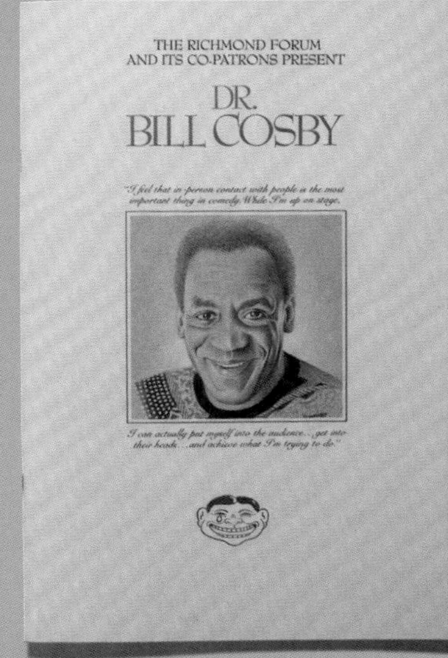

celebrities/speakers and maybe they'll want to buy their actual portrait. Neither of those ever happened. I didn't even get free tickets to those Forum events! But as I said, working with Doyle was payment enough."

The portraits would be ended a year after a new president took over the Forum following Krueger's death. The cover focus was shifted from the speakers themselves to their topics, represented in objects photographed by Tim Gabbert.

Program book covers from the 1992–93 season (upper) and from the 1993–94 season (lower), including a couple that were autographed afterward by the speakers. Right: Artist Bill Nelson also created a portrait of Krueger after his death. It was presented by Governor L. Douglas Wilder to Krueger's widow, Mary Jo, at the next season's opening program. The portrait today hangs in the Forum offices.

CHAPTER 6

PROFESSIONALIZING THE FORUM

THE RUCKER YEARS OF THE RICHMOND FORUM: 1993–2008

It takes a visionary to start an organization. Passion, big ideas, and an appetite for risk are the requirements. Organization, systems, even balanced budgets—those are details for others.

But dotting the I's and crossing the T's do matter eventually. For that it takes a leader who can ensure the visionary's creation will be sustained.

Finding a replacement for the inestimable Ralph Krueger was not necessarily easy but it was done quickly. After going through ninety applications and conducting six interviews, The Forum had its new man. Edward W. Rucker, forty-year-old director of development and government relations for the Virginia Foundation for the Humanities and Public Policy in nearby Charlottesville, was announced as the new president in September 1993, only four months after Krueger's death.

The new president knew The Forum. "I brought Ed Rucker to see Gorbachev at The Forum," says Barbara Fitzgerald, who would be on the search committee. "I thought Ed would be great because he was so well-organized. He applied and got the job."

Rucker promised to continue the work of his predecessor. "One of the things Ralph did here was to build a model, a national model," Rucker told the *Richmond Times-Dispatch.* "I think one of the challenges of the future—and I'm committed to this—is to uphold and extend the quality of the speakers and programs which Ralph set forth."

General Colin L. Powell, appearing November 19, 1994, became the first to speak at The Forum's temporary home at the University of Richmond's Robins Center.

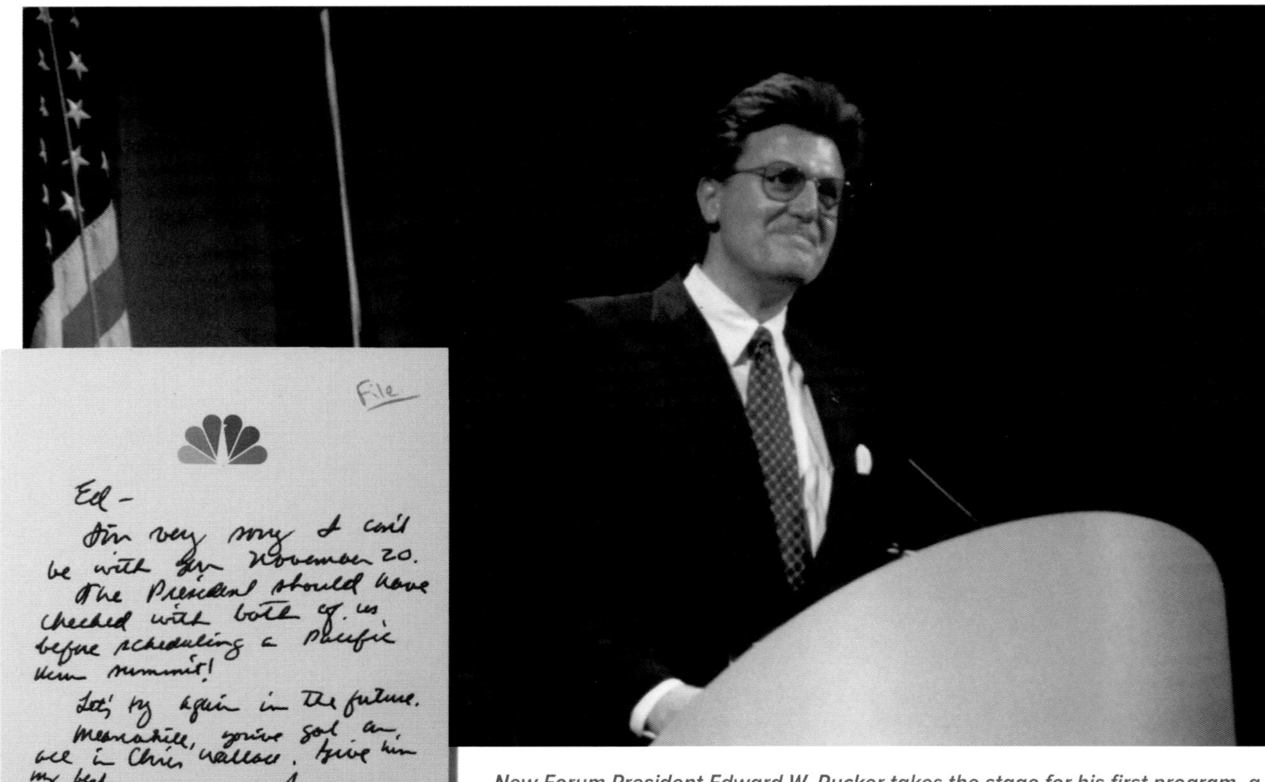

File

Ed –

I'm very sorry I can't be with you November 20. The President should have checked with both of us before scheduling a Pacific Rim summit!

Let's try again in the future. Meanwhile, you've got an ace in Chris Wallace. Give him my best.

Tom Brokaw

Tom Brokaw

New Forum President Edward W. Rucker takes the stage for his first program, a November 1993 panel discussion on "America in 2000," involving Forecasting International President Marvin Cetron, former Education Secretary Lamar Alexander, and former Senator Warren Rudman. ABC newsman Chris Wallace was the moderator, replacing Tom Brokaw who had to cover the Asia-Pacific Summit and who apologized for his absence in a personal note to Rucker.

He would also like to reach more people, Rucker said, noting The Forum sold out each year as it was. He hinted that television might beam programs across the state. He mentioned collaboration with local museums and universities. Nothing had been decided, he emphasized. Those were ideas to "simply spark discussion."

What he did not say publicly was that he also intended to make The Forum more of a professional organization. Rucker, who had served as the business manager and then general manager for TheatreVirginia for seven years in the 1980s, would tighten up the finances, improve production values, and reduce the role of volunteers.

During a sometimes tumultuous tenure, Rucker would leave his stamp on The Forum.

THE 1993–94 SEASON was already set, with a big-name lineup, highlighted by former President George H. W. Bush and comedian Bob Hope. The season kicked off with a special moment when former Governor L. Douglas Wilder took to the Forum stage to present a portrait of the late Ralph Krueger, drawn by artist Bill Nelson, to his widow, Mary Jo Krueger.

The transition to new leadership was visible in other ways that first night. Gone were the game-show style desks of the Krueger era and the wood lectern that had been inherited from the Unitarians, replaced by sleek podiums and conversational seating. Also gone was the old Q&A format that involved both a professional moderator and a questioning panel of three-to-four local personalities, another leftover from The Richmond Public Forum. In subsequent seasons, Rucker would continue

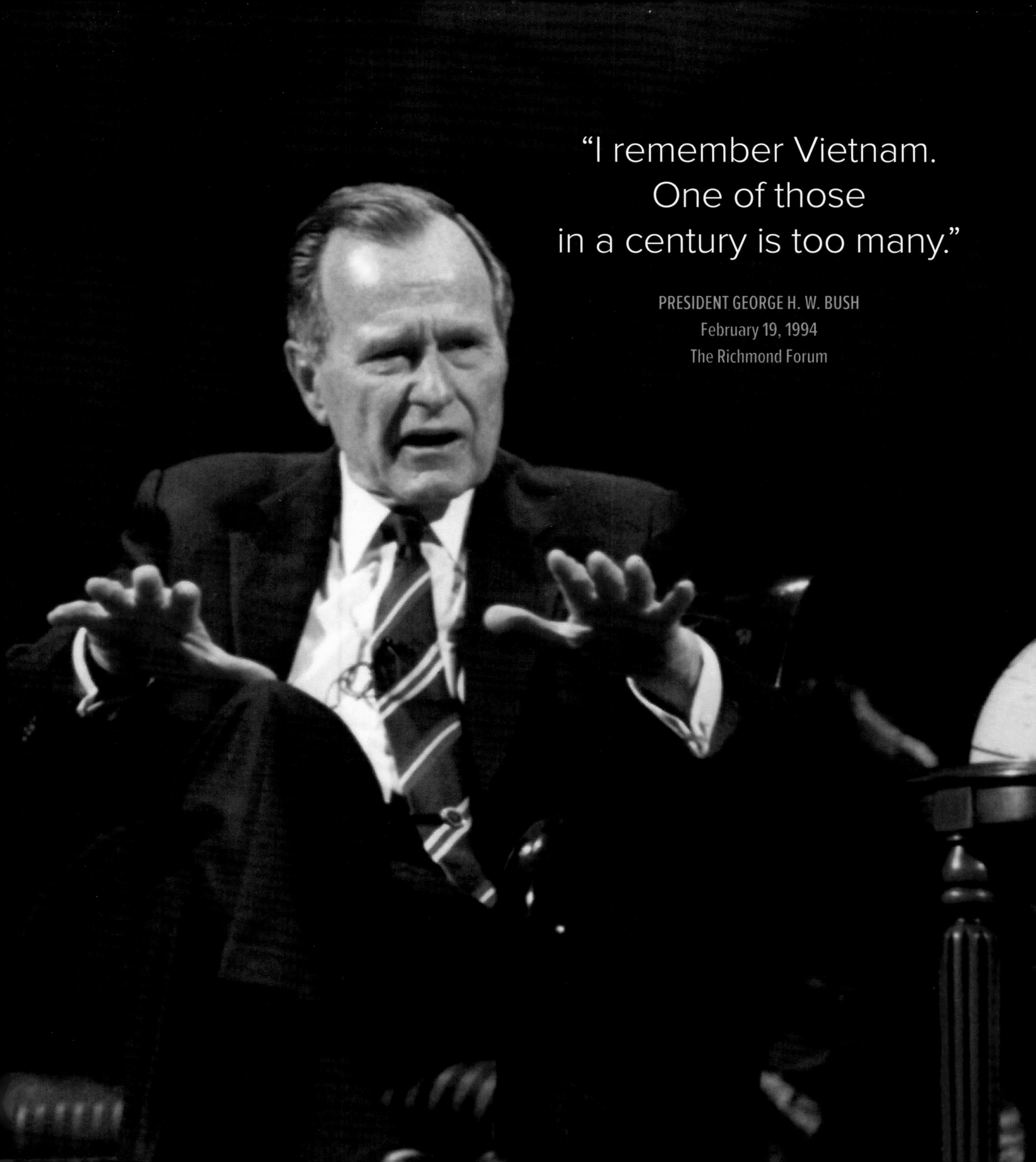
"I remember Vietnam.
One of those
in a century is too many."
PRESIDENT GEORGE H. W. BUSH
February 19, 1994
The Richmond Forum

to make enhancements: adding giant Ionic columns and greenery to the set, introducing live music before the programs and during intermission, and creating an opening video to set the stage. An evening at The Forum was to become a highly produced, first-class event.

Bush, the first former president to appear at a Richmond Forum, did so February 19, 1994. He said it was his third appearance in the city. He had first come with the Yale baseball team nearly a half-century earlier, to play the University of Richmond in either his junior or senior year. "I think we won, and that was fun." He came again to the university in 1992 for a presidential debate—"and that was not fun," he said, drawing laughs. The debate included Bill Clinton and Ross Perot; Clinton would defeat Bush in the 1992 election.

Actually, Yale records show his team lost 8–7 to UR on March 31, 1947, as well. But Yale had defeated the University of Virginia two days earlier in Charlottesville.

THE PRESIDENT AND THE FOURTH-GRADER

A former president's February 1994 appearance was a special evening for many at The Forum.

"George H. W. Bush, he was the nicest guy, of all the speakers," fundraiser Susan Rekowski says, looking back. "He had an aura. He was kind."

Dory Yochum, vice president of a technology company, sat at his table for dinner. "I was quite nervous," she said that evening, "but he was very easy to talk to."

Perhaps no one was as nervous as Jenna Shoaf.

Jenna was a fourth-grader at St. Edward-Epiphany School who had written Bush the previous fall. If the 1992 presidential election had been up to her school, she wrote, he would have won re-election.

Bush responded by inviting her to The Forum and reception.

"I had no idea what a big deal that was, but my mom was ecstatic," Shoaf, who goes by Jenna Shoaf Swann, says now. On the big day, she became increasingly nervous. "We were escorted to a private reception room where there were multiple Secret Service agents checking everything, which at the time I didn't understand at all." She became more nervous.

"He came in," she says of Bush, "and I just remember standing up and trying to make sure I shook with the right hand. The first thing he said as we shook hands was that he had a granddaughter named Jenna, and that made me feel special and much more at ease."

She says Bush engaged in small talk, asking her about school and playing sports. "He took the time to make me feel very important, which I appreciate more today than I did then."

The fourth-grader also was given a presidential stick

pin—but ended up breaking it when she got home. Her mother, Bonnie, repaired it twice but was told the crest would break with another attempt, so she wrote to Bush a year after his appearance. He had another one sent.

Jenna Shoaf Swann can't forget that evening at The Forum.

"Seeing him and his family on television and social media now just brings back such fond memories of an important person who took the time to meet a fourth-grader and make her feel special when he didn't have to," she says. "I think it speaks volumes of his character and good nature and I have always supported the Bush family since then."

Bush said he would avoid criticizing his successor, Clinton, that night. But he did claim credit for the improving economy and for Middle East Peace initiatives. He also defended his decision to abort Operation Desert Storm and declare victory, though American troops could have proceeded into Baghdad. He said he always used a three-point military test: "What's the mission? How do you do it? How do you get out? . . . I remember Vietnam. One of those in a century is too many."

Bush said he was happy in retirement. He could play golf without reporters around. "Now that I'm no longer president, it's amazing how many people beat me."

Meanwhile, Bob Hope, about to turn ninety, canceled. The Forum publicly blamed a scheduling conflict and contractual complications in making the announcement. Really, Susan Rekowski says now, Hope's health was the issue.

Another comedic icon, Bob Newhart, was the replacement. Newhart proved more than satisfactory. "He was awesome. He was a character," Rekowski says. Michael Bland agrees. "We hosted Newhart [at dinner]. He had the driest sense of humor of everyone. Very self-deprecating."

The following season, 1994–95, was the first of two moved to the University of Richmond's Robins Center, a basketball arena that could seat 5,200 Forum attendees, while the Mosque was undergoing renovations.

From a technical and logistical standpoint, the move was a tremendous undertaking that required Rucker, in only his second season, to reinvent nearly every aspect of producing a Forum evening. But it did have its upside. Even given that UR students received some 800 seats as part of the agreement with the university, revenue from additional ticket sales at the larger venue allowed The Forum to start a reserve fund that would provide financial stability and support for operations for years to come. Jacques Moore, whose decade-and-a-half with The Forum included stints as treasurer and board chairman, says the fund helps The Forum cover the fees of the most expensive speakers and provides financial stability for the series. The lack of such a safety net had contributed to the demise of Richmond's two earlier forums.

Ed Rucker and Dr. John Roush, the University of Richmond's vice president for planning, make plans to move The Forum to UR's Robins Center for two seasons.

podium

The Richmond Forum 1994-95 Season

The 1994-95 Richmond Forum Season Welcomes Nationally Known Speakers To The Robins Center

The leaders and the legends are waiting just offstage. The authors are ready with exciting tales to tell. The newsmakers and news media are poised for question and answer. And the politicians are about to take a stand.

Yes, it's another season at The Richmond Forum – and what a season it is! The topics range from world affairs and current events to arts and culture; from science and technology to business and the economy.

Whatever your special interest, somewhere along the way in the 1994-95 Season, The Forum is likely to touch upon it. So sit back, get comfortable, and prepare to be surprised, informed, entertained and fascinated as The Richmond Forum gets underway in the Robins Center at the University of Richmond.

A General idea of what's ahead

We hope that you'll be with us on November 19, 1994, for an evening with General Colin Powell, the former chairman of the U.S. Joint Chiefs of Staff. General Powell will speak on "The American Military and a Changing World Order." And could anyone possibly be more qualified to tackle that subject?

As Chairman of the Joint Chiefs from 1989 to late 1995, Powell served as the principal military adviser to both President Bush and President Clinton, as well as to the Secretary of Defense and the National Security Council. He also served President Ronald Reagan as the Assistant for National Security Affairs.

General Colin Powell's outstanding military career began inconspicuously enough, with his enrollment in ROTC as a student at City College of New York in the mid-fifties. Graduation in 1958 found him commissioned as an Army second lieutenant.

Attention!

The next step led to Fort Benning, Georgia, where Powell completed the Infantry Officer Basic Course, the Ranger Course, and the Airborne Course, before being stationed in Germany.

Subsequent assignments moved him, first, back to and all around the states and eventually to two tours of duty in Vietnam.

Powell also served in Korea and later commanded the 2nd Brigade, 101st Airborne Division (Air Assault) and V Corps, United States Army, Europe.

Along the way, Powell completed work on a master of business administration degree from George Washington University, served as a White House fellow in 1972, held posts in the Defense Department and briefly served as an Assistant to the Secretary of Energy.

Awards, Medals, Decorations, Honors.

General Powell has received numerous military awards and decorations, including the Defense Distinguished Service Medal (with three Oak Leaf Clusters), the Army Distinguished Service Medal (with Oak Leaf Cluster), Defense Superior Service Medal, Legion of Merit (with Oak Leaf Cluster), Soldier's Medal, Bronze Star, and the Purple Heart. He has received dozens of civilian awards as well, including two Presidential Medals of Freedom and an honorary knighthood from the queen of England.

General Powell is married to the former Alma Vivian Johnson of Birmingham, and the Powell family includes one son, two daughters and a grandson.

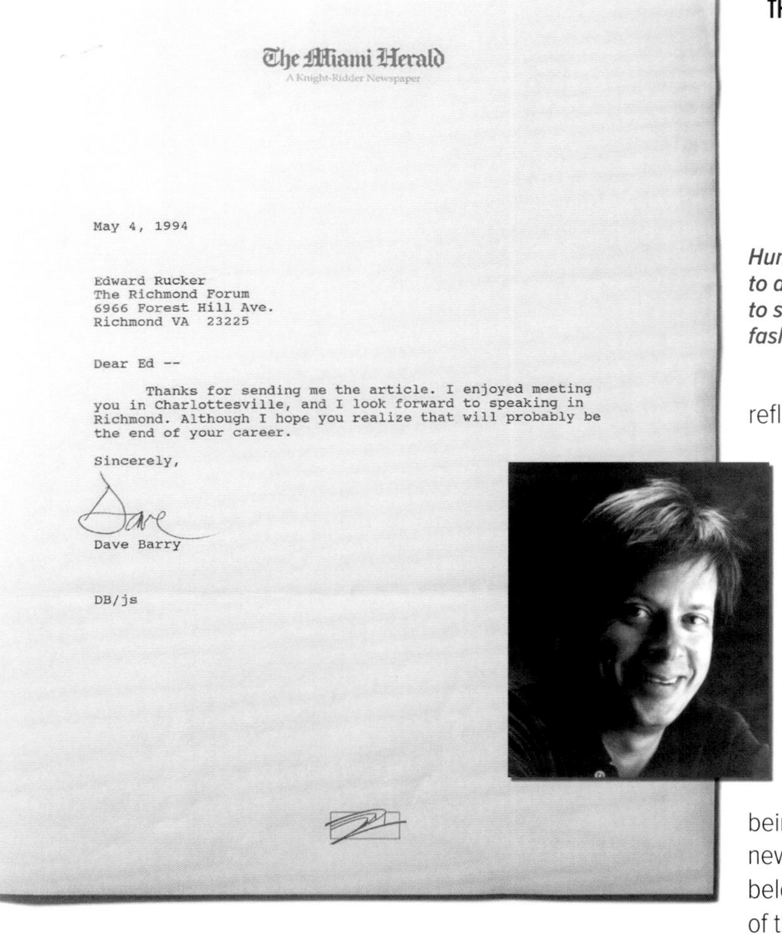

The Miami Herald
A Knight-Ridder Newspaper

May 4, 1994

Edward Rucker
The Richmond Forum
6966 Forest Hill Ave.
Richmond VA 23225

Dear Ed --

Thanks for sending me the article. I enjoyed meeting you in Charlottesville, and I look forward to speaking in Richmond. Although I hope you realize that will probably be the end of your career.

Sincerely,

Dave

Dave Barry

DB/js

Humor columnist Dave Barry was among the first to accept the new Forum president's invitation to speak in Richmond, doing so in typical Barry fashion.

The 1994–95 season had no trouble filling even the larger arena, being full of heavyweights, including General Colin Powell, newsman Walter Cronkite, humor columnist Dave Barry, novelist Tom Clancy, and retired politicians Jack Kemp and George Mitchell.

None was bigger than Powell, the recently retired chairman of the Joint Chiefs of Staff and rumored presidential candidate.

The general was making no declarations about running for anything. But *Times-Dispatch* reporter Tom Campbell witnessed a playful Powell as he walked into the Robins Center. The general spied photographer Alexa Welch and suddenly leaned toward her, just for a second, with a big Dwight Eisenhower grin and two V-for-victory hand signs. The pose was quickly withdrawn. "You missed the great shot," Powell joked.

Onstage, Powell talked about Mikhail Gorbachev's world-changing 1988 perestroika. Gorbachev had told Powell the end of the Cold War meant America had lost its enemy. "We lost something else," Powell reflected, solemnly. "We lost containment. We lost our strategy. . . . We have lost our unifying theory, and we have no new stars to guide by as yet."

Walter Cronkite, whose weather-disrupted appearance in 1966 had been one of the predecessor Forum's least-attended programs, appeared to a full house this time. The former CBS news anchor criticized Republican Newt Gingrich for over-reading the results of the previous year's election, Democratic President Bill Clinton for lacking "backbone," and tabloid news shows like *Hard Copy* and *Inside Edition* for being "despicable." But he also revealed his famed newscast-ending line, "And that's the way it is," was not beloved, either. "The first day, I was called to the office of the president of CBS," Cronkite said, where his boss expressed outrage over the line. "He hated it every day of his life."

Forum official Margaret Pace says offstage she and Cronkite talked about sailing and the Chesapeake Bay. But it was the evening's questioner, another newsperson, of whom she has the fondest memories.

"Judy Woodruff was probably one of the nicest, nicest people I ever met," says Pace, who picked her up at her hotel room that day for the evening's festivities. "When I went up to get her, she wasn't quite ready. She invited me in. I helped pick out her outfit. We sprayed perfume. We were like two college girls."

As the 1995–96 season was about to get underway, Rucker talked with a local magazine about the move to the Robins Center, which had turned the Forum focus somewhat away from performers because of the technical requirements. When The Forum would return to the Mosque, there needed to be a continuing emphasis on blending both content and stardom, he said.

"Getting to The Forum is like living the news. It's

important that The Forum's programs, while informative, are always entertaining," Rucker said. "We're a cultural and educational resource for the community, and there's a whole range of opportunities to schedule entertainers and satirical journalists within the Forum season."

Under Rucker, former board member Jacques Moore says now, "The Forum earned a reputation in Hollywood as being a friendly place to speak . . . Ed was very, very professional and very good at relationship building [with speakers]." In seasons to come, these relationships would bear fruit.

Behind the scenes, Rucker was reigning in the budget and often generating a surplus. Margaret Pace, working in the office with him, said the Rucker approach caused some friction. "Ed Rucker turned what was in my mind a community-based Forum into a business," she says. Whereas Krueger would spend every penny on speakers and programs, "Ed Rucker was more interested in building the Richmond Forum bank account. And he did a great job with that. And he alienated many people along the way."

Board member Jack Maxwell, a finance committee member, says, "He got us in good financial shape. . . . Rucker was the key guy. He really got things turned around." Rucker's budgets were balanced, his expenses were supported by revenue and his numbers were believable. "If he said somebody was going to cost $75,000, that was the number. I think without him, The Forum would not have been able to survive."

The February 1996 program, part of The Richmond Forum's 10th anniversary season, showed the logistical problems The Forum could face in winter. *New Yorker* and *Time* magazine humor essayist Calvin Trillin was on the bill. But a Friday snowstorm that walloped the East Coast prompted Trillin to cancel his flight from New York and instead catch an Amtrak train to Washington, where Forum officials picked up him and his wife for a drive to Richmond. Trillin was on time but some Forum attendees were not. The usually punctual Forum delayed its start by

CRONKITE'S "LIBERAL PAP"

FORUM FILES

The Walter Cronkite program of January 21, 1995, pointed up the unpredictability inherent in The Forum's Q&A session. One anonymous questioner wrote the following to Cronkite, read onstage by moderator and newswoman Judy Woodruff:

I am thoroughly unimpressed with tonight's presentation. If I wanted to hear this kind of liberal pap, I could have stayed home and watched TV instead of paying $30 to hear this. If there are any more presentations like this I will no longer continue to support this forum.

Times-Dispatch **columnist Randy Fitzgerald, who had been backstage sorting questions, revealed Woodruff insisted on taking that one. It was one of half a dozen questions about being "liberal," Fitzgerald wrote, but by far the rudest. (Fitzgerald's** ***Times-Dispatch*** **headline the next morning: "It's Not Very Richmond to Ask Rude Questions, and It's Even Worse to Mention Them in Public.") Woodruff did agree to read a balancing letter from an audience member thanking Cronkite for his "middle-of-the-road approach" and asking why he didn't run for president.**

Onstage, Cronkite listened to the "liberal pap" question, then took the card and read the question silently. "You know, God, America is a great country," he finally responded, receiving a roar of applause. He asked the woman to come talk to him after the talk.

He also put the card in his coat pocket.

University of Richmond Junior Michael Nickson said afterward he was surprised. "I liked the speech," he said. "I didn't think it was 'liberal pap' at all, but I guess even moderates don't fly in Richmond."

fifteen minutes to allow them to negotiate slick area roads.

Both Trillin and the following month's speaker, newsman and writer Charles Kuralt, making a return Forum appearance, brought humor to the Robins Center.

Kuralt, after noting "I'm staggered by the size of the crowd," jokingly took on Trillin himself. The topic was barbecue. "I like it served on a hamburger bun with cole slaw," Kuralt said to thunderous applause. But Kansas City native Trillin, Kuralt teased, "comes from a culture that slathers ketchup on beef and calls it barbecue. They don't know any better." More thunderous applause.

BY THE START of the 1996–97 season, the five-and-a-half million dollar renovation was concluded at the Mosque, which now sported a name intended as less offensive, the Landmark Theater. The Forum was going home.

"You really shouldn't have refurbished this whole place just for Carl and me," talk show host Dick Cavett said at the opening event. "This place is really stunning, isn't it?"

The Landmark, at capacity, sat fewer people than the Robins Center had. All 3,600 seats were full for the opening program, which featured a conversation between two of television's more thoughtful comedians and storytellers, Carl Reiner and Cavett. Reiner, who famously created *The Dick Van Dyke Show,* told the audience he had done so in one summer, writing an episode every four days. He did so only after his wife said he surely could write better scripts than those being prepared for shows he was producing.

There is a commonality among most Forum speakers, say those who get to spend time with them. Almost without exception, they are gracious and self-effacing.

A few are more complicated.

British theater composer Andrew Lloyd Webber was interviewed by David Frost in March 1998 in one of The Forum's more unusual productions. The two sat at a grand piano, with a background of six mammoth columns rising out of a jungle of greenery. (Colin Powell once quipped that The Forum's on-stage greenery made him feel like he was back in Vietnam.) Five videos of Lloyd Webber's songs were interspersed during the program—and Frost led the audience in singing *Happy*

FORUM FILES

THE SOUNDS OF LOVE

Times-Dispatch **columnist Randy Fitzgerald—he and his wife, Barbara, were Forum volunteers—was behind the scenes for the Carl Reiner-Dick Cavett program.**

Fitzgerald had been going through audience questions backstage, he wrote afterward. Suddenly, Reiner showed up. "Are there any about my wife?" he asked. He clearly wanted some. Reiner had already told the audience Estelle and he had been married nearly fifty-two years—because he had found someone who could stand him.

After intermission, Reiner told the story he had been waiting for—that his wife had been singing to him for that half-century. At a friend's suggestion, she recorded a compact disc. It was not in stores yet.

When Reiner saw The Forum's sound system, he kicked himself for not bringing it. The closest copy he knew of was in Washington, D.C., but that friend had guests and couldn't leave. So Reiner paid a limo driver $300 to go north, pick up the CD and bring it back—just in time. Reiner had it played to the Forum crowd.

Estelle Reiner proved to have a sweet, clear, old-fashioned blues voice, Fitzgerald wrote. The audience loved it. Reiner, projected on the large screen above, settled back in his chair and closed his eyes. He moved his head slightly in time. A smile played on his lips. Throughout the theater, teary-eyed men and women smiled back.

Andrew Lloyd Webber (left) at the grand piano in March 1998. David Frost interviews him.

Birthday to the composer, who turned forty-nine that day. Lloyd Webber, in turn, led the audience in singing *Happy Birthday* to fellow composer Stephen Sondheim, whose birthday he shared.

Michael Bland, whose company was a host sponsor, found Lloyd Webber distant off-stage, however. In 2000, Bland, who served a total of fifteen years on the board, had introduced Desmond Tutu at the pre-program dinner, as he did with Lloyd Webber. "Tutu never wanted to talk about himself. He helped change the world, is known worldwide, helped stave off a civil war and was a part of history—and was not selfish at all. . . . At the opposite end was Andrew Lloyd Webber . . . who insisted he come over on the Concorde, which is a bit more than The Forum thought it would be; he was coming here, anyway, for the Oscars. Not an approachable guy. Very standoffish."

Susan Rekowski adds, "There was only one Andrew Lloyd Webber photo taken at the reception. His handler kept the photographer away."

But Lloyd Webber also was a nervous wreck backstage, say several who saw him that night. Margaret Pace witnessed this different side of the man. "Andrew Lloyd Webber, he was such a musical genius but such a shy individual," she says. "At one of the receptions, he walked into the room. 'Margaret, do I have to go in there?' Scared to death. I said, 'Absolutely.'" Linda Warren was in attendance that night—she would later become Forum board chair. "Andrew Lloyd Webber was my favorite speaker," she says. "To have him on our stage was amazing—and he was scared to death. He was. He admitted he was."

As Lloyd Webber had, Jazz trumpeter and composer Wynton Marsalis worked music into his presentation in January 1998. Jazz, he said, while playing occasionally, was the art form closest in spirit and function to the ideals of America. "Louis Armstrong did not have full United States citizenship when he was born, but he believed in it. And that belief is what makes this music."

The Pulitzer Prize-winning musician drew audience raves. "People all around me were exclaiming it to be the best Richmond Forum ever," W. Baxter Perkinson, Jr.

Above: Trumpeter Wynton Marsalis shares philosophy and music in a January 1998 Forum appearance that some called the best ever. Below: Mary Tyler Moore waits in the Landmark Theater green room with a friend in March 1998.

wrote to the editor of the *Times-Dispatch.* "Men and women from ages 20 to 80 all seemed to know they were in the presence of a very special man. When Mr. Marsalis spoke, it was as quiet and reverent as a church. His ability to calmly articulate difficult subjects from music theory to racism showed wisdom and maturity beyond a normal man born in 1961. His prescription for society's ills went far beyond music and his view of the big picture was enlightening."

The Forum shifted from music to the Mideast when former Israeli Prime Minister Shimon Peres followed Marsalis in February. Peres, the 1994 Nobel Peace Prize winner for his role in the Oslo Peace Agreement between Israel and the Palestine Liberation Organization, dealt with a variety of questions—but tensions in Iraq dominated the somber evening.

Peres praised the 1991 military strike against Iraq by a U.S.-led coalition of forces. "If not for Desert Storm, Saddam Hussein would today possess nuclear weapons," he said. Peres hoped talks between the United Nations and Iraq would be successful because Hussein needed to be stopped, he said. "He is a killer. He has killed more people

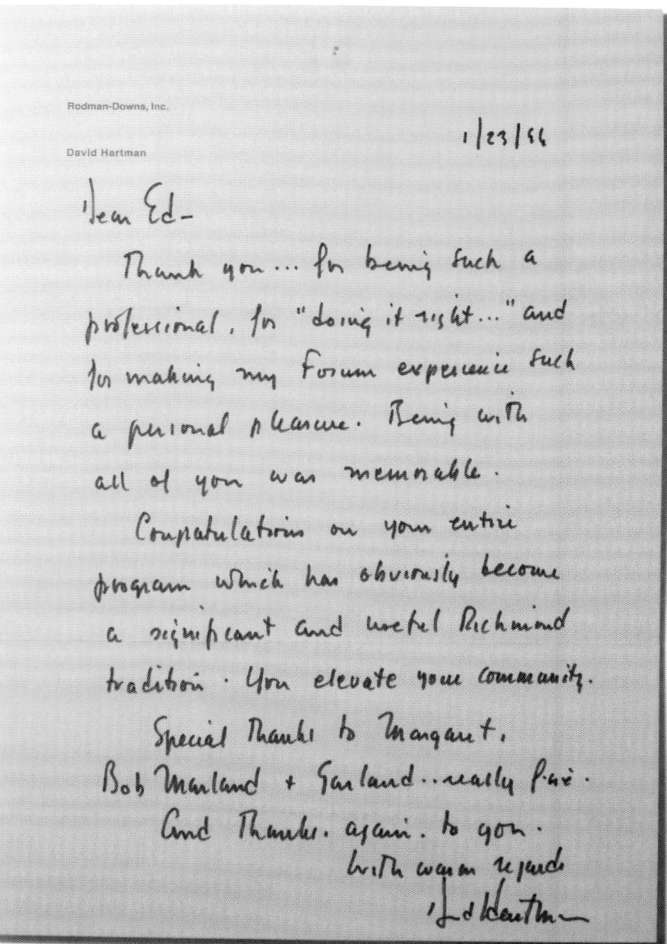

Rodman-Downs, Inc.

David Hartman

1/23/96

Dear Ed-

Thank you... for being such a professional, for "doing it right..." and for making my Forum experience such a personal pleasure. Being with all of you was memorable.

Congratulations on your entire program which has obviously become a significant and useful Richmond tradition. You elevate your community.

Special Thanks to Margaret, Bob Marland + Garland.. really fine.

And Thanks again to you.

With warm regards

David Hartman

"(The Forum) has obviously become a significant and useful Richmond tradition. You elevate your community."

DAVID HARTMAN // ABC newsman

Moderator of the January 1996 program featuring astronauts Neil Armstrong and Eugene Cernan, with *Voyager* pilot Dick Rutan

than any other leader that is still alive." But if Hussein did not comply with U.N. resolutions, "there is no alternative than to teach him a lesson in a different way," Peres said.

One interested listener in the sold-out Landmark crowd of 3,600 was the Most Reverend Walter Sullivan, bishop of the Catholic Diocese of Richmond, who had publicly denounced the Clinton Administration's threat to bomb Iraq. Though Peres had said he would support such military action, Sullivan said he admired Peres as a man of peace. "He also is hoping for diplomacy," he told Carrie Johnson of the *Times-Dispatch*. "I just think he has a broader world view than some of our own leadership."

For the next program, The Forum continued its shift: from music to the Mideast—to Mary. The headliner was Mary Tyler Moore, star of what are considered two of television's best situation-comedies: *The Dick Van Dyke Show* and her own *Mary Tyler Moore Show.* Stepping up to the lectern, she quickly sized up the situation.

"I think I know what you want from the story of my life.

"You want smut."

The audience roared.

As is usually the case with stars, what everyone really wanted was behind-the-scenes stories, which she delivered.

Her first TV role was as Sam, a sexy switchboard operator on *Richard Diamond, Private Detective* whose legs and lips were all that was shown, but Moore became a women's role model. Even as a suburban housewife in *The Dick Van Dyke Show,* she said, "I wore pants. TV wives didn't do that. TV wives wore full-length floral frocks with high heels—usually while they were vacuuming." Then as the star of her own show, she was a single, independent career woman.

Not every role on her show was so positive, she revealed.

Popular Ted Knight, who played bumbling

anchorman Ted Baxter, grew so tired of playing an idiot that he broke down in tears in front of the producer, Moore confided. "He said, 'I can't play Ted Baxter anymore. People think I'm stupid and I'm not. I'm an intelligent, well-read man and people think I'm a schmuck.'"

The producer had nearly persuaded Baxter to return to the role as it was when a staffer came in and clapped Knight on the back, Moore said. "He said, 'Ah, Ted. America's favorite schmuck.'"

THE EVENING OF SATURDAY, January 16, 1999, was one of those creative pairings that Rucker and The Forum would now seek from time to time.

Robert Bennett was representing President Clinton in a sexual harassment case and impeachment proceedings. His younger brother, William, was a conservative commentator and author of *The Death of Outrage: Bill Clinton and the Assault on American Ideals.* This was the first time the famous siblings had met publicly to talk about Clinton, adultery, perjury, and impeachment.

Tim Russert, host of NBC's *Meet the Press* and moderator that evening, said he was looking forward to learning about "the DNA, the genetic mutation that created both William and Robert Bennett." *USA Today* made their friendly-but-serious program national news by sending a reporter to Richmond and printing a lengthy play-by-play under the headline,"Bennett Brothers Begging to Differ."

Former British Prime Minister John Major fulfilled The Forum's self-imposed requirement of an annual world leader with his November 1998 appearance. Major told the audience he thought Britain should wait a few years before adopting the Euro, the European currency that was to come into effect the following January 1: "Not now, because the risks are too high."

Major also shared a story about Russian President Boris Yeltsin's visit to his country estate. The two men went for a walk but Yeltsin quickly tired. Major suggested a visit to a local pub. The pub was closed when they reached it, however, so a Yeltsin aide began banging on the door. "Open up!" he demanded. "It's the president of Russia." From inside came a doubting Britisher's voice, Major said: "'Oh, yes? And this is the Kaiser.'"

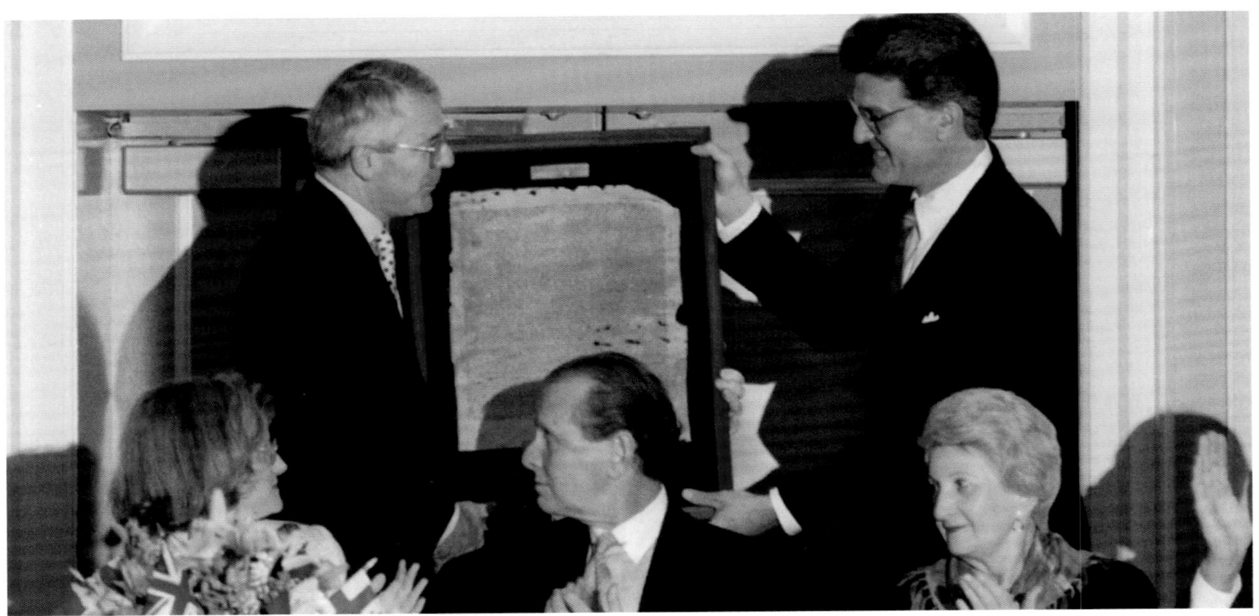

At the dinner before the November 1998 program, Ed Rucker (right) presents former British Prime Minister John Major with a framed reproduction of the Magna Carta.

At one time or another, almost every word has been uttered from the stage during the current Forum's 300 hours of programs. But actress Julie Andrews no doubt is the only one to attempt "suoicodilaipxecitsiligarfilacrepus." She pulled it off, too, it being an exact-backwards variation of the non-word she famously sang in the *Mary Poppins* movie, "supercalifragilisticexpialidocious."

It's hardly the only unexpected word Andrews ever let fly. As she told The Forum in November 1999, the film's director, Robert Stevenson, saved all the dangerous flying stunts for *Mary Poppins* until the final day. She was suspended from the ceiling when, suddenly, a wire slipped. She abruptly fell a foot—and immediately sent word to lower her slowly. Instead, she came crashing to the stage. "I let fly with several Anglo-Saxon four-letter words that Disney has not heard before or since," she said.

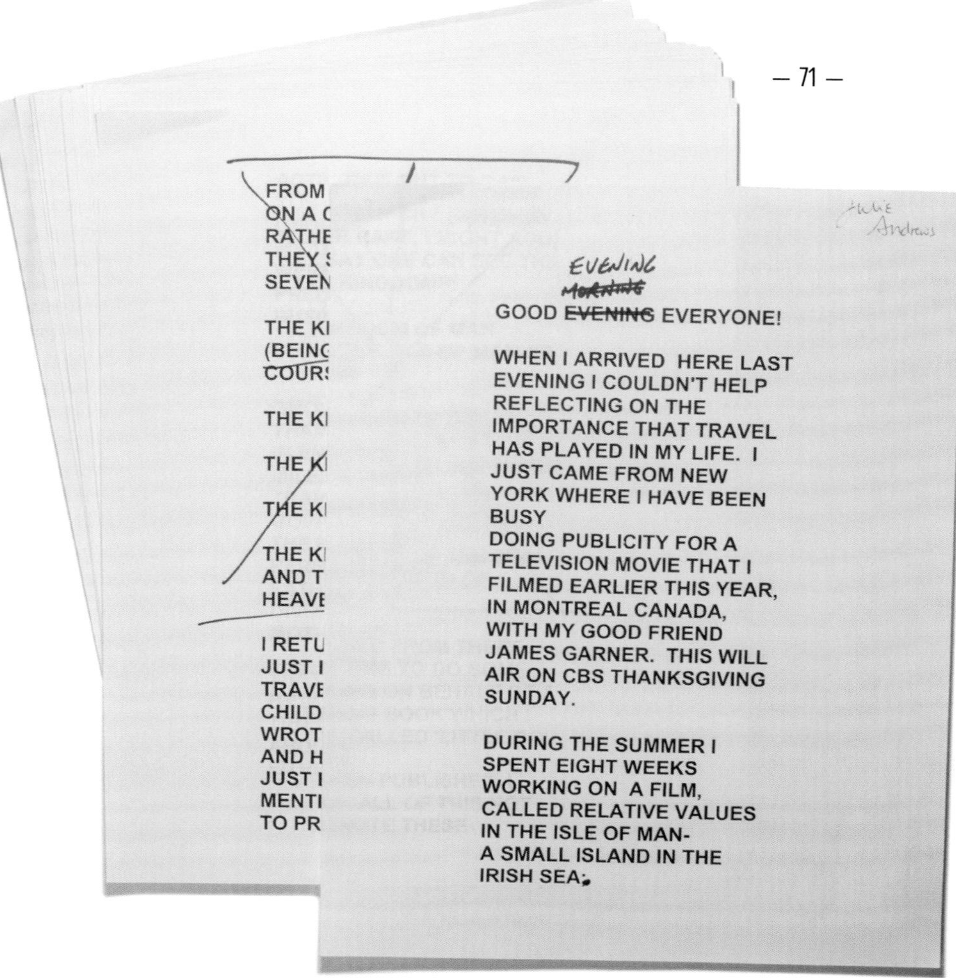

Julie Andrews

EVENING

~~MORNING~~

GOOD ~~EVENING~~ EVERYONE!

WHEN I ARRIVED HERE LAST EVENING I COULDN'T HELP REFLECTING ON THE IMPORTANCE THAT TRAVEL HAS PLAYED IN MY LIFE. I JUST CAME FROM NEW YORK WHERE I HAVE BEEN BUSY DOING PUBLICITY FOR A TELEVISION MOVIE THAT I FILMED EARLIER THIS YEAR, IN MONTREAL CANADA, WITH MY GOOD FRIEND JAMES GARNER. THIS WILL AIR ON CBS THANKSGIVING SUNDAY.

DURING THE SUMMER I SPENT EIGHT WEEKS WORKING ON A FILM, CALLED RELATIVE VALUES IN THE ISLE OF MAN- A SMALL ISLAND IN THE IRISH SEA;

Julie Andrews' Forum stage script.

On January 15, 2000, ABC-TV news anchor Peter Jennings and former *Life* magazine writer Todd Brewster brought 100 years of perspective when they came to talk about *The Century,* the title of both their book and a History Channel series.

They did not hesitate in answering an audience member's question on what they saw as the 20th century's most important event: World War I, for the changes it brought in the hierarchy of government in Europe and the massive death toll.

But the pin-drop moment came when Jennings read a book excerpt from the words of Clara Hancox, a Depression-era child. She had put nickels and dimes in her piggy bank when she had any.

"One day I came home and grabbed hold of my piggy bank, just to give it a shake, and discovered that there was nothing in it . . . and my father took me in his arms and said, 'I'm sorry. I had to have money. But it's a loan. I'll pay it back to you.' He never did. . . . That's what was bad. It wasn't the piggy bank; it was to see this happen to the man who in my eyes could do no wrong."

BY 2000, MORE CHANGES were underway at The Richmond Forum.

That year, Rucker hired Dee Raubenstine as director of development, a position she still holds today. The Forum also purchased an office that summer, a 1,500-square-foot, two-floor structure in a small office park off Forest Hill Avenue in South Richmond. The office, which cost $89,500, was next to one The Forum had been renting for twelve years.

FORUM FILES

WHAT THEY'RE REALLY LIKE

Jeff O'Flaherty, former treasurer and board member, estimates he has been to more than 75 percent of programs during The Richmond Forum's 30 years. He has met many of the speakers. His assessments of some:

"**ANDREW LLOYD WEBBER** wouldn't shake hands.

"**DAVID GERGEN** offered to help my son get into Duke (he was fourteen at the time).

"**JAMES CARVILLE** had a tough time talking about anything but politics.

"**MIKHAIL GORBACHEV** pretended he didn't understand English when I asked him for an autograph.

"**MIKE WALLACE** once interviewed my father on *60 Minutes;* I told him about it and he feigned remembering it. But I remember his question to me: 'Do you think I was fair?'

"**GEORGE MITCHELL** and I laughed about being 'Maniacs' (my birth state).

Robert Redford (left) poses with Paula and Jeff O'Flaherty at a November 2005 Forum reception.

"**ROBERT REDFORD** knew how to take a picture. The large majority of his shots were profiles, not directly looking at the camera. . . . The largest ticket request I had was to meet Robert Redford. A lot of women wanted their picture with him. When they did get to meet him, there was complete silence!"

FORUM FILES

THE MOST FAMOUS GAFFE

Forum speaker Neil Armstrong delivered his most famous speech on the moon in 1969.

The appearance of four astronauts at The Forum in January 1996 gave the most famous of the four, Neil Armstrong, a chance to explain what may have been one of history's most famous misstatements.

Armstrong, who in 1969 became the first to walk on the moon, uttered the famous line: "That's one small step for man, one giant leap for mankind." As linguists the world over soon pointed out, it made no sense: "man" and "mankind" are synonyms here.

Armstrong told moderator and TV newsman David Hartman that he had intended to place the necessary "a" in front of "man"—and actually thought he had.

So, Hartman asked, did the radio transmission drop the "a"?

He didn't know, Armstrong answered. "I think everybody will forgive me if I missed it," he added, however. "It was a pretty exciting time."

Most years, The Forum showcases politics in some fashion. Perhaps it has never been showcased so colorfully as during the April 2000 program with former Republican Speaker of the House Newt Gingrich and Democratic strategist James Carville.

Meet the Press moderator Tim Russert returned to . . . referee. In his introduction, Russert borrowed an assessment originally made by former first lady Barbara Bush of John Sununu, chief of staff to her husband, President George Bush. Sununu had once asked her, "Why do people take an instant dislike to me?" The first lady's response: "Because it saves time."

Gingrich, who helped orchestrate the House of Representatives' vote to impeach President Clinton, said: "It came out exactly right. The House sent a signal to the president that a severe penalty will be paid, but the Senate took notice of the fact that this was not a case large enough to justify vacating the office and repudiating the vote of the American people."

Carville saw it in opposite fashion. "We spent $52 million to find out that a grown man misbehaved with a young woman and didn't want anybody to know about it."

Tom Brokaw, who had been interviewing President-elect George W. Bush in Midland, Texas, earlier in the day, barely made his pre-program dinner in January 2001. He had to be flown in on an NBC plane.

Onstage, Brokaw recounted his career highlights but called writing his best-selling book about his parents' World War II generation, *The Greatest Generation,* his most important professional achievement. Martha Tiller, a Richmond woman whose husband was lost in World

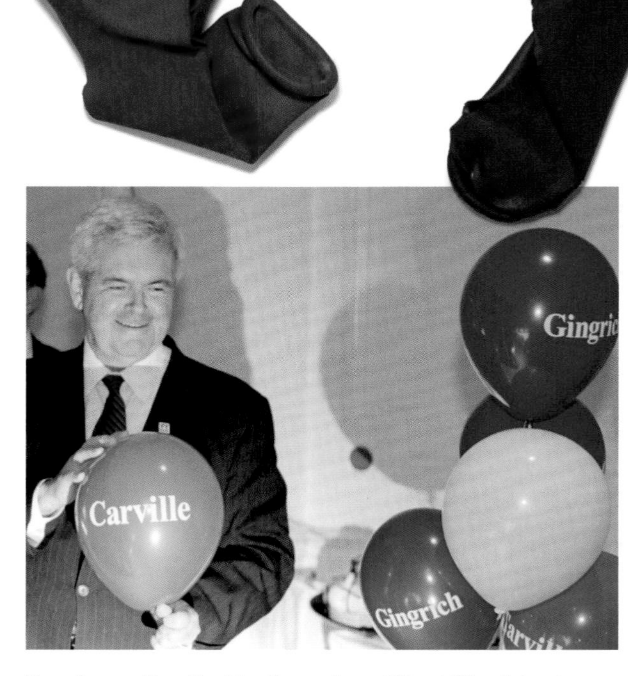

Top: James Carville, Tim Russert, and Newt Gingrich, plus shriveled proof that The Forum never throws anything away. Bottom: The photo The Forum promised Gingrich it would never show anybody.

NBC Nightly News *anchor Tom Brokaw meets up with Martha Tiller at the post-Forum dessert reception at The Jefferson Hotel. The Richmond woman's late husband, killed in World War II, was portrayed in Brokaw's book,* The Greatest Generation.

Right: The once and future prime minister of Israel, Benjamin Netanyahu, is interviewed by NPR journalist Daniel Schorr in February 2001.

War II and was portrayed in the book, was on hand at The Forum. Brokaw and she got together at a reception.

The only unnerving moment of the feel-good evening with the man from Yankton, South Dakota, came from a Forum questioner who wanted to know if Brokaw's parents had been members of the Communist Party. Brokaw's eyes watered as he responded with irritation: "That is an insult to my family and what I stand for. If it weren't so outrageous, I would probably work up a pretty good anger about it." A few days later, Mechanicsville resident Martin April wrote to the *Times-Dispatch:* "After a wonderful evening at the Richmond Forum . . . we can only hope that [Brokaw's] memory of Richmond is not [of that question]. Let's hope he remembers Richmond as a place where the auditorium was filled to capacity with a welcoming, appreciative, attentive, and warm audience."

Forumgoers had the chance to hear another newsworthy if controversial speaker in February 2001, former Israeli Prime Minister Benjamin Netanyahu. As they arrived, they saw sixty-five protesters across the street, most of Palestinian descent, chanting vigorously, though in orderly fashion: "One-two-three-four, stop the killing, stop the war. Five-six-seven-eight, Israel is a killing state. End the occupation now."

Netanyahu, defeated for reelection in 1999 after being "portrayed as an obstacle to peace," made news by saying he might run again. He drew more attention by criticizing the Clinton Administration's "deep intervention" in the peace process.

DON'T LEAVE HOME WITHOUT THEM

Queen Noor of Jordan with Douglas Nabhan.

Douglas M. Nabhan, The Forum's lawyer and former board member and chairman, has something he takes abroad that's even more important than an American Express card: photographs.

"My passion is traveling in the Middle East and whenever I travel I carry two pictures with me," Nabhan says. "One has me with Queen Noor of Jordan and the other has me having cocktails with Benjamin Netanyahu." The photos were snapped at the two speakers' Forum appearances in 2003 and 2001, respectively.

So do they help?

"If I pull out the picture of me with the Queen when I am Jordan, the driver usually drives his car off the road," Nabhan reports. "But whenever I try to curry favor in Israel, it doesn't do a thing because my passport has too many Arab stamps."

FORUM FILES

A SOLITARY MOMENT

Not all important moments of The Richmond Forum take place on stage.

On March 18, 2000, Archbishop Desmond Tutu, winner of the 1984 Nobel Peace Prize, gave an inspiring and wide-ranging speech on spiritual values, materialistic possessions, Mother Theresa, the human spirit, the Tiananmen Square Massacre, Nelson Mandela, God's creation of human masterpieces, equal respect for all religions, the Dalai Lama, and the ordination of women. It was an emotionally exultant speech that brought the Forum crowd to its feet in sustained applause and left the moderator to remark: "Tonight, I have been standing on holy ground."

But Tutu himself had had a special moment in Richmond, unknown to most in the audience.

That afternoon, Tutu had slipped away virtually alone to visit the statue of Arthur Ashe on Monument Avenue. Richmond's Ashe, who had overcome racism in his hometown, had gone on to become a world-renowned humanitarian, scholar, and, of course, tennis champion. He had died seven years earlier of AIDS contracted from a blood transfusion. This statue had, with great controversy, been erected on an avenue previously dedicated only to Confederate war heroes.

Tutu stayed for a moment. Then he returned to his car, with three quick photographs snapped by The Forum's driver the only indication he had been here.

MEETING JOHN GLENN

When astronaut John Glenn spoke at The Forum in November 2000, two guests were especially thrilled to meet him.

One was six-year-old Jack Bland. "My son came dressed in a NASA outfit," former board member Mike Bland remembers. "Glenn signed it." He wanted to be an astronaut some day, the boy proudly told Glenn, "'cause I'll get to float around."

The other thrilled guest was Mil Hayes, widow of William Hayes, and her story was more poignant.

Her husband had led the recovery phase of Project Mercury in 1962, during which Glenn became the first American in space. Glenn was plucked from the ocean and brought onboard the USS *Randolph* after parachuting into the sea. Her husband was waiting.

Now, Mil Hayes, her son, and three grandchildren were at The Forum. She carried a large photograph that evening. It showed her husband welcoming Glenn onboard the deck of the *Randolph* that day nearly four decades earlier.

Glenn signed it: "To Mil with best regards. This is a great day. Best always, John Glenn."

Young Jack Bland donned a helmet for the famous visitor, and their photo (above) made the next day's Times-Dispatch. *Right: John Glenn speaks while footage of a Space Shuttle launch plays on the video screen above him.*

THEY SAID IT AT THE FORUM

As her character Chrissy, "All my life, I always knew I wanted to be somebody. I see now that I should have been more specific."
LILY TOMLIN // March 1999

"We are supposed to be like God. Perfect like God, loving not just our friends—because sinners do that—but those who are not. . . . We have an extraordinary God, a God who has a soft spot for sinners."
ARCHBISHOP DESMOND TUTU // March 2000

"One of the sad things about modern life is that [teenagers] have been deprived of their dreams. Today, all the images are supplied for them—television, movies, the Internet. They don't have any images of their own. They're a spectator generation."
FRANK McCOURT // March 2001

On Monsignor Thomas Hartman and he, co-Forum speakers, describing their duties since the September 11 attacks on the World Trade Center, "We just finished thirty funerals and memorial services between us. We didn't have a single body."
RABBI MARC GELLMAN // January 2002

On finding the truth of an historical subject, "It's hard work. Sometime it's daunting. You try to get below the surface. . . . That's what all writers of biography and history are trying to do: make me see and make me feel what's happening and why."
DAVID McCULLOUGH // March 2002

"The world was pretty much the same before September 11 as it was after September 11—the same risks, the same people plotting what they were plotting, the same forces of terror. What had changed is, we now have had the curtain lifted and we can see what existed. And we can't go back to where we used to be."
RUDY GIULIANI // January 2003

On being different from her TV *Murphy Brown* character: "She's a much more confident woman, much more ambitious. . . . There's a price for that kind of mono-focus on your career. I'm just for balance."
CANDICE BERGEN // February 2004

"We tend to be creative when we are scared, when we're threatened."
BURT RUTAN // November 2006

"At first, when I heard people calling me a legend, I thought they were 'playing the doubles.'" (Referencing a game of trading insults.)
B. B. KING // February 2007

"Iran wants to develop a ballistic missile that can reach the Eastern Seaboard. You're in Richmond. Think about it."

BENJAMIN NETANYAHU // February 2001

"There are right-wing chat shows and blogs, and there are left-wing chat shows and blogs. They are often covertly and openly designed to generate heat and not light."
JIM LEHRER // March 2007

"I think the United States should withdraw as soon as possible from Iraq."
VICENTE FOX // November 2007

"My family is first, whatever humanitarian work I can do is second, and my career is third."
MICHAEL DOUGLAS // February 2008

EMORY UNIVERSITY
Candler School of Theology

May 10, 2000

Mr. Edward W. Rucker
President
The Richmond Forum
6966 Forest Hill Avenue
Richmond, VA 23225

Dear Friend:

Thank you very much for your kind letter and especially for the very beautiful pictures that will be a splendid memento of a memorable visit.

I enclose a copy of a letter you could send to the His Holiness, the Dalai Lama when you write to invite him. I know that his schedule is hectic, but I hope that we will be able to persuade him one day to address your Forum, because I am quite certain that all your members will be thrilled with the encounter with a remarkable man.

God bless you richly.

Yours sincerely,

Desmond M. Tutu
Archbishop Emeritus
William R. Cannon Visiting Distinguished Professor of Theology

DMT/jls

2.30 postage

Benjamin Netanyahu

26.2.2001

Dear Ed,

Many thanks for hosting me at the Richmond Forum. You were unfailingly kind, and I was delighted with the program and the audience.

Best wishes,

GEORGE BUSH

February 28, 1994

Dear Ed,

Many thanks for your wonderful hospitality during my recent visit to Richmond. I hope from your perspective everything went as well as it did for me. Please convey to all those involved with my visit my very best wishes and my thanks for a job well done.

Warm regards,

Sincerely,

Mr. Edward Rucker
Richmond Forum
6966 Forest Hill Avenue
Richmond, Virginia 23225

COLIN L. POWELL 12 FEB

Dear Ed,

A great evening, again! Thanks for inviting me and for the splendid hospitality.

See you in 11 years!

Cheers, C.

Successful people often take the time to write thank-you letters and notes, and the Forum files are full of them. Some, like Archbishop Desmond Tutu's, even offer to help bring other speakers. Tutu did write that letter to the Dalai Lama. But as of yet, His Holiness remains one big name The Forum has not been able to land.

Forum subscribers making speaker suggestions either loved Bill Clinton or hated him.

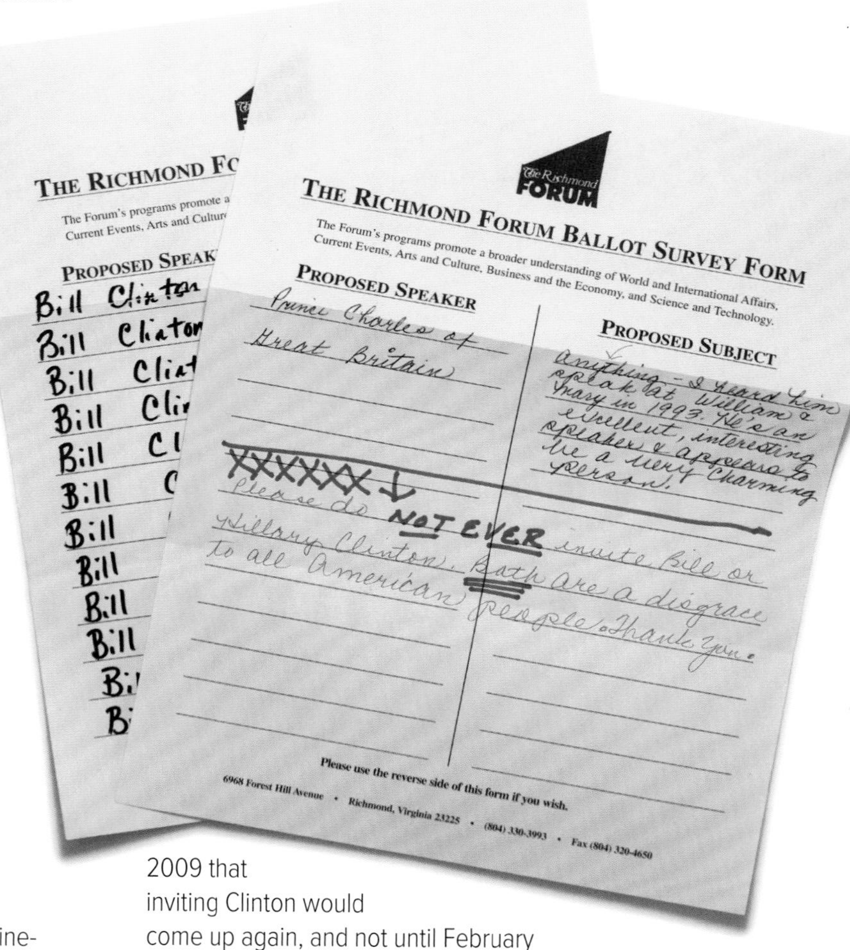

THE RICHMOND FO

The Forum's programs promote a
Current Events, Arts and Cultur

PROPOSED SPEAK

Bill Clinton
Bill Clinton
Bill Clint
Bill Clin
Bill Cl
Bill C
Bill
Bill
Bill
Bill
Bi
Bi

The Richmond FORUM

THE RICHMOND FORUM BALLOT SURVEY FORM

The Forum's programs promote a broader understanding of World and International Affairs, Current Events, Arts and Culture, Business and the Economy, and Science and Technology.

PROPOSED SPEAKER	PROPOSED SUBJECT
Prince Charles of Great Britain	anything - I heard him speak at William & Mary in 1993. He's an excellent, interesting speaker & appears to be a very charming person.

XXXXXX Please do NOT EVER invite Bill or Hillary Clinton. Both are a disgrace to all American people. Thank you.

Please use the reverse side of this form if you wish.

6968 Forest Hill Avenue • Richmond, Virginia 23225 • (804) 330-3993 • Fax (804) 320-4650

IF NETANYAHU WAS BOTH newsworthy and controversial, he had nothing on Bill Clinton.

Subscriber surveys in the fall of 2000 included many requests to bring the soon-to-be-former president to The Forum. There were also very pointed requests to not dare bring him. To some Richmonders, he was an anathema: a left-of-center Democrat, and one who had left the White House under a moral/ethical cloud. To others, he was a former president, so of course, he should be invited to The Forum.

The board took up the question November 15, 2000, as meeting minutes reveal: "Overall, the Board agreed that as the premier public forum in the country, The Forum should invite Bill Clinton to speak to The Forum next year. A few members acknowledged the potential controversy and wondered if a year out of office would be enough elapsed time. Others suggested pairing Clinton with other speakers. Mr. Rucker explained that with former heads of state there is less opportunity to direct or shape the content and format of the program." Nonetheless, the board "encouraged Mr. Rucker to pursue Clinton as a possible speaker in the future."

It didn't happen. Rucker took to the Forum stage four months later to make a unique announcement, intended to assure subscribers who had been asked to begin renewing their subscriptions for the next season without the full line-up of speakers having been announced: "We will announce our plans for next season during next month's program . . . However, to somewhat clear the air at this time, our plans for next season do NOT include a Forum that will feature former President Bill Clinton." The announcement was met with applause and even whistles.

Mike Bland, board chairman at the time, remembers that "the controversy associated with the Clintons regarding the way they left the White House and the controversial pardons made him a controversial pick for anyone" at the time, including other institutions. "We decided to wait until the smoke cleared."

Nevertheless, it apparently would not be until 2009 that inviting Clinton would come up again, and not until February 2013, a dozen years after leaving office, that the former president would appear.

"We never intended on waiting twelve years," Bland says. "We always wanted him as we have a tradition of having ex-presidents come on board."

The 2001–02 season did include two of America's favorite entertainers, Hal Holbrook and Dick Clark.

Holbrook, who had performed as Mark Twain for forty-seven years, had to forgo the pre-program sponsors dinner, spending those hours having his makeup applied. That sort of attention to detail was not surprising. Holbrook's contract included seventeen pages of highly specific requirements for his November 2001 appearance.

Under the section, "Rug," were these instructions:

Mr. Holbrook's playing area is an Oriental style rug 24' long and 12' feet wide. This must be secured first. Ask for Oriental, Persian, or Eastern patterns. ***Avoid white or beige backgrounds.*** *Measurement is most critical. Do not believe the measurements on the tag or promises made by the dealer. Do not be conned;* ***measure it yourself!*** *American-made reproductions are O.K. If a 12'x24' rug cannot be found,* ***choice #2*** *would be three matching, machine-made 9'x12' reproductions. (The width of these is usually at 8'4" after binding, which when laid side by side gives us 12'x25'.) These may be found at Home Depot, Builders Square, Wal-Mart, etc. If you find only 2 identical, a third may be of similar colors, with a medallion center pattern. Keep in mind that these stores may not have three identical rugs in stock. You may have to order ahead or go to several branches of the same store.* ***Again, avoid white or beige backgrounds.*** *DO NOT get 3 – 9'x12' old rugs from a dealer because they will not match and will not be of exact measurement to each other.* ***Choice #3*** *is to have a rug made. Commercial carpet companies who install carpet in hotels and restaurants can cut an 'Oriental' pattern to 10'x22' and add a solid 1' border to make a 12'x24' rug.*

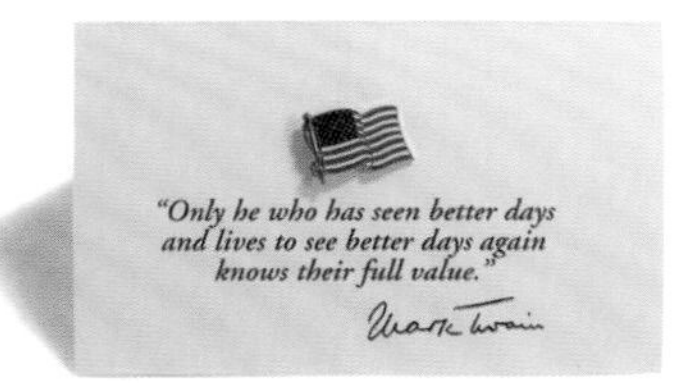

Above: Flag pins and a Mark Twain quote awaited dinner guests at the first Forum after the September 11 attacks. Below: Hal Holbrook is Mark Twain. Superimposed is his later thank-you to The Forum.

Holbrook also had the routine perfected for the Forum audience—and his may have been the perfect program to be staged as The Forum's first after the attacks of September 11. Twain's witticisms about the daily press, lawyers, organized religion and racism seemed uncannily timely in the perfectly delivered, cigar-puffing performance.

So, too, did his comment about mankind's general atrocities: "It is inexplicable that God would endure all this," Twain/Holbrook offered, "with lightning so cheap." The audience rose to a roaring standing ovation at the evening's end.

In an effort to develop original programming for The Richmond Forum, Ed Rucker had been working behind the scenes for two years with Dick Clark, the popular host of *American Bandstand,* and his staff. The effort proved worthwhile, both for the Forum audience that night who were treated to a rare public presentation by Clark, and for those who saw the Forum content transformed into a television special later.

While videos played behind him of performers like The Crystals, Neil Sedaka, Van Halen and even a young rapper, Will Smith, Clark told the Richmond audience that nothing has changed since he began *Bandstand.* "Kids like what their parents don't like. It's no different today than it was in 1956."

One thing had changed, however, and it came out

To The Richmond Forum
"Always do right. This will please some people and astonish the rest."
Mark Twain Hal Holbrook

Above: Dick Clark (second from right) meets with members of local band Carbon Leaf: Terry Clark, Carter Gravatt, and Barry Privett. The band had won the American Music Awards' first-ever New Music Award the previous month, and Clark added his public congratulations from the stage. Right: A portion of Clark's February 2002 Forum speech.

…ond Forum Presentation 12

That's when the "payola" hearings began.

I immediately felt like I was wearing a target. I wasn't immediately called by the committee to testify, but my name kept coming up all the time.

Before I was summoned to testify, my boss, Leonard Goldenson, the head of ABC, called me into his office. He asked me if there was any thing that the politicians could reveal about me, something that would reflect badly on "American Bandstand" and ABC. I told him the only thing I could think of was I was the part owner of two little record companies, a couple of music publishing ventures, a talent management firm and a record pressing plant.

These days probably nobody would bat an eye. Today the media conglomerates own TV networks, TV production companies, cable networks, record companies, movie production companies, movie distributors, record distribution companies, music publishing companies and CD manufacturing plants … the tentacles are all over the place. These days, that's called horizontal and vertical integration. In my early days, I was told I had a "potential conflict of interests".

Mr. Goldenson told me I had twenty-four hours to choose between continuing in broadcasting or a career as the owner of record and music publishing companies. It didn't take me that long to decide. I knew my future was in broadcasting. I divested myself of my music interests and continued to host "American Bandstand."

A few months later, I was called to come from my home base in Philadelphia to Washington, D.C., to explain why I was playing rock 'n' roll and promoting rock 'n' roll artists.

There I was, all of twenty-nine years old, being hauled before a tribunal backed by big money music interests. They were a lot more interested in presuming my guilt than in letting me prove my innocence. It was a real scary and a career-threatening moment, let me tell

But the bottomline was: I WAS innocent. I never ac
Nobody needed to give me money to play rock 'n' ro
what I told the Congressmen.

In the end the payola hearings fizzled out. There was
average person to get up in arms about. Even the man
bought rock 'n' roll music because they liked it.

Ironically, after the payola hearings "American Bandsta
to always watch my back, because somebody might be
reason.

By the end of 1960, there wasn't much steam in the anti-
was coming to accept rock 'n' roll as part of the overall m
who once battled rock 'n' roll were now jumping on the ba

The Richmond FORUM
Presents
Dick Clark
Saturday
February 16, 2002
at 8:00 p.m.
Landmark Theate
at 6 N. Laurel Street
Richmond, Virginia
$34 Sub-$40 S
ORCH C S
SEC ROW
Dick Clark

during a question from the audience. Clark had hosted his thirtieth annual *New Year's Rockin' Eve* from Times Square six weeks earlier. The attacks of September 11 had come just months before that. "I honestly had the feeling that this might be the last go-round," Clark said. "But I was so angry at what happened on 9-11 that I felt like we had to do it, because if we didn't, [terrorists] would have won."

THE FORUM HAS HAD REPEAT speakers from time to time, though appearances are often decades apart. The popular duo of historians David McCullough and Doris Kearns Goodwin returned in March 2002, just five years after their first appearance.

Through a fluke of timing, Goodwin was on the hot seat in the weeks before The Forum.

Her recent biography, *The Fitzgeralds and the Kennedys,* had included thousands of words directly taken from another book. Charges of plagiarism swirled around Goodwin. She would settle a lawsuit and make changes to the book—and she had taken leave from her roles as *PBS NewsHour with Jim Lehrer* contributor and as a Pulitzer Prize judge. She also lost speaking invitations, including one from James Madison University—but The Forum made a decision to go forward.

"Since I know you are all aware of the media maelstrom that has enveloped me, you are entitled to an explanation," Goodwin said. Her handwritten notes, which she thought she had already paraphrased from other books, were actually direct quotes. "Never for a single

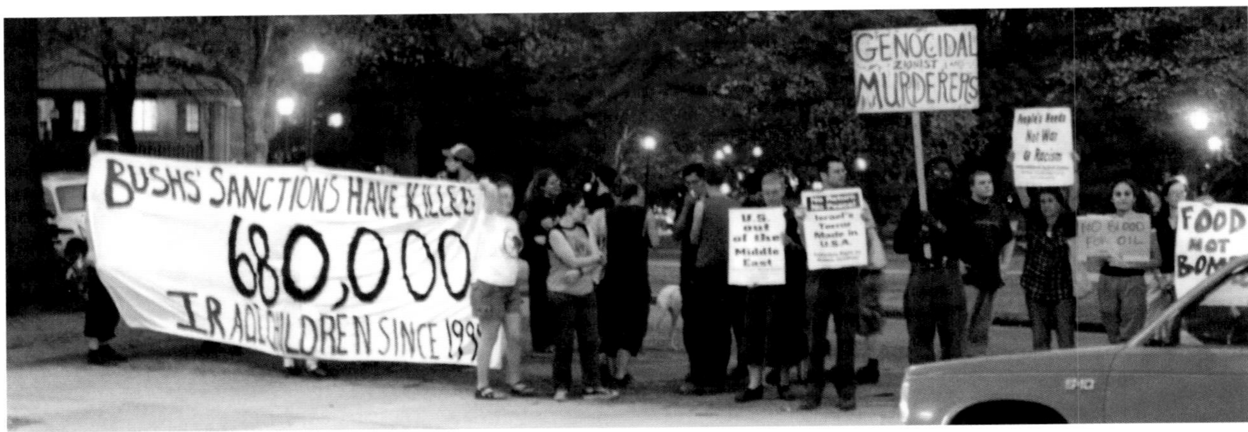

Above: Protesters march in Richmond's Monroe Park as former secretaries of state James Baker and Madeleine Albright arrive to speak in April 2002. Below: Forum subscribers who braved a winter storm in February 2003 were part of a special evening with Queen Noor of Jordan (left) and the former Prime Minister of Pakistan, Benazir Bhutto (right), moderated by Gwen Ifill.

moment did I intend to adopt another writer's words as my own," she said.

After her explanation, the audience applauded for almost thirty seconds.

The season's finale paired two former secretaries of state, Madeleine K. Albright and James A. Baker III, to discuss terrorism and the Middle East. Once again, protesters lined the sidewalk across the street from the theater in Monroe Park.

The February 2003 program included what was frequently an interesting Forum concept: the pairing of speakers not usually paired. This time it was former Pakistani Prime Minister Benazir Bhutto and Queen Noor, widow of King Hussein of Jordan.

It also included what was occasionally a winter Forum problem: bad weather. This time it was a treacherous mix of freezing rain, sleet pellets, and snow that closed most shopping centers, canceled many events and led Governor Mark Warner to declare a state of emergency throughout Virginia. (It did not lead to a

Forum rescheduling, however, something that would occur with David Plouffe in 2010 and again with General Keith Alexander and Robert Mueller in 2015.)

Those who successfully overcame the weather—and two-thirds of the Forum audience did—heard Bhutto say that as prime minister she had to stand up to extremists in trying to make a strong democracy. Bhutto, whose father, a former prime minister, was assassinated, would herself be assassinated less than five years later.

The appearance of actress Candice Bergen in February 2004, represented a first for the five-time Emmy winner best known for her *Murphy Brown* TV series. Forum President Ed Rucker invited her not to talk about her acting career, but rather to share her little-known 1970s photographs taken for NBC's *Today Show, Life* magazine, *Ladies Home Journal* and other clients. Unsure at first, Bergen relented. She scoured her archives to select more than fifty forgotten shots to share on The Forum's big screen, including Paul Newman ("you couldn't take a bad picture of this guy"), Muhammad Ali ("Ali had that unbelievable power and presence; he was so gorgeous, and he knew how gorgeous he was"), family friend Charlie Chaplin, personal hero Jane Goodall, the Ku Klux Klan, Black Panther Party member Huey Newton, bodybuilder Arnold Schwarzenegger, and Sonny and Cher.

There was also Frank, a blind beggar from Harlem who stood in front of Tiffany's jewelry store in New York with his dog. "I was very moved by him and his dog and very curious about someone's life like that." After the attention, Frank earned a lot more money, she said.

During the Q&A, moderated by gallery owner Bev Reynolds, Bergen said she regretted not having a photo of Sean Connery despite making a movie with him. She was also asked whom else she wanted to photograph. The answer: Osama Bin Laden.

The breakout event had not been perfect. Bergen's plane arrived 28 minutes early, and The Forum wasn't there to pick her up. Instead, she went on her own to the Reynolds Gallery, where thirty-two of her photographs were being exhibited for a month in conjunction with her Forum presentation.

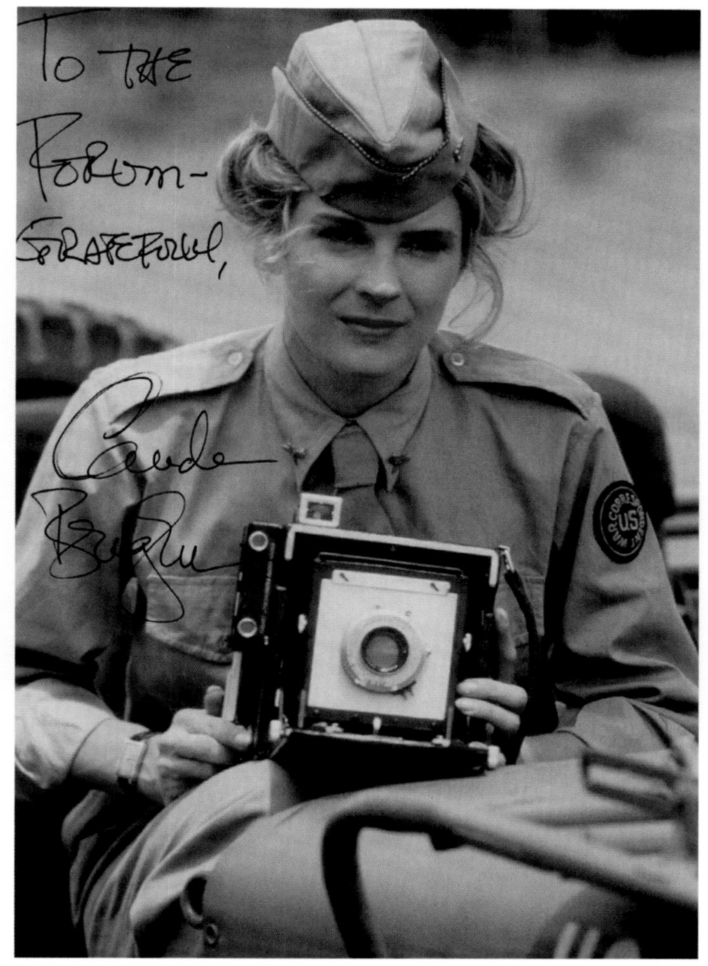

In the 1982 film, Gandhi, *Candice Bergen portrayed photo-journalist and war correspondent Margaret Bourke-White. In 2004, Bergen shared her own photography at The Forum.*

Still the event—a risky one for The Forum—had come off well.

"Every once in a while, we produce a program that goes beyond presenting a great speaker that patrons [hear] expecting to be informed and to simply hear another point of view," Forum President Ed Rucker wrote to Bergen's agent afterward. "I think our group was very supportive and wanting Candice to succeed in so many ways. . . . I do know that this program took guts—courage—because it was new, she was talking about a part of her life that she had not discussed before, and because of the scale of our audience. She did great, and she did it with finesse."

***NEW YORK TIMES* PULITZER PRIZE**-winning columnist Thomas L. Friedman came close to being a no-show in April 2004, says Douglas M. Nabhan, The Forum's lawyer, who was also then in the midst of nearly two decades on the Forum board, including a term as its chairman.

The near cancellation was the fallout of a 2003 scandal involving plagiarism and fabrication by a *Times* reporter, Jayson Blair. "The publisher called all of the writers in from around the world. The idea was they needed to focus on what they were paid to do, write," Nabhan says. Friedman's agent called and said the journalist would need to cancel. "I told him that was ridiculous as his engagement was at least a year off. He told me that was final. I told him that if that were the case, then I wanted him to tell Tom Friedman that he would always be the holder of an unusual distinction in The Richmond Forum's history: He would be the only speaker who had canceled." Friedman appeared.

Someone who no doubt was torn about coming for his 2005 appearance was Tim Russert, moderator of NBC's *Meet the Press.* Russert, making his third appearance, was this time the headliner, talking about Washington, ethics in journalism, and his new book about his father, *Big Russ and Me.* Russert and Richmond loved each other but his beloved Boston College was playing basketball against Syracuse University that evening in a matchup of two of the nation's top ten teams. The solution: The Forum got him into the backstage stagehands lounge, where there was a TV set. Fortunately, B.C. won.

"We consider Tim to be a member of our 'Forum Family,'" Ed Rucker wrote Russert's agent afterward. "There were references to his appearances here in 1999 and 2000 to moderate other programs. I hope that there will be an opportunity to bring him back in the future." Sadly, three years later, the fifty-eight-year-old Russert would die of a heart attack.

General Motors CEO Rick Wagoner, a Richmond area native, spoke in April 2006, for The Forum's twentieth anniversary season. Wagoner, joined onstage by two cars, said he realized what people must be thinking of his returning to his hometown to talk up GM's future: "Isn't that kind of like George Bush going to a military base to talk about his Iraq strategy?" The moderator was Geoffrey Colvin of *Fortune* magazine, who

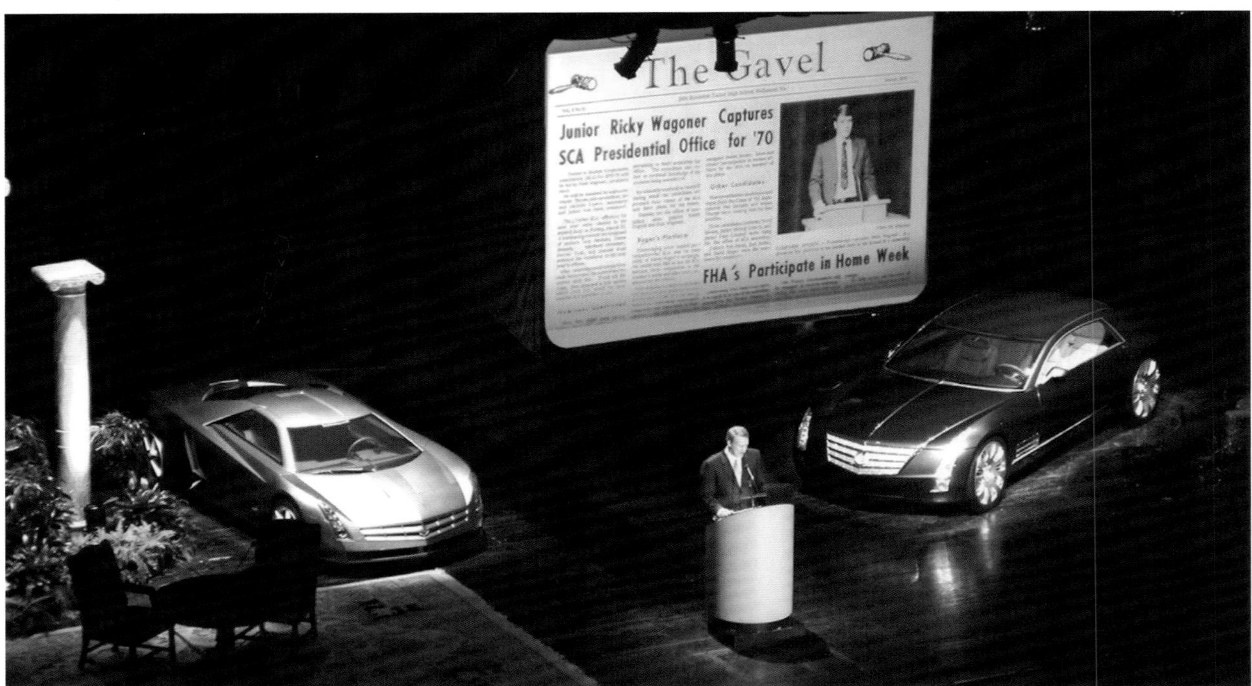

General Motors CEO Rick Wagoner, a Richmond area native and brother of Forum board member Judy Pahren, returns home to speak in April 2006. Joining him onstage were two other very large GM representatives.

THE LEGEND AND THE LEGEND-TO-BE

Cal Ripken, Jr., the Baltimore Orioles' legendary "Ironman" who broke baseball's consecutive-games streak, was the first sports star ever to appear at The Richmond Forum. (Unless, that is, one counts playboy football star Joe Namath, who in what can only be called a masterstroke of programming, had moderated a conversation with famed television psychologist Dr. Joyce Brothers at The Richmond Public Forum in 1970. Their topic: "Love.")

The range of Ripken's appeal could be seen outside the Landmark Theater that evening in November 2003, noted Ed Kelleher of the *Times-Dispatch:* lined up was a bus from Chesterfield County Public Schools and two smaller ones from retirement homes. Inside, Ripken regaled the crowd with video highlights, stories of life and leadership, and an engaging sense of humor.

Earlier, Ripken had met with local Little League All-Stars, as well as players from a local high school, Collegiate. "My son played on Collegiate's baseball team at the time and I had four extra tickets," explains Jeff O'Flaherty, a Forum board member. "I invited Sanford Boisseau, the baseball coach, to choose three [other] players he would like to invite."

For the little-known high schoolers, it was a thrill of a lifetime.

Almost. One of the three was a two-sport athlete who went on to have a few thrills of his own as a football star. Indeed, Russell Wilson would become the first quarterback ever to reach the Super Bowl in two of his first three years in the National Football League.

Nearly a dozen years later, during The Forum's thirtieth anniversary season, he would be part of another example of Forum synchronicity: Russell Wilson himself was booked to appear at The Forum. ❜

Above, left to right: Fourteen-year-old Russell Wilson; Cal Ripken, Jr.; Evan Bronson; Sanford Boisseau; and Evan Ocheltree

WHEN THE KING CAME TO TOWN

Legendary bluesman B. B. King, who appeared in February 2007, was not a typical Forum speaker. Indeed, Forum officials had anticipated a discussion of the blues, with some playing interspersed. King, however, let his guitar, *Lucille,* do most of the talking. King and his eight-man band played a full concert before he took questions from the audience, with Ed Rucker serving as moderator. Perhaps appropriately, for a photo shoot with *Living Blues* magazine, King himself was seated on an actual throne stored backstage by the Virginia Opera.

Those who were there often say it was among their favorite Forum experiences.

"My favorite memory is B. B. King rocking the house," says subscriber April Cain. "I mean REALLY rocking the house. I remember people on their feet screaming, clapping, laughing along to his singing. I actually bent the back shank of my antique engagement ring clapping along so hard to that presentation and had to have it fixed."

King's focus on music did not deprive the evening of relevance. "I loved that he told stories of his own life, which was SOOOOO relevant to American history, but still wove in songs as an illustration of that remarkable life," Cain says. "I'll never forget it as long as I live. This was not only my favorite Richmond Forum; it's the favorite live presentation of any kind that I've ever attended in my 58 years."

What most in the enthralled house did not realize that evening was that this was one of the more unusual Forum offerings offstage, as well.

King's contract demands rivaled those of Hal Holbrook's—but with a more personal flair. They included nineteen rooms in the Omni Hotel, bottles of alcohol, and whole chickens for his band, says board member Mike Bland. The really surprising part: "I saw the contract. We paid him in cash," Bland says. The payment included $50,000 in cashier's checks, the equivalent of cash, along with $25,000 in actual U.S. currency. "He paid his entire crew every night in cash," Bland says. "We literally had to get him a bag of cash as part of his contract."

Richmond Forum President Ed Rucker facilitating the audience Q&A with B. B. King.

reported on the event afterward, another instance of The Forum being national news. He noted Wagoner had been making the rounds talking to news media but this was not part of the campaign; Wagoner had agreed to the Forum gig a full year earlier after his sister persuaded him.

His sister was Forum board member Judy Pahren.

That family connection led to a memorable opportunity for board funnyman Henry Fine. Fine, a financial planner specializing in special needs planning, was blind in one eye, deaf in one ear and not quite movie star-handsome. But when Ed Rucker told the board that superstar actor Robert Redford would be appearing that season, Fine deadpanned:

"Hey, great, my brother's coming, too."

The room exploded in laughter.

"He loved The Forum . . . everyone on the board loved him," Judy Pahren says of Fine. "A great guy. His sudden death, while serving as The Forum's treasurer, really shocked everyone." Fine died of a heart attack at age fifty in 2009.

The following season, 2006–07, led off not only with aeronautical genius Burt Rutan, designer of both *Voyager* and *SpaceShipOne,* but also with a newly produced opening video. The exciting two-minute video used iconic images, if not Forum speakers—Gandhi, Elvis, Ronald Reagan, the Statue of Liberty, Martin Luther King Jr., JFK's funeral, the burning World Trade Center—connected by a series of graphics and strategically deployed words. The music, composed by In Your Ear studio president Carlos Chafin, started slowly, then built dramatically.

The audience applauded at the video's conclusion.

"Richmond is very humble about this kind of thing," said Joe Alexander, a creative director for The Martin Agency, the ad agency that was among several organizations to help create the film. "We should celebrate things like the Forum. They're talking about big stuff."

> "Richmond is very humble... We should celebrate things like the Forum. They're talking about big stuff."
>
> **JOE ALEXANDER // The Martin Agency**

IN 2007, ED RUCKER SUDDENLY announced he was leaving.

It was a shock, says The Forum's longtime art director, Doyle Robinson. The news came during a routine meeting about the program book for the next event.

"We met one day to talk about the upcoming issue; we used to go to the Thai Room to have lunch," Robinson remembers. "He announced that the next two copies he was doing would be his last ones and he was going to Charlottesville. That was the last we heard of him. Everyone was surprised."

Rucker had had rocky relationships with some members of the Forum board and staff who saw him as authoritative and secretive. Mike Bland, a board member during nearly all of Rucker's tenure and chairman for four of those years, saw both sides of the leader. "Ed Rucker was really professional and lifted the organization. . . . But he was a different egg," Bland says. "At the end, he was extraordinarily difficult to get along with."

In announcing his departure, Rucker noted that during his tenure The Forum had grown to be more financially stable: It had the safety net of a reserve fund, its own building and a balanced budget.

Bland agrees. He says Rucker stepped into "an extraordinarily difficult situation: Ralph [Krueger] was loved by a lot of people. I think Ed didn't get the credit for the things he did."

Like many on the board, Judy Pahren saw the yin and the yang of Rucker. "Without Ed, I don't know where

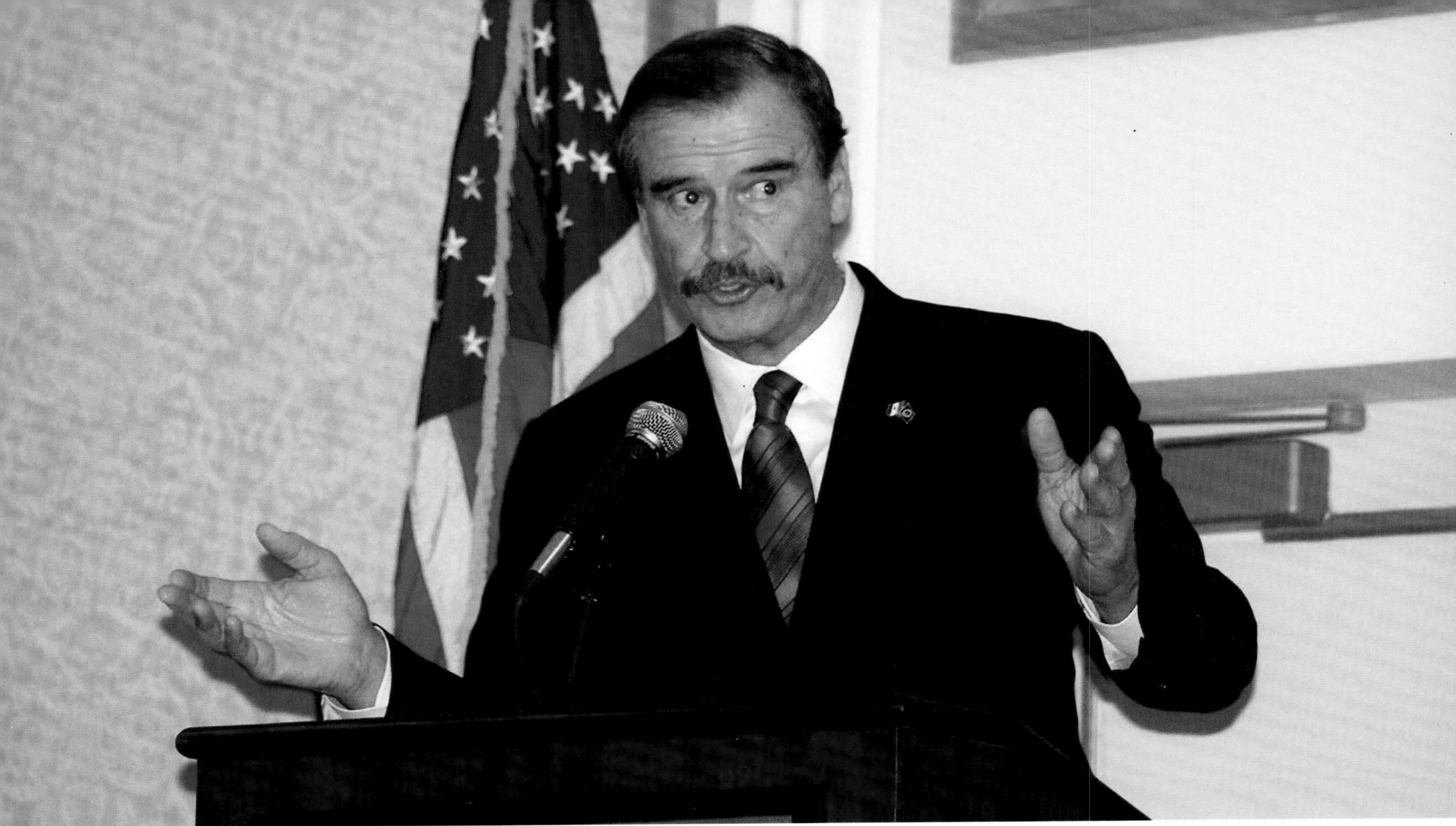

Vicente Fox, President of Mexico from 2000 to 2006, addresses dinner guests before his November 3, 2007, presentation to The Forum. Earlier that day, Fox and his wife, Marta Sahagún, had ditched their security detail to go shopping in Carytown.

The Forum would be," she says. "But I think it was time to make a change."

As promised, Rucker stayed involved with logistical planning for the November 2007 speaker. Former Mexican President Vicente Fox, appearing less than a year after leaving office, was known as a friend of President Bush—but he quickly offered up an area of disagreement.

"I think the United States should withdraw as soon as possible from Iraq," Fox said. The United Nations, not the United States, should take the lead in resolving conflicts with Iraq. The sold-out audience at the Landmark Theater applauded.

Meanwhile, with The Forum seemingly on solid ground, the president's position was left vacant during the 2007–08 season. Dee Raubenstine helped keep day-to-day operations continuing. An occasionally fractured board of directors was left to make major decisions. Board chairman Jacques Moore stepped in to handle program-night duties previously left to Rucker.

"I had a lively conversation with Michael Douglas backstage," Moore recalls. Calling Douglas "very gracious," he said the actor had lived near John Lennon, who had been gunned down. "He was curious about how a message about gun control would be received by The Richmond Forum audience."

Douglas also joked about a problem he had making *One Flew Over the Cuckoo's Nest,* a movie that had become among Hollywood's most honored—but whose cast had not included his legendary father, Kirk Douglas. "He wanted to know, 'How do you tell 'Spartacus' he can't be the star?'"

Meanwhile, the search for a successor to Rucker was continuing. For only the second time in its twenty-two years, The Richmond Forum was looking for another leader.

The Forum's temporary move to the University of Richmond's Robins Center for the 1994–95 and 1995–96 seasons brought what would become a new tradition of live pre-program music. Russell Wilson, a classical and jazz pianist with the Richmond Symphony Orchestra and member of the UR faculty—and not the star football player of the same name booked for 2016—was the go-to performer over the next few years.

Since then, the musical prelude has become an important part of a Forum evening, with a different performer each time, appreciated by both audience and speakers.

Susan Greenbaum, a former Forum board member and a well-known local singer, has been called on a couple times to perform. "I'll never forget Tim Russert giving me a thumbs-up, after hearing us play during the intermission, and calling out from across the backstage area, 'Hey! Great music! Great Carole King! Love it!'" Greenbaum says.

Performers, when possible, are themed to the evening's topic. Singer Kelly Kennedy, with other Irish musicians, performed at the Frank McCourt program on St. Patrick's Day in 2001, as well as on three other occasions, including for former Irish President Mary Robinson in 2004. The Fort Lee Army Band and the Fort Lee Army Band Brass Quintet played before the programs of General Tommy Franks (2004) and former Secretary of Defense Robert Gates (2012), respectively.

For Tony Blair's 2008 appearance, The English Channel played "British Invasion" music. For Smokey Robinson's in 2009, Bak N Da Day played Motown hits; for Liberian President Ellen Johnson Sirleaf's in 2010, Ban Caribe played West African music; and for Quincy Jones' in 2012, the Richmond Public Schools All-City Jazz Band performed.

The Federal City Brass Band, the country's leading performer of Civil War-era music, appeared for a 2013 panel on the movie *Lincoln,* with Steven Spielberg, Doris Kearns Goodwin, and Tony Kushner. The Saltanah Ensemble played traditional Middle Eastern music for an Islam panel in 2013. Andy Vaughan and the Driveline played "Texas swing" for former President George W. Bush's appearance in 2013. (Bush joked that their music momentarily made him think he was in Richmond, Texas, instead of Richmond, Virginia.)

The touring Steep Canyon Rangers performed a mini-concert before a 2014 program featuring friend Steve Martin, the evening's headliner, who joined in later on his banjo.

Bio Ritmo played Cuban Salsa for the 2014 appearance by Cuba-to-Miami swimmer Diana Nyad. The performance was obviously captivating: Nyad herself went on stage during intermission to Salsa with the band.

Clockwise from top left: Winton Marsalis thanks director Billy Dye and the members of the Richmond Boys Choir in 1998; Tony Blair, who played in a rock band in his teens, runs from a backstage invitation to sit in with the band from English Channel member Julie Quarles in 2008; The Federal City Brass Band performs before the Lincoln *panel in 2013.*

CHAPTER 7

EXPANDING THE FORUM

THE CHAPMAN YEARS OF THE RICHMOND FORUM: 2008–

The search for a new Forum leader, one might have thought, should have gone more quickly.

The position, after all, seemed a wonderful opportunity. For the right candidate, this would be the chance to steer a storied and beloved Richmond institution.

And what a bonus . . . hobnobbing with world leaders, opinion shapers, and five-star celebrities—in short, the most interesting people in the world. What was not to like?

One possibility was Bill Chapman, whose term on the board of directors had ended just before the announcement of Rucker's departure. Like Forum founder Ralph Krueger, Chapman had been an advertising man before selling his interest in the sixty-person RightMinds agency he co-created. He knew The Forum from a number of perspectives, as well: as attendee (he and his then-fiancée Gay Chafin attended their first program, to hear Mike Wallace, in 1990), as sponsor, and as board member. He considered applying. But the timing was wrong. Chapman and his wife were in the midst of restoring their 250-year-old home, doing most of the work themselves.

The 2007–08 season opened without a new leader and with the Chapmans in their usual seats in the audience. Dee Raubenstine, The Forum's longtime director of development, was temporarily overseeing daily operations while the board's executive committee made key decisions.

From left: Screenwriter Tony Kushner, director Steven Spielberg, and historian Doris Kearns Goodwin discuss the movie Lincoln *with moderator Tim Reid. The January 2013 panel discussion became the first Forum program in more than three decades to be broadcast on television and the first ever to be shared in full online.*

The new year came and went. Still, nobody. Late that winter, the board extended its search nationally by hiring a New York headhunter.

Chapman, by now well enough along on the home restoration, decided to apply. "What took you so long?" one director asked. He was quickly hired, though as the Forum's executive director, not its president, as his two successors had been. The board had seen the sometimes troubling power that went with the president's title and, besides, most nonprofits were led by an executive director. Former board chairman Mike Bland, who had nominated Chapman to the board in 2001, considered him perfect, whatever the job was called. "When I knew Bill was the guy, I was thrilled," Bland says.

Chapman's first day, June 1, 2008, was an eye opener.

It was Sunday, but he came in to the office to get a handle on things, pulling the speaker contracts for the upcoming season—former British Prime Minister Tony Blair highlighted a high-dollar roster that included musical superstar Smokey Robinson and football players-turned-announcers Terry Bradshaw and Howie Long. Putting together an impressive lineup had been intended as reassuring to subscribers and sponsors in the absence of a Forum leader. It meant, however, that more money had been spent than ever; Blair himself would become the Forum's highest-paid speaker ever. Chapman found The Forum would end the season, his first, with an operating deficit of well over $200,000 that would have to be covered by the reserves left behind by Rucker—at that time, nobody foresaw the beating that the reserve fund would take when the stock market imploded later that year. The deficit came as news to many on the board of directors, and new policies were put into place that would make speaker fees known and approved beyond only the executive committee to ensure greater financial transparency. Over the course of the next four seasons, the Forum would eventually recover the 2008–2009 deficit.

The arrival of a new leader with an advertising background brought changes to the look of The Forum. The stage was redesigned—gone were the Ionic columns and greenery, replaced by bold graphic panels surrounding an enlarged video screen. In his initial letter to Forum attendees, printed in the season's first program book, Chapman also noted the Forum's new logo, with converging quotation marks. Developed by circle S studio, "[It] reflects an idea that we heard over and over again: The Richmond Forum can be about more than listening to great speakers, it can also be about a continuing community conversation once the speaker has left the stage. The truth is that The Richmond Forum audience is a community with a unique set of shared experiences. . . . We want to provide more opportunities to bring this community together and to enable dialogue."

Bill Chapman, who attended his first Forum event in 1990, takes the stage as the Forum director 18 years later.

TONY BLAIR KICKED OFF the season. Upon their meeting, the former British prime minister said, "I understand this is your first program." Chapman kidded, "Yes it is. So, don't let me down." Tickled, Blair shared the

The Office of Tony Blair

From the Rt Hon Tony Blair

2 November 2008

Dear Bill,

Thank you for so generously hosting me at the Richmond Forum. It was an honour to address it, and a privilege to join such a distinguished list of speakers.

Everyone at the Forum was incredibly kind and the event is a real credit to the talent and dedication of your team and the volunteers who work day in and day out to put on the lecture series. Please pass on my sincere thanks to the Governor, and everyone who worked hard to make the event such a success.

With best wishes,

Yours sincerely,

Tony Blair

www.tonyblairoffice.org

Former British Prime Minister Tony Blair becomes the Forum's highest-paid speaker with his appearance in November 2008—a distinction he still would hold at the publication of this book seven years later. Left: Blair expressed his appreciation in a letter after The Forum.

directive during his dinner remarks. Blair, the season's most anticipated speaker, did not disappoint with his personable presentation. During the Q&A, moderated by former Governor Gerald L. Baliles, Blair said global alliances based on the U.S. and British values of freedom and justice are necessary to solve the world's problems. "Don't stop leading. People expect America to lead."

After the program, The Forum canvassed subscribers on their views—a first—getting a forty percent response rate. Most judged the program either excellent (eighty-four percent) or good (fourteen percent). Only the Landmark Theater itself came in for real criticism, both for its increasingly dilapidated condition and lack of cleanliness.

Bill Chapman and moderator Daphne Maxwell Reid visit with Smokey Robinson in the green room backstage. Right: Robinson enjoys dinner with Forum patrons before the program.

Smokey Robinson wowed the Forum crowd in February 2009 with stories of Motown hit-making. Wearing a cream-colored suit and copper tie, Robinson looked natty and younger than his sixty-nine years, *Richmond Times-Dispatch* writer Melissa Ruggieri wrote. She watched him at the pre-program reception at the Omni Hotel, Robinson working the small room with a smile, an extended hand and the simple greeting, "Hi, I'm Smokey."

Local R&B tribute band Bak N Da Day had the sold-out crowd singing to classic Motown beforehand, including hits of Smokey Robinson and the Miracles. But Robinson, the performer of thirty-seven Top-Forty hits, didn't perform at The Forum, though moderator Daphne Maxwell Reid tried to persuade him. Robinson told the stories, however. He was a month into college, at age eighteen, when his first hit, *Get a Job,* was released. "That killed my college career," he grinned. He was grateful for success, though. "I have seen thousands of people come through showbiz. With the bulk of them, people get to the point of getting a hit record out and they start to portray this person who feels like, 'Showbiz cannot possibly survive without me.' Showbiz is a very fickle place."

At a reception afterward, reported the *Richmond Free Press,* a musician from Mathews County, Virginia, Herbert Carter, brought a promotional photo of Smokey's band from the early 1960s. The band had played on the "chitlin' circuit" for African-Americans in the days of the segregated South. Carter, who used to play in a band called the Dynatones, had met Robinson at a small Gloucester County venue on the circuit, the Wagon Wheel at Ordinary. "When I showed him the picture he had a fit," Carter told the paper.

March 2009 brought fellow football-stars-turned commentators Terry Bradshaw and Howie Long. Athletes have been a rarity at the Forum and humorous athletes more of a rarity still. The longtime cohosts of *Fox NFL*

***Above:** At The Jefferson Hotel, Howie Long makes sure Terry Bradshaw is presentable for the March 2009 Forum.*
***Below:** April 2009 speaker Michael Pollan joins Forumgoers at a farmers market in the ballroom at the theater.*

Sunday did make serious assessments of the game of football, including the long-term health effects on retired players. But it was their fast-moving repartee that kept the audience laughing.

"I'm from Boston; he's from Louisiana," Long said. "He grew up Baptist, I grew up Catholic. Villanova . . . Louisiana Tech. [Bradshaw was a] quarterback . . . defensive lineman. Steeler . . . Raider. We couldn't be any more different. To say we're like friends—it's like family. He's the older brother I never wanted." Bradshaw, putting down the needle for a moment, said the TV friendship is genuine. "You can't fake that. It's a trust factor now . . . plus we hang out all the time. We truly enjoy each other's company."

Forum attendee Susan Cruse calls it the funniest program she's seen. Fellow attendee Jim Albertson calls it his favorite: "Bradshaw-Long were very entertaining." Then-board member Mike Bland got an up-close look that night. "Backstage it didn't change," he says. "That is who they are. They were laughing, poking fun at each other. Terry Bradshaw, in particular, is a pedal-to-the-metal kind of guy. The energy he had was amazing."

Following the high-profile appearances of Tony Blair, Smokey Robinson, and Bradshaw-Long, the season-ending program of writer Michael Pollan and food studies professor Marion Nestle was lower-key, but nonetheless noteworthy. Onstage, the pair talked about the emerging trends of eating local and changing food culture. Below stage, The Forum had partnered with the Virginia Department of Agriculture to set up an actual farmers market in the theater's ballroom, allowing Forumgoers to connect with local growers.

It was the first of a number of occasions when The Forum would now extend programs beyond the presentation on the stage.

THE SECRETARY OF STATE . . . AT THE PIANO

Former Secretary of State Condoleezza Rice appeared at the Forum in April 2010, a year after leaving office. The Richmond Forum's invitation had been one of the first she accepted.

To no one's surprise, she still commanded a grasp of the world scene, talking of the need to deal with nuclear proliferation and to help failed states heal. She said the war in Afghanistan will "take extraordinary patience and it's going to take a long time."

Returning to the stage after intermission, however, Rice surprised everyone by exhibiting a firm grasp of . . .

The concert piano.

Rice, an accomplished pianist, sat down and gave an unannounced performance of the *Brahms Violin Sonata in D Minor.* Karen Johnson, concertmaster with the Richmond Symphony Orchestra, accompanied her. It would become one of the first such deliver-beyond-expectations surprises orchestrated by Executive Director Bill Chapman.

The performance drew gasps from the audience.

Only board members had any idea what was coming. "We had kept it secret for nearly a year," Forum Director of Development Dee Raubenstine says.

Rice, a fourth-generation pianist who had once intended to have a music career, frequently played chamber music with a small group. But she mostly did so privately.

In the weeks before her Forum engagement, Rice began to have second thoughts about the agreement, made a year earlier, to include a performance. The challenge was switching between the cerebral and the artistic—a left-brain/right-brain dichotomy—not to mention between the different outfits generally required for giving a speech and for giving a concert piano performance. The solution came in performing immediately following the fifteen-minute intermission, giving her time to mentally switch gears.

The performance came off without a hitch. The audience was thrilled.

Rice also received high marks for her speech and her personality. (Afterward, the audience would judge her Forum presentation the second best among thirty during a six-year period, edged out only by Robert Gates.) Board member Judy Pahren had the opportunity, with her husband and daughter, to talk with Rice. "I would have thought of her as cool and a little reserved," Pahren says. She was anything but. "She is so warm and engaging."

Condoleezza Rice performs at the piano, accompanied by violinist Karen Johnson, in one of The Forum's biggest surprises.

THE FORUM IN NOVEMBER 2009 got an early look at astrophysicist Neil deGrasse Tyson, not yet as famous as he would become but regaling nonetheless. Tyson's combination of science and entertainment was a winner. He seemed at home, taking his shoes off onstage, then staying at the post-program reception until the wee hours of the morning, being interviewed by a high school student and being timed as he solved a Rubik's Cube.

"I'd seen Neil deGrasse Tyson on *The Daily Show* a few months before he was to appear at The Forum, and he'd noted on the show how much he'd appreciated that they'd left him a Rubik's Cube in the green room," says Susan Greenbaum, who was a member of the Forum's board. "I asked if I could meet him briefly before everything started. I presented him with a Rubik's Cube, saying I wanted him to enjoy his visit to RVA at least as much as he'd enjoyed that Rubik-enhanced visit to *The Daily Show.*"

Tyson's appearance was the first at which the Forum's new Student Viewing Room was used. About 100 Boy Scouts and astronomy students from Monacan and Godwin high schools watched a closed-circuit presentation of Tyson's remarks, the first of some 650 students to see Forum programs during that season. (The season also saw a revitalization of the Ralph Krueger Memorial Fund that had been established in 1993 to fund student initiatives.) As would become Forum custom, Tyson went to the room to talk with the students before the program and again during intermission.

Tyson gave the night a thumbs-up afterward. "The hospitality was a delight (although I'm told that's just normal for Virginia!)," he wrote The Forum. He credited the series for its regional support, legacy, and new viewing room with enthusiastic students—"I can see that concept growing in the future."

But Tyson had one lament in an era when America's science lead had dwindled. "I notice from the list of past speakers that scientists are uncommon. Carl Sagan, exactly 20 years ago. And just a few others since then." The allure of performers, statesmen, and the like was undeniable, he conceded, but "if even one in ten of your invitations [went] to a scientist or technologist, that would go a long way in serving this desperate social need."

***Left:** Astrophysicist Neil deGrasse Tyson kicks off his shoes onstage. **Right:** Earlier in the evening, Tyson conducts an impromptu science demonstration in The Forum's new student room.*

MAKING A FORUM A FORUM

The question-and-answer period that constitutes the second part of an evening's program is, in a very real sense, what transforms a "speech" into a "forum."

It can define the evening. It was during her November 2010 appearance, for instance, that Liberian President Ellen Johnson Sirleaf, responding to an audience question, first talked publicly about the purge she had conducted of her political cabinet just days earlier. Her comments were international news.

There's also a personal aspect.

For many Forum attendees, there's nothing quite like hearing their own questions, submitted in writing during intermission, then selected backstage by volunteers, asked of the evening's famous speaker.

Susan and Woody Tucker attended the Margaret Thatcher program in January 1992 with her sister, Carol Mahoney. Mahoney, always on top of the news, submitted this for the former prime minister: "Are you considering joining up with Reagan and Gorbachev to develop an international think tank?"

Mahoney looked at Tucker, wondering what her sister had written. The answer: "In light of the recent scandals with the House of Windsor, do you think the Royal Family will cease to exist in our lifetime?" Mahoney was unimpressed. The royals?? "She felt I was reading too many *People* magazines at the hairdresser," Tucker says.

As the Q&A session was winding down, "The moderator says, 'And now for our last question: Mrs. Thatcher, in light of the recent scandals . . .' My question!!!

"I must admit I looked rather smugly at sister."

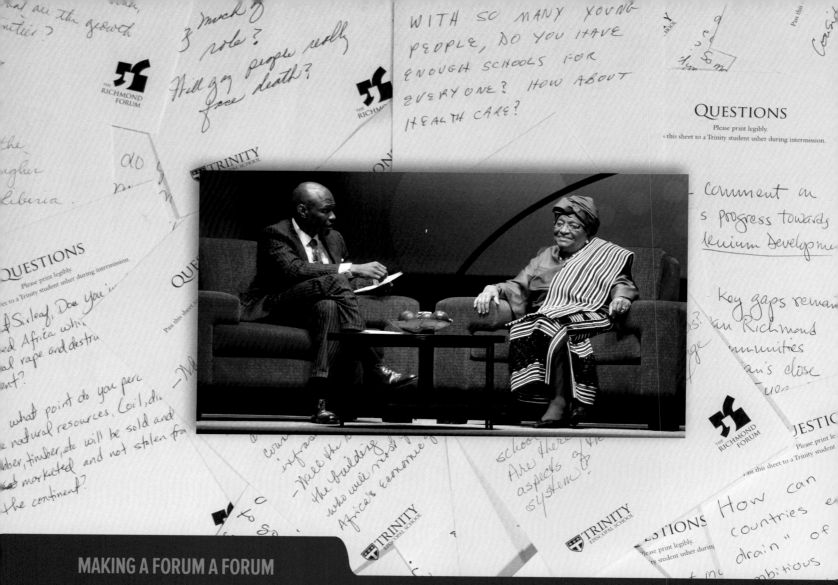

Christopher Howard, president of Hampden-Sydney College, poses questions submitted by the Forum audience

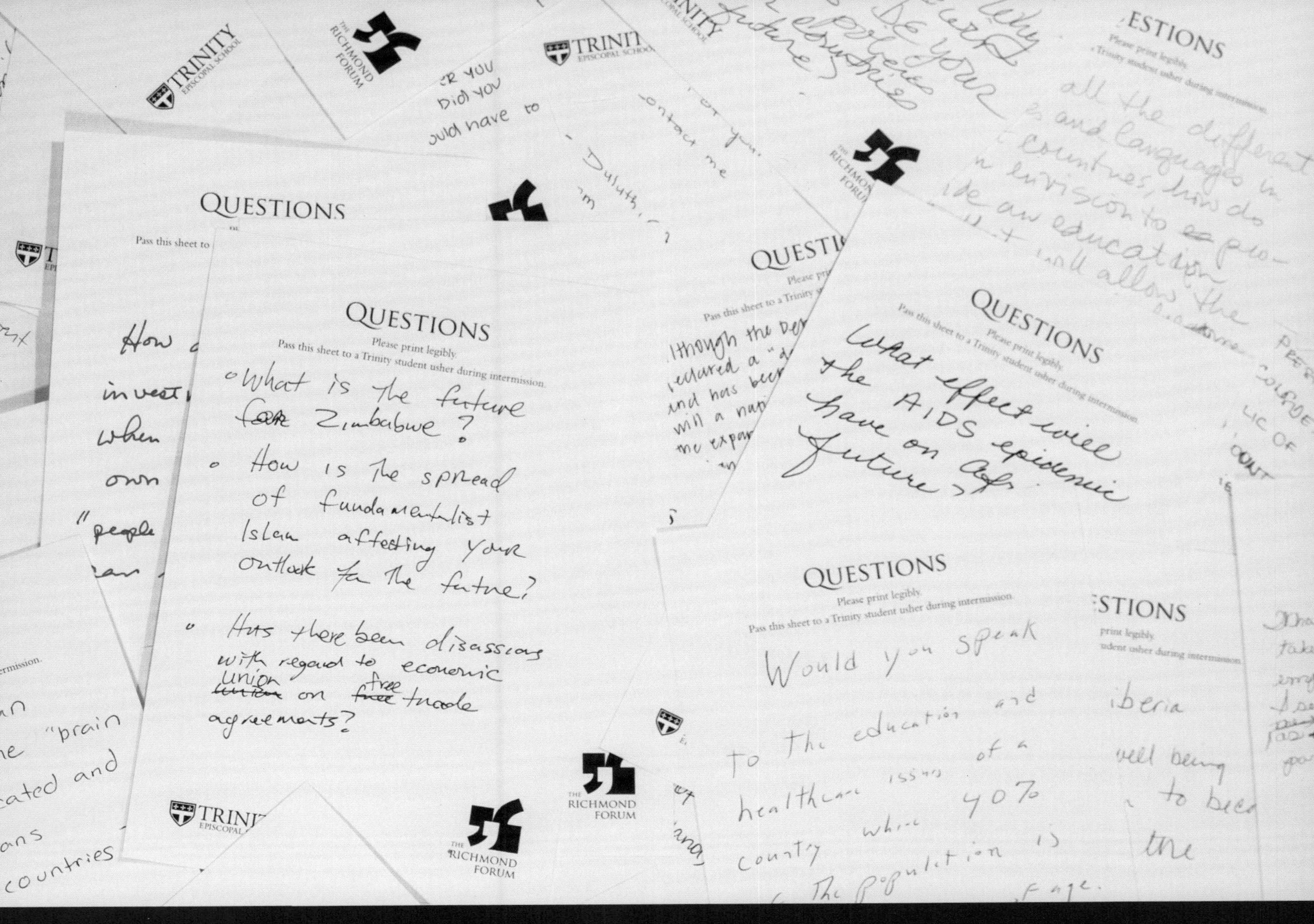

Often, the actual answers are unexpected—and insightful. "The Q&A is usually where the evening's surprises come," Forum Director Bill Chapman says. "The speakers are off their script—and on their toes."

Susan Greenbaum had moved to Richmond in 1996. A Boston transplant, she had felt isolated in Richmond, having met few other Jews in her eight months in the city, she says. Through her employer, she received tickets to The Forum, to hear Carl Reiner and Dick Cavett. She discovered the blank sheet for questions and submitted one. "This was the only time one of my questions has been selected, and it was quite a thrill to hear Dick Cavett read my words to Carl Reiner: 'Why is it that the funniest people at the party are always Jewish?' And it's signed, 'A pretty funny Jew.' The whole place laughed, and I felt like I'd been elected king."

The response was more serious than she or anyone may "Carl Reiner answered my question with a long and very interesting story about his time in the military, facing all kinds of anti-Semitism and racism," says Greenbaum, who would go on to become a member of The Forum board of directors.

Reiner told of confronting a Southern white soldier who was threatening a black soldier for using the same latrine as the whites. Reiner, known as a skilled marksman, tried to defuse the situation, to little avail. Finally, Greenbaum recalls, Reiner said: "Well, you're the only one who has a problem with this man using the latrine. If you're not going to walk away from this, I guess there's only one solution: We're going to have to have a duel, you and me. You know what a good shot I am, and we both know who will win that duel. You're going to die in that duel. That's going to be very embarrassing for you, going off to war, dying in a duel over a toilet. Think of your family, how upset they'll be—that you're dead, and that

MAKING A FORUM A FORUM (Continued)

The Forum audience exploded in laughter.

Reiner continued the story: The soldier was quiet for a few minutes. He then said (and Reiner launched into a Southern accent): "Reiner, you're a Jew, ain'tcha?" Reiner said he was. "I know some Jews back in my town in Alabama. They own the store. They're all-right people." And that was that.

Reiner said that Jews, persecuted for centuries in various regions of the globe, naturally sought to develop humor as an entrée into social settings, often a self-deprecating humor that helped dispel myths and preconceptions, especially for people who may never have met Jews.

As insight-revealing as Reiner's answer was, few Forum answers are more often recalled by subscribers than one given by former Defense Secretary Robert Gates, who appeared in January 2012. W. Taylor Reveley III, president of The College of William & Mary, moderated the Q&A and put to Gates a question submitted by a subscriber identified as Marybeth: "What one word or phrase would you use to describe each of the eight presidents for whom you've served?"

"Oh, geez. This is a family audience, right?" Gates said, laughing.

But Gates was game. He took on Marybeth's question, his assessments revealing more insight—and no doubt honesty—than many may have expected:

On Lyndon B. Johnson: "Tragic. He wanted to do so much domestically and couldn't extract himself from his fear of taking the country out of Vietnam."

On Richard M. Nixon. "Probably our strangest president. I'll leave it at that."

On Gerald R. Ford: "Vastly underestimated. A man of extraordinary courage and intelligence."

On Jimmy Carter: "Couldn't figure out what his priorities were. Tried to do too much and, therefore, accomplished relatively little."

On Ronald Reagan: "I think one of our greatest presidents. . . . Ronald Reagan restored the confidence in the American people and confidence in the American dream."

On George H. W. Bush: "Again, vastly underestimated."

On George W. Bush: "Confident. A man of strong convictions and confident in those convictions."

On Barack Obama: "Far more courageous than anybody would have expected when he was elected." Gates called Obama's decision to launch the attack that killed Osama bin Laden "one of the gutsiest calls I have ever seen a president make" and his decision to approve the politically unpopular military surge in Afghanistan very courageous. ❞

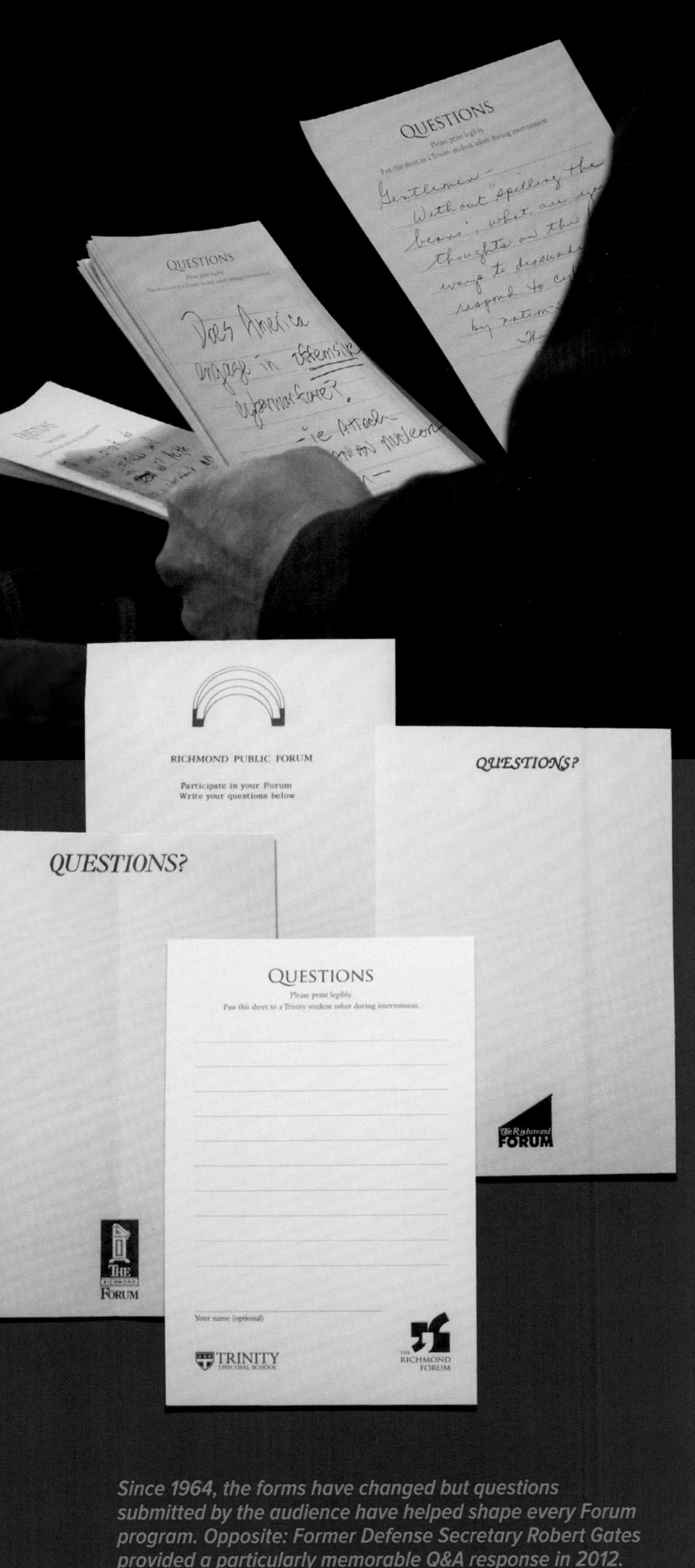

Since 1964, the forms have changed but questions submitted by the audience have helped shape every Forum program. Opposite: Former Defense Secretary Robert Gates provided a particularly memorable Q&A response in 2012.

THE TWENTY-FIFTH ANNIVERSARY SEASON of 2010–11 brought a number of Forum firsts.

Liberian President Ellen Johnson Sirleaf, the first female head of state in Africa (known as Liberia's "Iron Lady") would become the first head of state to address The Forum while still in office.

In the months leading up to the president's visit, Chapman met frequently with the small but vibrant Liberian diaspora in Richmond, and ideas were developed for the types of program extensions and outreach that The Forum now sought: Two weeks beforehand, The Forum co-sponsored a companion lecture at the Virginia Historical Society by Marie Tyler-McGraw, author of *An African Republic: Black and White Virginians in the Making of Liberia.* During the Q&A, questions veered to the long and bloody civil wars in Liberia; being a 20th century history matter, Tyler-McGraw deferred to the Liberian Americans in the audience who shared often heart-wrenching personal accounts.

The Forum night dinner was marked by a special meal for Sirleaf and Forum patrons, a Liberian feast planned by Richmond Liberian chef Ida MaMusu and prepared by the chef at The Jefferson Hotel. The Forum audience that night included members of the Liberian community, in their colorful traditional attire.

Adding to the news value of her Forum speech, the seventy-two-year-old president had abruptly dissolved her cabinet the day before boarding a flight from Monrovia to Richmond, replacing all members but one.

"Complacency had set in a bit," Sirleaf explained at The Forum, her first public statement on the startling housecleaning. The Harvard-educated economist told the audience that her country needed maximum results; she wanted cabinet members to reflect and set new goals. "The way to do that was something drastic." She said she expected many of the "young, dynamic, and vigorous" cabinet members would be back. "The others, I don't know about."

The following morning, Sirleaf attended a private worship service at Virginia Union University, hosted by the Liberian Association of Virginia. Later that day, the Liberian ambassador to the United States attended a wreath-laying ceremony in Petersburg at the monument to Joseph Jenkins Roberts, a Petersburg native and the first president of Liberia.

Welcome, President Sirleaf

Africa's first woman head of state in Richmond B1

Richmond Free Press

FREE

© 2010 Paradigm Communications, Inc. All rights reserved.

VOL. 19 NO. 44 | RICHMOND, VIRGINIA | www.richmondfreepress.com | NOVEMBER 4-6, 2010

President of Liberia to visit Landmark, VUU this weekend

Welcome

Free Press staff report

Liberia's celebrated president, Ellen Johnson Sirleaf, is coming to Richmond this weekend.

Africa's first and only female head of state is scheduled to address The Richmond Forum on Saturday night at the Landmark Theater.

She also is to participate in a Sunday worship service at Virginia Union University, which will recall Virginia's ties to her nation and pay tribute to Liberia's first president, Joseph Jenkins Roberts, who was born in Norfolk and grew up in Petersburg before he emigrated to Liberia.

President Sirleaf may touch on those ties, but her speech at the forum will focus "on Africa and its place in the world," said Bill Chapman, forum executive director.

"Part of her emphasis will be on the fact that there are real success stories, rather than what we see in the headlines," he said.

President Sirleaf will be the first sitting head of state to address the forum in its 46 years of bringing nationally and internationally renowned individuals to the city.

He said the forum invited President Sirleaf more than a year ago at the request of subscribers.

Richmonder Antoinette Essa, a former Miss Liberia, was among those who made the request and she, like other Liberian émigrés, is thrilled the leader of her native country will be in her adopted city.

"I'm very excited," said Ms. Essa, a TV and radio personality.

She called President Sirleaf's visit an opportunity "to raise awareness about Liberia and President Sirleaf's accomplishments" since her election in 2005.

President Sirleaf has gained international recognition for leading a turnaround of the previously war-racked nation. Among other honors, in 2006, she was awarded the U.S. Medal of Honor by President Bush and had the distinction of addressing a joint session of Congress that year.

She is credited with slashing foreign debt and bringing stability to Liberia, which had been embroiled in upheaval and civil war for nearly 20 years before she took office.

Her visit brings back warm memories for Ms. Essa, now 52, who has not been back to Liberia in more than 30 years. She reigned as Miss Liberia in 1976 just before she came to the United States to begin her studies at her alma mater, the University of Bridgeport in Connecticut. Now an American citizen, she came to Richmond 21 years ago to pursue her broadcast career.

"Her visit is so important, and I'm looking forward to being a part of it," Ms. Essa said.

So is Ida MaMusu, another Liberian émigré who owns and operates Chef MaMusu's restaurant in Downtown that offers Liberian-style dishes.

She will be preparing the meal for the invitation-only dinner that The Richmond Forum will host for President Sirleaf at the Jefferson Hotel before she speaks at 8 p.m.

Liberian President Ellen Johnson Sirleaf

"I'll be preparing a traditional menu," Ms. MaMusu told the Free Press Friday, including jollof rice, smoked turkey, collard greens, bread pudding and akara, a fried bean cake, along with a ginger-based drink.

Ms. MaMusu, who has lived in Richmond since 1980, said she's proud The Richmond Forum selected her to make the meal. She said she is working with the hotel's kitchen staff in seeking to make the dinner a success. "Everyone has been very cooperative, and I'm very happy to be able to do this," she said.

Garway Bright of the Liberian Association of Virginia has worked with Virginia Union President Claude G. Perkins in arranging Sunday's 90-minute service that is to start at 9:30 a.m. (VUU announced Monday the doors will open at 8 a.m., but people desiring to attend need to be inside by 9 a.m. Admission will be barred after 9 a.m. due to security concerns, according to a statement the school issued Monday.)

He said about 300 Liberian families live in the Richmond area, and he is expecting a large turnout at the service to welcome President Sirleaf, who is esteemed "as the best thing that has happened to Liberia in a long time. For most of us, this is the first time we will be able to see her in person."

He said that President Sirleaf has agreed to spend time responding to questions from the audience at the conclusion of the service.

However, he said he has been notified by her staff that her itinerary will not allow her to travel to Petersburg to take part in a wreath-laying ceremony at the monument to Mr. Roberts, who was elected Liberia's first president in 1848. The association has scheduled the ceremony for around 12:45 p.m. Sunday after the service.

Mr. Bright said he has been told that President Sirleaf will leave Richmond after the VUU program, but he said he has not been told where she will be going after that.

Mr. Bright, a regulatory compliance team leader for Richmond-based Genworth Financial, said there had been hopes President Sirleaf would take part in the wreath-laying ceremony, but said the timing did not work out. "We're so happy, though, that she will be part of the service."

This article is based on reporting by Jeremy M. Lazarus.

Richmond schedule

Saturday, Nov. 6
Address to The Richmond Forum
Time: 8 p.m.
Location: Landmark Theater, 6 N. Laurel St.

Sunday, Nov. 7
"Celebrate Liberia 2010"
Time: 9:30 a.m.
Location: Coburn Hall at Virginia Union University, 1500 N. Lombardy St.
(Doors open at 8 a.m., but admission will end at 9 a.m. sharp, VUU has announced, due to security concerns.)

Ellen Johnson Sirleaf's November 2010 visit to Richmond for The Forum received front page coverage in the* Richmond Free Press. *The Forum helped Richmond's Liberian community invite Sirleaf to the private Sunday worship service she attended.

Laura Bush's appearance in January 2011 was another first, the first by a former first lady. When it had been announced the previous year, one subscriber wrote: "It is tacky to have Laura Bush without having her husband the past president first. It shows bad manners. Then again, Bush should not be invited before Clinton has been." Any possible bad manners aside, Laura Bush became an audience favorite.

"It was funny to hear her talk about life after leaving the White House," Mark Hourigan says now. "'George, pick up your towel off the bathroom floor. There isn't a maid or Secret Service here.'" Afterward, she sent Hourigan and several others handwritten thank-you notes on personal stationery. "Laura Bush was so kind, so warm, a very regular person," Hourigan says. Tim Butturini, a regional president for a bank sponsoring the Forum, agrees. He keeps Forum pictures on his desk of himself with George W. Bush and with Laura Bush.

Laura Bush's appearance may also have been the first to result in the changing of the Forum's onstage furniture. The large red chairs, selected by the Forum's set designer to fit the massive scale of a seventy-foot-wide stage, seemed to swallow her up. Afterward, Chapman reported to the board, "there were many survey responses, phone calls, notes and in-person comments that Mrs. Bush looked very uncomfortable in her chair."

For a while, the chairs became a Forum topic of conversation and even urgency. By September, Chapman reported, the crisis was under control. Everyone could breathe again. "After much research, investigation and angst, I have purchased new chairs." He believed the "updated traditional" style chairs, tracked down in Georgetown, would be more comfortable for guests of all sizes. Introduced at the start of the next season, the new chairs, in the same "Forum red" color, even received a round of applause.

The season's third speaker, Anderson Cooper, also recorded a Forum first by speaking not only Saturday night but also to a second audience on Sunday afternoon. It was a Forum foray into series-expanding options to meet increasing demand; Sunday tickets were made available to the public. The popular CNN news anchor

(Continued on Page 106)

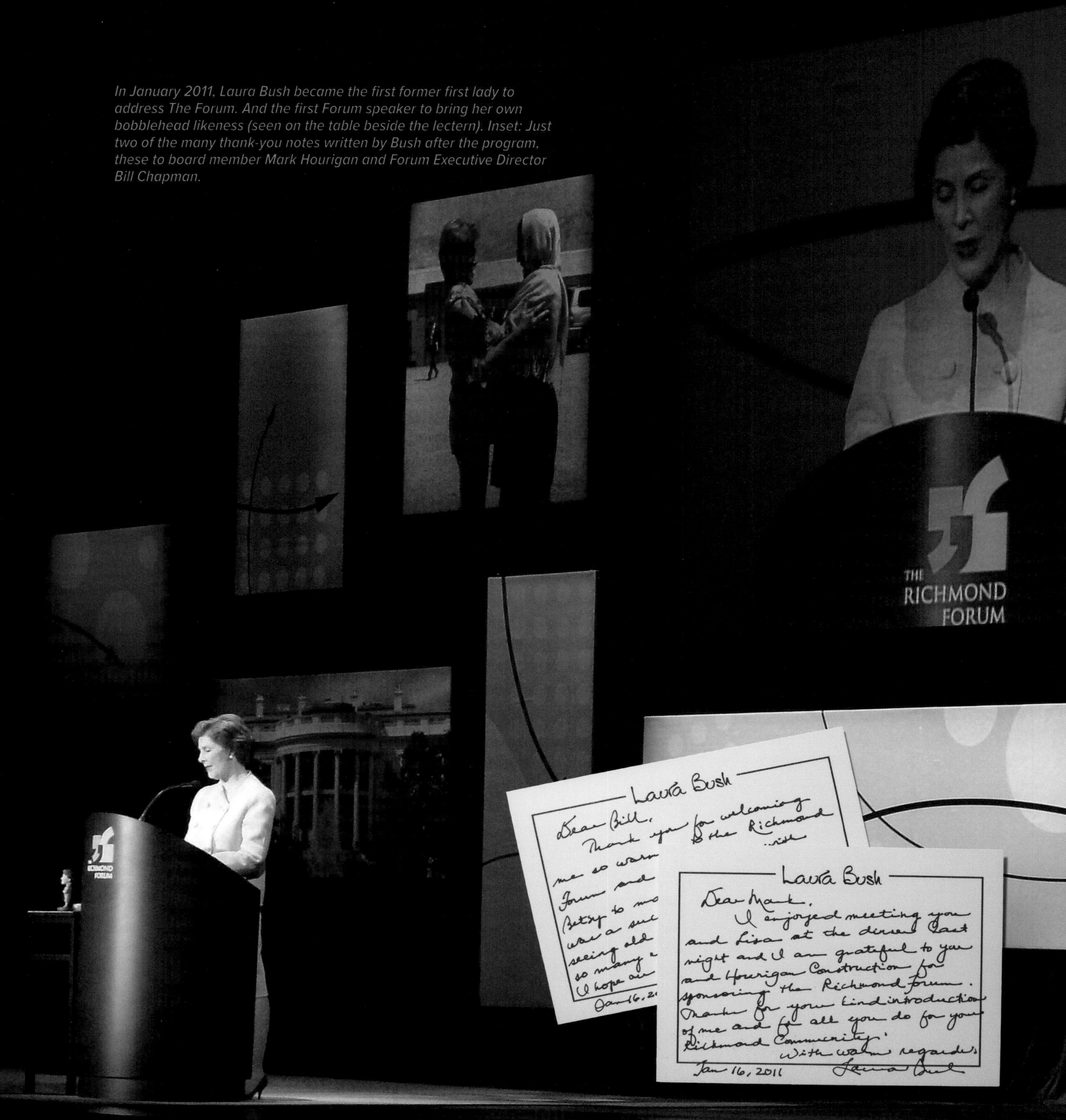

In January 2011, Laura Bush became the first former first lady to address The Forum. And the first Forum speaker to bring her own bobblehead likeness (seen on the table beside the lectern). Inset: Just two of the many thank-you notes written by Bush after the program, these to board member Mark Hourigan and Forum Executive Director Bill Chapman.

MY NIGHT AT THE FORUM: DAVID BLAINE

David Blaine's appearance in April 2011 required an additional day's rental of the Landmark Theater for rehearsal.

It also required engineers to ensure that the stage would support a massive water tank, custom made for this presentation.

And it required Blaine to be underwater in that tank for more than eight minutes—holding his breath, of course—before emerging to talk.

All of that was a first for The Forum. But this was a first for the illusionist and endurance artist, as well.

"This was the first time I put together a talk with a performance," Blaine says. "It was a great learning experience."

It was not part of the initial concept for the program. But the idea of combining the two elements began to take shape as The Forum's director, Bill Chapman, met with Blaine in his New York City studio to plan the presentation. One problem would be eight minutes of dead air while Blaine was submerged. "When he arrived in Richmond on Friday, I took him to In Your Ear studio to record a voiceover," Chapman says. That short biographic talk played while Blaine was underwater and gave way the final two minutes to the sound only of Blaine's heartbeat. "There was incredible tension in the theater as he passed seven minutes, and then eight," Chapman recalls.

Above: David Blaine using playing cards in his New York studio to outline his Richmond Forum speech. Small photo above: In a Friday night rehearsal that ran into the early morning hours of Forum day, Bill Chapman and Blaine work out the details of the water tank stunt onstage.

It is not likely that any future Forum speaker will top the entrance made by David Blaine, who spent the first eight minutes and forty-two seconds of his time onstage underwater (left). He's also the only Forum speaker known to bleed onstage after taking a bite out of the Forum's water glass—which he later autographed.

Blaine surfaced to thunderous applause and, after changing into dry clothes, began his speech. His stories took the audience behind the scenes and into the science and physical and mental effects of his headline-making endurance stunts.

During the Q&A with longtime local television personality May Lily Lee, Blaine shared a story about the time he took a bite out of a wine glass belonging to the president of Kazakhstan. The story was better told, he decided, by taking an unscripted bite out of a Forum water glass. Blaine's microphone filled the theater with the sound of crunching as he ground the mouthful of glass into bits—and finally swallowed.

The program was a hit.

"It was a lot of fun to put it together," Blaine says. "We had to put it together from scratch. . . . It was an ambitious task."

Ambitious for Chapman, too, who professes that the program was fun to create but also gave him a few gray hairs. "With Blaine, every detail needs to be not only perfect, but also amazing. So, he's always thinking of a better idea, changing things up. As he was onstage in the tank, I was backstage replacing slides in his presentation because he had a better idea right before he went out."

Blaine explains his rationale: "As a magician, it's very easy to do magic." Combining that with a talk was a professional stretch. "That was my reason for doing it."

CNN newscaster Anderson Cooper poses with Richmond area high school and college students in The Forum's student room—right after absentmindedly throwing his speech in a backstage trash can.

and reporter was one of the few speakers who could draw a large enough audience for two events—and was willing to do so.

But would he get to Richmond? Less than a week earlier, reporting on the Egyptian revolution, Cooper had been caught with his producer and cameraman in a crowd of supporters of President Hosni Mubarak. The three were repeatedly punched and kicked. Footage of the attack played over and over, on air and online. Cooper and crew escaped but, for a while, The Forum wondered if CNN would allow him to depart the news event; fortunately, it did.

Cooper did make it to Richmond, strolling in unaccompanied, carrying just one bag. Onstage, he talked of the world's tragedies, urging the audience to confront them. "I think it is important for us not to look away, but to look directly at the things that frighten us most." He had time for levity, as well. The Yale University graduate, who had focused on communism while studying political science, said he graduated in 1989, just as the Soviet Union was crumbling. "When the Berlin Wall came down, I was pretty much screwed," Cooper said. "It was hard not to take it personally."

Cooper was confronting his own fears. What the charmed audience did not know Saturday evening—or Sunday afternoon—was that the seemingly confident newsman had actually taken the double Forum gig in part because he was not comfortable as a speaker. Speaking onstage, he said, was a muscle he wanted to exercise.

Saturday night, though, any Cooperian discomfort was experienced only by him. Perhaps feeling a sense of relief after his speech was so well received, Cooper tossed that speech into a large backstage trash can at intermission—apparently forgetting all about Sunday. Chapman saw him do it. So later, while the audience was watching Cooper answer questions onstage, the executive director of The Richmond Forum was upside down in a trash can, digging out the speech.

"Oh yeah!" Cooper laughed when he got the pages back.

Robert Gates was another impressive catch for The Richmond Forum, which became the first series to land the former U.S. secretary of defense after he left office. Indeed, when Chapman announced the following season's schedule in March 2011, there was a conspicuous gap in the January 2012 slot. That date was being left open in the hopes of landing Gates, who would leave the Defense Department June 30. The strategy paid off. The Forum announced Gates as a speaker on July 4.

Gate's talk the following January, which decried partisanship in Washington, D.C., was enthusiastically received in Richmond. "We have lost the ability to execute even the most basic functions of government," he said. Gates blamed deep partisanship for "the ongoing dysfunction of our political system." He also blamed changes in the news media, now giving even the most extreme viewpoints the chance to fuel a "coarsening and dumbing down of our national political dialogue." He called for an overhaul of the districting system, "more humility in victory," and more compromise.

Afterward, *Times-Dispatch* reader H. D. Penzler, in a letter to the editor, called Gates a "giant among the men of his era. . . . It is too bad that Congress and 250 million Americans were not at the Landmark Theater to hear and reflect on his talk." Gates would receive the highest rating ever from Forumgoers, with ninety-nine percent rating his presentation excellent or good. Several years later, a lecture series in California presented Gates, and its director mentioned The Richmond Forum. "I was their highest-rated speaker ever," Gates boasted.

BY NOVEMBER 2011, the possibility of a blockbuster 2012–13 season was beginning to take shape. Both President Bill Clinton and film director Steven Spielberg were being pursued, though Chapman was under no illusion The Forum could get both. Either one would be a coup.

By January 2012, however, Clinton was on board. And, after an initial "no thank you," conversations with Spielberg's office had gotten serious—so much so that Chapman went to the board to seek approval of an increase in the speaker budget . . . just in case. The board enthusiastically agreed.

After several more months, and with the deadline of the season announcement looming, Spielberg, too, would finally commit. Chapman later would tell the *Times-Dispatch:* "This season is an embarrassment of riches. We've raised the bar—maybe a little bit too high."

The previous year, The Forum had a near-record eighty-percent renewal. This season—featuring Platon, Spielberg (with Doris Kearns Goodwin and Tony Kushner), Clinton, Mark Kelly with Gabby Giffords, and Jane Goodall—100 percent of seats were renewed by subscribers. Even when told no tickets were available, more than 1,000 people added themselves to an email list for tickets. Beginning in January 2013, with the Spielberg program, the Forum would open a Simulcast Room in the theater's downstairs ballroom, showing the program on two large HD screens and seating 460.

The new seats sold out in less than ten minutes.

Speaker series around the country wanted to know how The Richmond Forum had gotten Spielberg. The truth is, Chapman says now, they had an "in." Historian Doris Kearns Goodwin, who appeared twice before—and who was the author of *Team of Rivals,* the basis for Spielberg's movie, *Lincoln*—was a fan of The Forum. After being pitched the idea of a program in which the director and historian could discuss the process of bringing the Civil War president to life on screen, she became an advocate. Goodwin visited the movie set when Spielberg was filming in Petersburg and Richmond, planted the seed, and eased the way for Chapman to take it from there.

August 19, 2011

Bill Chapman
6968 Forest Hill Avenue
Richmond, VA 23225

Dear Mr. Chapman,

Thank you for your letter to Steven Spielberg regarding The Richmond Forum.

While we appreciate your request, unfortunately, Steven is unable to participate due to his tight filming schedule at the time of your event. For much of the production, they will be shooting 6 day weeks which would prevent him from being able to do this.

Additionally, he rarely does speaking engagements and the few times that he has, they were for his own foundations.

Thank you again and we wish you all the best.

Above: Screenwriter Tony Kushner, director Steven Spielberg, historian Doris Kearns Goodwin and moderator Tim Reid in January 2013, discussing the making of Lincoln. *Below left: Backstage after a succesful program, Reid, Forum board member Daphne Maxwell Reid, Spielberg and Kearns Goodwin prepare to leave the theater for a Forum-hosted dessert reception. Longtime stage manager John Carter Hailey can be seen packing up in the background. Below right: The companion piece to the rejection letter: Spielberg's thanks for a replacement for his lost Boy Scout knife and for "a fantastic day and evening."*

February 22, 2013

Dear Bill,

Thank you for your very thoughtful gift of the pocket knife. If anybody comes up with the one I lost in Richmond, I will be very happy to trade!

With great memories of a fantastic day and evening,

SS/sb

The panel of Spielberg, screenwriter Tony Kushner (added at Spielberg's suggestion), and historian Goodwin—moderated by actor/producer Tim Reid, a key figure in Virginia's growing film industry—was one of the best received and most publicized in Forum history. It was also the first Forum since the series re-founding in 1987 to be broadcast in its entirety on local public television and the first ever to be shared online.

"There was such affection between the three of them, and they hadn't seen each other in a while. So, our subscribers got to enjoy an onstage reunion between very good friends," says Chapman. "It was also really interesting to watch as they learned things about and from each other as the conversation unfolded."

Few had expected the director to visit The Forum.

"I said, 'It'll never happen. Steven Spielberg is not going to do this type of program,'" Harry Rhoads, CEO of the Washington Speakers Bureau, says now. But Chapman knew Spielberg had an affinity for Richmond, Rhoads says, and "that was his way of thanking the people of Richmond." Rhoads, whose firm represents Goodwin, just had to come down to Richmond for this event. "In walks Steven Spielberg," he says. "He couldn't have been nicer. He had that Bill-Clinton-look-you-in-the-eye-style that made you feel special."

Rhoads says most series around the country require speakers to be on-site only for three or three-and-one-half hours. "Now, I gotta tell you: Bill's programs go on for a very long time. There's a reception, a dinner, the speech and another reception. . . . I never once saw Steven Spielberg look at his watch. He was the happiest man in Richmond that night."

Onstage, Spielberg said local help in filming earlier movies led to considering the area again. In addition, he said, Virginia offered tax incentives and then-Governor Bob McDonnell talked with him about the "healing process" necessitated by slavery in the former Confederate capitol. Moreover, because there's more respect for history on the East Coast than on the West Coast, it's easier filming historical pieces here, Spielberg said. Except for digitally taking out overhead wires, the Petersburg of today performed without alteration as the Petersburg of yesterday.

The director revealed one personally disheartening moment during the shoot. "I dropped a pen knife in Petersburg," said Spielberg, who attained the rank of Eagle Scout as a Boy Scout. "It said, 'Boy Scouts of America, Troop 294, Roosevelt Council.'" He clearly missed the knife. Following the program, the Heart of Virginia Council of the Boy Scouts, headquartered in Richmond, provided a new knife, engraved "Richmond Forum 2013" to be sent to Spielberg as a gift.

The season's third program featured Space Shuttle commander Mark Kelly and his wife, Gabby Giffords, the Arizona congresswoman who was the victim of a near-fatal assassination attempt.

The booking had been completed shortly after Giffords had been forced by her health to leave Congress—and before it was fully known what her condition would be. Kelly was to be the evening's main speaker with Giffords joining him onstage for the Q&A, participating as best she could. Several weeks before appearing, however, Kelly let Chapman in on a secret: As part of her therapy, Giffords had been working on her own remarks. It was another Forum surprise. When the moment came, and Giffords spoke, the audience rose as one in appreciation.

"It's been a long, hard haul but I'm getting better," Giffords said, charming the audience with her determination and smile. "My spirit is stronger than ever."

Former Congresswoman Gabrielle Giffords, the survivor of a horrific gun assault and brain injury, used her Forum appearance as a goal in her recovery. For months, she worked with husband, Mark Kelly, and therapists, so she could deliver her own remarks.

A DAY IN THE LIFE OF THE FORUM: QUINCY JONES

Forum days are not for the easily tired.

For Quincy Jones' appearance in February 2012, the Forum gave Richmond's *Boomer* magazine full access to the day's proceedings, resulting in an eight-page cover story by Editor Ray McAllister. A few highlights:

Stagehands begin loading equipment into the Landmark Theater at 7 a.m. It is all set when Executive Director Bill Chapman, who has arrived at 9:30, begins run-throughs at one o'clock. The huge photos are in place onstage, the audio and visual equipment is hooked up and . . . the microphone doesn't work. Then Gabriel Dixon, a high school honors student who will introduce Jones, stumbles during his rehearsal. He has to restart twice. These glitches will be worked out, though another will come that evening—which Dixon will also work out.

By 2:15, the All-City Jazz Band, made up of Richmond public school students, is rehearsing. Actor/producer Tim Reid, who will moderate the evening's event, has arrived.

At 3 p.m., still five hours before the official event, Quincy Jones arrives. This is the first of six—yes, six—Forum engagements to which the seventy-eight-year-old musical genius has committed. The band is playing some of Jones' tunes back to the master, who is seated, smiling. The students are uncommonly talented, perhaps none more so than Drew Anderson, a fourteen-year-old trumpet player. "That was impressive," Jones says.

Jones heads off to an interview with *Boomer,* sharing reminiscences—he has been to Richmond once before, touring as a teen with Lionel Hampton in the early 1950s, and remembers being fascinated by the architecture—and his hopes for projects ahead—"We've got to reinvent the record business, because it is finito. Everywhere on the planet, [there is] ninety-eight percent piracy . . . And that's not good for young kids and all. It just tears me up."

Richmond Open High School student Gabriel Dixon (right) welcomes Quincy Jones to the Forum stage in February 2012.

Jones then is ushered into a small reception with the evening's patrons and then into the already-filled banquet hall at the Omni Hotel, where he gives a five-minute off-the-cuff talk, eats and is whisked off in a limo to the theater. At 7:35 p.m., he enters a side room at the Landmark to talk in person with 120 students who will see his presentation on a closed-circuit screen.

He moves to a backstage room, waiting with Reid. Following the National Anthem and the Forum's opening video, Chapman goes onstage at 8:05, introducing Tim Butturini, regional president of the evening's sponsoring bank, who chooses to hand off the introductory honors to young Gabriel Dixon. "I wanted to impact a young man's life," Butturini says now of Dixon. "The audience loved him. . . . He hit a home run."

Dixon did, indeed. After he finishes, and, after a five-minute video on the guest, he introduces Quincy Jones . . .

Who does not appear.

The waiting continues. Jones, it seems, has decided on a last-minute bathroom break. The young Dixon takes to the microphone again. "No, no, keep clapping," he urges the appreciative audience. "They're coming, I promise."

Jones' presentation, steered artfully by Reid, shares his stories of working with Frank Sinatra and Michael Jackson—Jackson and he reviewed 800 songs before deciding on the nine that would make *Thriller* the largest-selling album of all time. Jones, who has had a stroke and sometimes speaks quietly, jumps from topic to topic while often mixing slang from three generations. He is not easily understood. But for those who are able to keep up—and thanks to Reid's assistance, many are—it has been a whirlwind evening. It ends with a standing ovation.

"With Quincy, you have to try to bring him back sometimes," Reid says now. "He goes all over. He's free-form. He's a musician."

It's not over for Jones, who retires to an after-event reception back at the Omni, posing for photographs and talking with guests. It will be after midnight before the evening ends. Susan Greenbaum, a former board member says. "He was ready for fun and loved talking with the few folks who were still hanging out. How thrilling to interact with a true musical genius—and discover that he is kind to random strangers and admirers, with no hint of arrogance or ego."

BEHIND THE SCENES, CHAPMAN frequently joked that he should have retired immediately after announcing the blockbuster 2012–2013 season. Could the expectations for the followup season be met? Another former president was to be part of the solution—this time a Republican.

George W. Bush accepted few invitations to speak publicly, but The Forum was able to leverage Bush's Richmond family connections (his youngest brother, Marvin, married Margaret Molster of Richmond, and his daughter, Jenna, married Henry Hager, also from Richmond), as well as his father's and wife's appearances at The Forum to gain his acceptance.

It had taken twelve years to bring Bill Clinton to The Forum without backlash. The announcement of Bush, another controversial president, just six years after leaving office, however, came too soon for some. "We did lose a few subscribers who gave up their Forum seats in protest," says Chapman. "That's unfortunate, but as a public forum, we're not in the business of presenting only people who everybody already agrees with. And we certainly should be pursuing any past president."

The season would begin with a provocative panel discussion of Islam and end with a counterbalancing evening of silliness with comedians Steve Martin and Martin Short—the yin and yang of The Richmond Forum. (Steve Martin later called the Forum audience "sublime.")

The November 2013 Islam panel would provide another opportunity for outreach to the larger community. The panel discussion was broadcast on public television WCVE, part of Central Virginia's "Community Idea Stations," followed by a discussion by leaders of Richmond's interfaith community. It was not the first such effort. Spielberg's January 2013 *Lincoln* panel had been broadcast on WCVE. And an April 2012 presentation by Rafe Esquith and Sir Ken Robinson on "Revolutionizing Education" had spurred organized community conversations about how their ideas might be put into play in Richmond schools.

The March 2013 speaker was former British Prime Minister Gordon Brown, who explained the significance of a penholder he gave to incoming President Barack Obama in 2009. The penholder was created from what had been reported to be a sister ship to the HMS *Resolute,* the historic ship found abandoned in Arctic ice, restored by the U.S. and given back to the British in 1856

(Continued on Page 120)

THE
RICHMOND
FORUM

"The last election was not a mandate for dictatorship of Democrats, just like the 2010 election was not a mandate for dictatorship of Republicans.

. . .

Our system was set up for honorable, dignified compromise."

PRESIDENT BILL CLINTON
February 8, 2013
The Richmond Forum

A PRESIDENT COMES TO TOWN

The list of former heads of government who have visited The Forum is a long one: American presidents George H. W. Bush, Bill Clinton and George W. Bush; British prime ministers Margaret Thatcher, John Major, Tony Blair and Gordon Brown; Soviet President Mikhail Gorbachev, Israeli prime ministers Shimon Peres and Benjamin Netanyahu; German Chancellor Helmut Schmidt; Canadian Prime Minister Brian Mulroney; Pakistani Prime Minister Benazir Bhutto; Irish President Mary Robinson; Mexican President Vicente Fox; and Liberian President Ellen Johnson Sirleaf.

Getting Bill Clinton, the man The Forum had temporarily eschewed years earlier, meant making concessions. In September 2010, Chapman reported to the board that presidents always come with restrictions and Clinton, especially so. The Forum would be getting less of a time commitment than with most speakers—and spending more.

By January 2012, Clinton had agreed to speak to The Forum, but his appearance would have to be on a Friday instead of a Saturday—Friday, February 8, 2013. And, though he would be The Forum's second highest-paid speaker—after Tony Blair—there would be no dinner, no student room visit, and no dessert reception following. In total, Clinton would spend twenty minutes with the evening's sponsors before the program and just sixty minutes on stage—a forty-minute speech, followed by twenty minutes of Q&A with questions that had been submitted in advance by subscribers.

It was how Congress could best work together that the audience most wanted to hear. Though impeached by the House of Representatives during what became known as the Monica Lewinsky scandal, Clinton had come to be seen as someone who worked well with political opponents.

Success comes from treating people, and their ideas,

with respect, Clinton implied. "Virtually a hundred percent of those people who don't work together believe they're doing the right thing," he said. "That's a lesson I learned in eighth-grade science from a teacher named Vernon Dokey, who, to put it charitably, was not a handsome man. And he knew it.

"And he told us a story one day. . . . 'Every morning, I get up and I go into my bathroom and I throw water on my face, and then I put the shaving cream on and I shave, and then I wash the shaving cream off, and I dry my face. And I look in that mirror and I say, 'Vernon, you're beautiful.' And he said, 'You just remember that. Everybody wants to believe they're beautiful. And when you start by treating them like they're not, you're not gonna get a good result.'"

The Forum audience agreed.

Clinton continued:

"Interesting, huh? And fifty-three years later, I still remember it. But I think that we have—we live in such a complicated world—we have changed in so many ways that are positive: We're not as racist or sexist or homophobic as we used to be. [But] we just don't want to be around anybody who disagrees with us."

As it turned out, Clinton's time on stage was not much truncated at all. Snow around New York would slow his plans to return home that evening. "Ask me more questions," a relaxed Clinton had said to Chapman upon arriving at the theater.

"When we finally came off stage after forty minutes of Q&A, his handler was shooting daggers at me," Chapman says. "She didn't realize that he had told me that."

Above left: Bill Clinton greets Production Manager Dan Hitchcock and other members of the video team backstage. Right: Bill Chapman listens as the former president drives a point home during the Q&A.

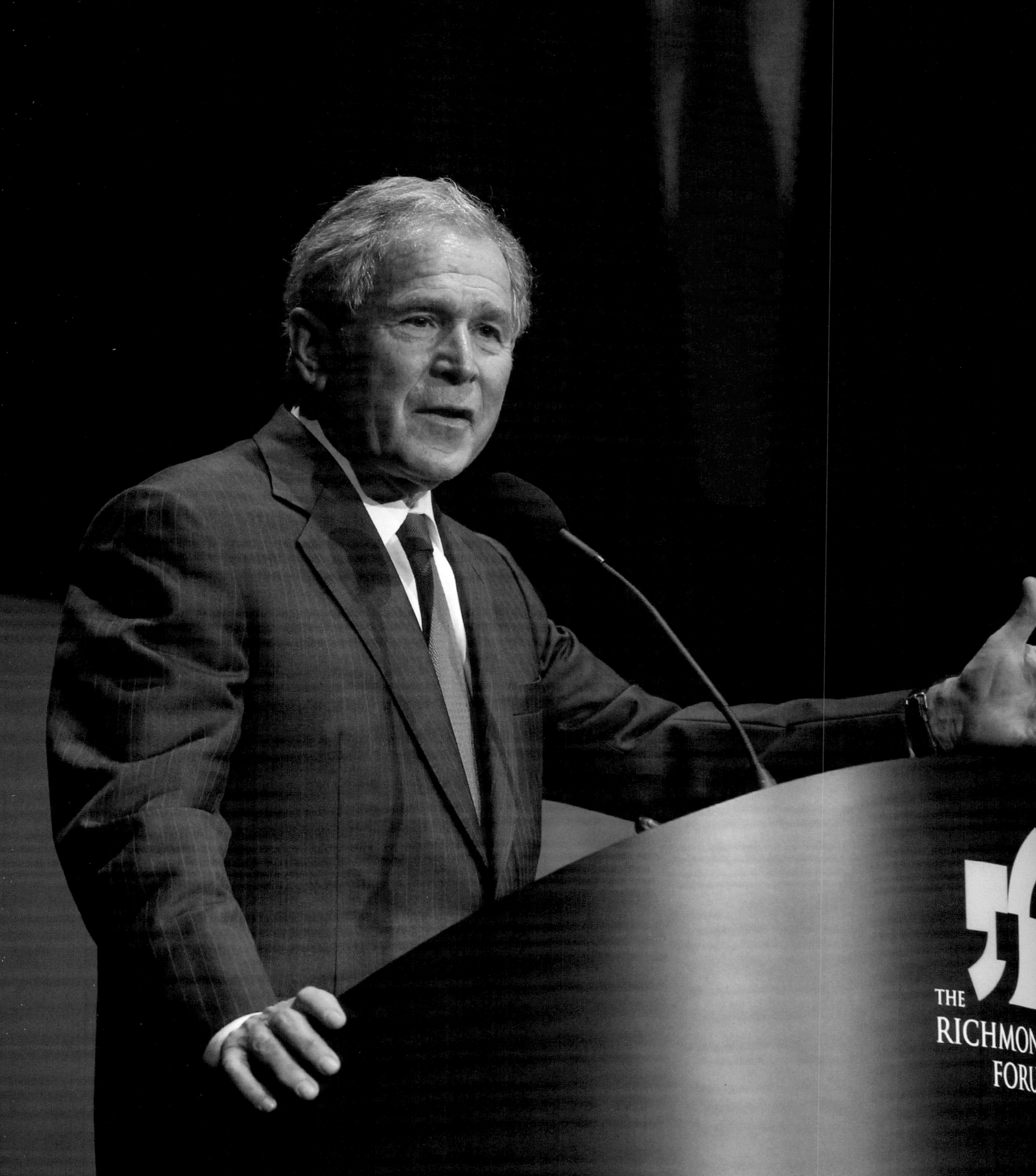
THE
RICHMOND
FORUM

"It's not a great revelation,
but it dawned on me, of course,
that [today,] 9-11 is like
Pearl Harbor to some kids.
It's just a moment.
And yet the lessons are real.
Evil exists."

PRESIDENT GEORGE W. BUSH
February 22, 2014
The Richmond Forum

AND ANOTHER PRESIDENT

George W. Bush became the second president in as many years to speak at The Forum, coming to the hometown of the in-laws of his daughter, Jenna Bush Hager.

"I'm honored to be here," Bush opened. "I understand I'm following in some important people's footsteps, namely my wife. You had the A team, now you have the B team."

Unlike Bill Clinton the year earlier, Bush took full advantage of all aspects of an evening at The Richmond Forum, including having dinner with 440 Forum patrons before the program and spending time with 100 local high school students before he went onstage, answering their questions and posing for photos.

Not surprisingly, security was tight. Subscribers were told that the doors to the beautifully restored theater—known for the first time that February 2014 night as the Altria Theater following a sixty-three million dollar renovation—would close firmly at 7:45. Everyone must be seated by 8 p.m.

Bush himself seemed less constrained by formality, even outlining his speech on an envelope moments before going onstage. He continued his post-presidency policy of avoiding partisan politics, focusing instead on foreign affairs and behind-the-scenes stories as he regaled the audience with his personal warmth and humor. Time and again, he went back to his belief that people's inherent desire for freedom will lead to more democracies, even if those will struggle.

Bush said Russian leader Vladimir Putin had sniffed dismissively at the Bush family dog, a Scottish terrier named Barney. When Bush visited Putin, the latter made a point of presenting his powerfully built hound, "bigger, faster and stronger than Barney." It was a telling look into the Russian mind-set, Bush said.

Bush also shared a little-known decision. Once he became president, he said, he had to choose which president's portrait would go up with Washington's in the Oval Office, which he called a "shrine to democracy." He opted for Lincoln, for his having kept the nation together. His father, too, had held the office, of course. But George H. W. Bush, he said, would have to settle for being his son's choice "in his heart."

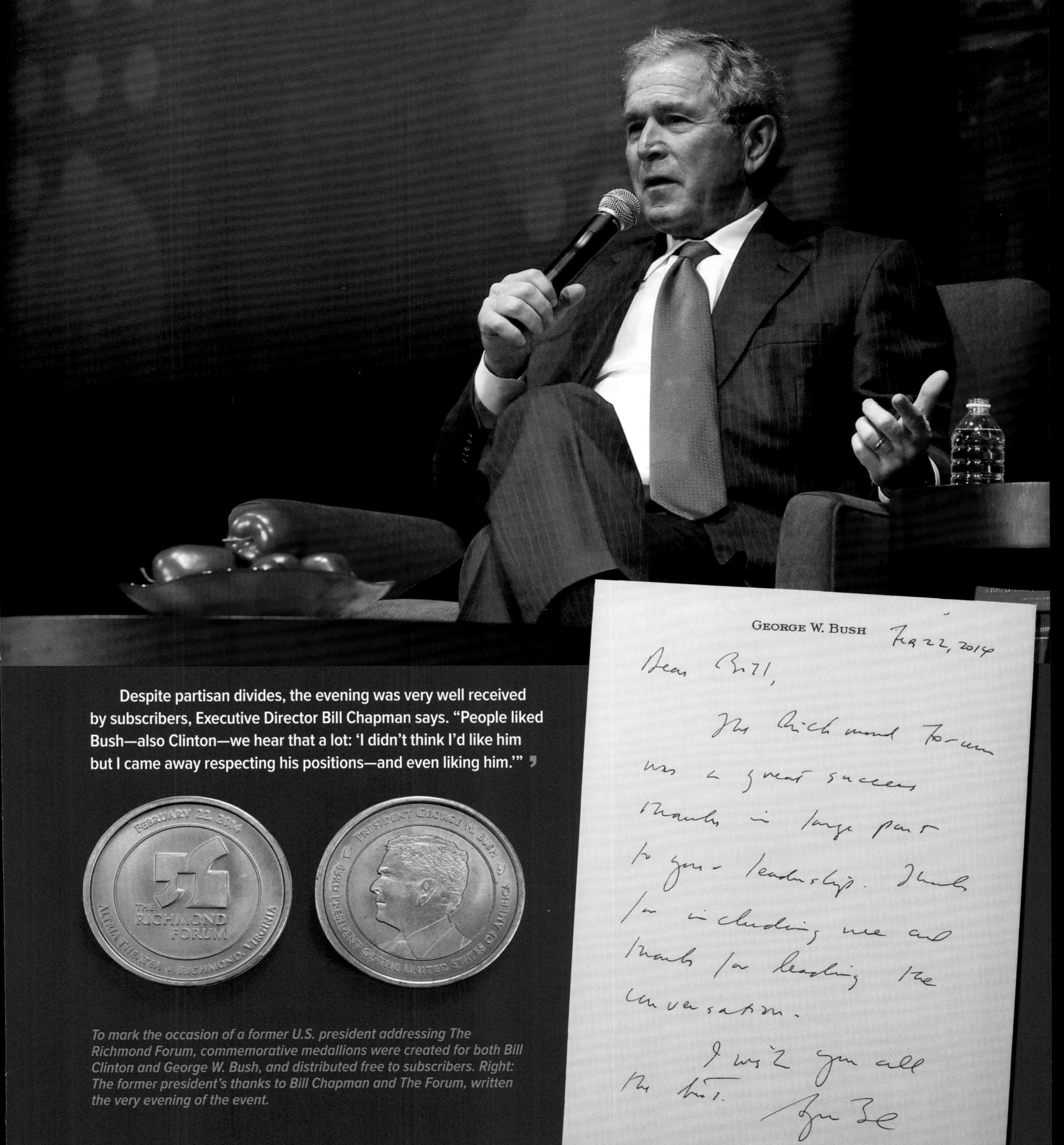

Despite partisan divides, the evening was very well received by subscribers, Executive Director Bill Chapman says. "People liked Bush—also Clinton—we hear that a lot: 'I didn't think I'd like him but I came away respecting his positions—and even liking him.'"

To mark the occasion of a former U.S. president addressing The Richmond Forum, commemorative medallions were created for both Bill Clinton and George W. Bush, and distributed free to subscribers. Right: The former president's thanks to Bill Chapman and The Forum, written the very evening of the event.

GEORGE W. BUSH

Feb 22, 2014

Dear Bill,

The Richmond Forum was a great success thanks in large part to your leadership. Thanks for including me and thanks for leading the conversation.

I wish you all the best.

George Bush

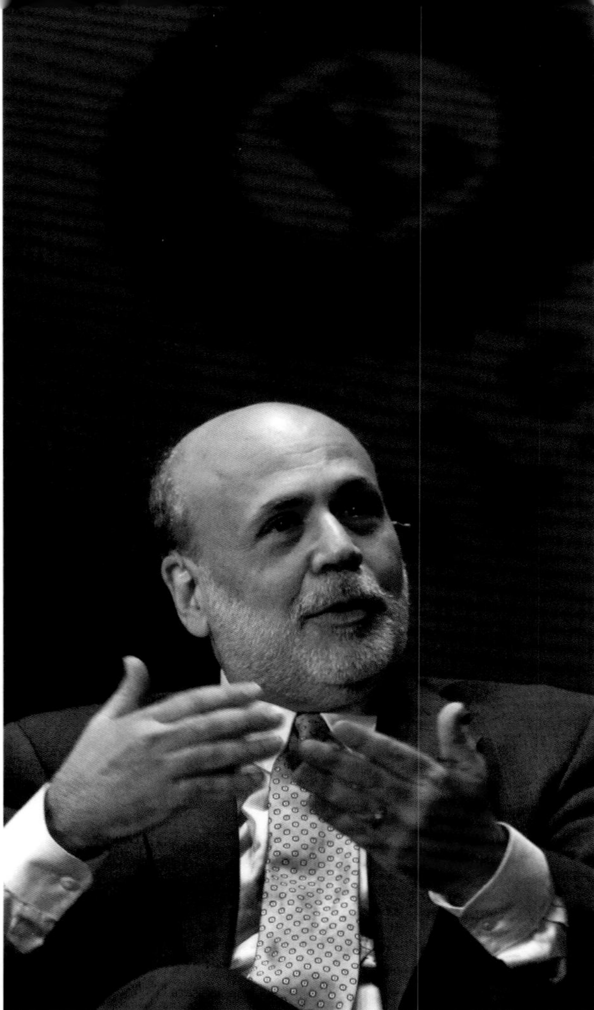

Gordon Brown (left) becomes the fourth British prime minister to address The Forum when he appears in March 2013. Former Federal Reserve Board Chairman Ben Bernanke (right), in March 2014, discusses his decision-making during the global financial crisis. While in Richmond, both men also addressed the student delegates of the Governor's School Model United Nations conference, a new partnership designed to further expand student exposure to Forum speakers of international importance.

as a gift. When the *Resolute* was finally decommissioned decades later, Queen Victoria had a desk made from its wood and gave it to the Americans for the Oval Office. The penholder given by Brown was made to fit The *Resolute* Desk. As required, the U.S. government officially reported the gift.

"And they valued it at $16,000," Brown said. "I don't know who did the valuation. . . . In the British press, they immediately ran a story: 'Brown, the British prime minister, [is] so anxious to ingratiate himself to President Obama, he's given him a $16,000 gift, a penholder, that has cost a huge amount of British taxpayers' money. And why should Brown be spending that money on the American president at the time of crisis?'

"And I didn't have the nerve to tell the truth: It actually cost us $300." The audience broke into laughter. "We had the wood, we had the ship, we had a carpenter who wanted to do it free of charge," Brown continued.

"And I had to decide: Would I tell the British press that I was so mean that I'd given Barack Obama a present that was only worth $300, or did I allow myself to continue to be accused of being so anxious to ingratiate myself to the American president that I'd spent $16,000?"

Brown's punchline: "So I just left it at $16,000. You know what we British are like."

The former prime minister's more serious point during the February 2014 appearance was that changing world economics mean America and Europe will go from being the world's dominant manufacturing and consuming markets to falling behind Asia. "You will see it initially as a threat and not an opportunity," he told the audience. But his travels have convinced him consumers in China and elsewhere want the best and most innovative American and British designs and products.

“You can blame companies, but if people are buying their products, why should they change?”

JANE GOODALL // April 2013
Urging the purchase of organic foods and clothing not made with child labor.

THEY SAID IT AT THE FORUM

“When visiting Colonel Gaddafi in his tent, the correct answer is ‘Yes, I have had camel’s milk many times.’”
TONY BLAIR // November 2008

“It’s a great pleasure to be here in Richmond, especially to be here at the Mosque!”
ISLAM EXPERT REZA ASLAN // January 2009

“When we eat from this modern industrial food system, we are eating oil and spewing greenhouse gases. . . . I can’t help but think that if we spend a little bit more on food, we could spend a lot less on health care.”
MICHAEL POLLAN // April 2009

“Blaming greed for the recession is like blaming gravity for an airplane crash. It doesn’t explain much.”
STEVE FORBES // March 2010

“By 2016, certainly by 2020, people are going to be completely untethered [from traditional information sources, using fast mobile devices instead.]”
DAVID PLOUFFE // May 2010

“You cannot win the hearts and minds of the Afghan population until you secure their bodies.”
CONDOLEEZZA RICE // April 2010

“Islam is not a religion of violence. But it’s also not a religion of peace. . . . Like all other religions on this planet from time unknown, it’s been interpreted, like Christianity has in the past, to cause much devastation on this earth. And it’s also been interpreted towards peacefulness.”
MAAJID NAWAZ // November 2013

“Freedom is transformative, . . . freedom is powerful, . . . freedom yields to peace, and . . . a former enemy can become an ally in the keeping of peace. And I think the same thing will happen in the Middle East over time so long as the United States of America does not shirk its duty, pull in its horns, and not help those who are desirous to have their voices heard in the public square.”
GEORGE W. BUSH // February 2014

“I’m just a citizen of the world who refuses to let this one wild and precious life quietly slip by.”
DIANA NYAD // November 2014

Do you know that the Fed has paid the U.S. government over the last five years over $400 billion of profit? It comes to about $1,500 a person in America. But, anyway, you won’t hear that on the news.”
BEN BERNANKE // March 2015

“You’re a better singer at fifty than you are at thirty because your whole life shows up in your voice.”
ROSANNE CASH // April 2015

Moreover, he said, alluding to America and Europe, "it's the countries that have the skills and the educational strength that are obviously going to be most successful, as well."

In advance of Ben Bernanke's March 2015 appearance, The Forum—no doubt suspecting "the Fed" might not be the easiest of topics for lay people to understand—partnered with the Federal Reserve Bank of Richmond to host an "Evening at the Fed" for subscribers. Jeffrey M. Lacker, president of the Richmond Fed, and himself a Forum subscriber, presented a history of the central bank, priming the pump for Bernanke's appearance two weeks later.

When Bernanke took the stage, the former chairman of the Federal Reserve first revealed something from his forthcoming book: He confirmed he had worked for a summer (to help pay his way through Harvard University) at South of the Border, the kitschy tourist mecca along Interstate 95 in South Carolina, near his home. The roadside attraction was promoted with billboards featuring a Mexican-style bandit, Pedro, as mascot. Bernanke did not put bumper stickers on cars, he assured the audience. "Actually, though, on a couple of occasions, I did play Pedro," he said. "Can you see it? Can you see the look?"

Bernanke also shared a story of being chairman of the Council of Economic Advisors, in essence President George W. Bush's chief economic adviser, before he was Fed chair. During a weekly meeting, "I was about to start my presentation, and the president comes over, and he pulls up my pant leg. He notices that I'm wearing a gray suit like this one, but [with] tan socks. And he says, 'Ben, this is the White House; we have certain standards here. What the hell is going on?'

"And I said, 'Well, Mr. President, I got those socks four for ten dollars at The Gap. And aren't we about budget-cutting and everything here at the White House, and fiscal responsibility?' He kind of looked at me, and he laughed." The next day, Bernanke was back in the Oval Office for another meeting. "The president comes in, and every man in the Oval Office, including Vice President Cheney, is sitting like this—tan socks."

Bernanke discussed at length what has been termed "the Wall Street Bailout." He said that, although the perception was that the Fed had allowed the Lehman Brothers security company to fail financially, actually yeoman-like efforts had been made to save it and find a buyer for it. Fearing another such collapse, the Fed decided it had to lend AIG, the world's largest insurance company, money to pay its bills, taking the company as collateral. "They're still unwinding the bankruptcy of Lehman Brothers, and this is six-and-a-half years later," Bernanke said. "Imagine if there had been ten firms that had collapsed. And that was where we were. We were getting very close to that. Again, I think it would have been a very, very serious, very persistent, deep recession. But thank goodness we won't get to run the experiment."

The 2014–15 season also brought more of the creative pairings that have become unique to The Forum: In April 2015, Grammy-winning singer/songwriter Rosanne Cash discussed "Music and Your Brain" with neuroscientist Daniel J. Levitin. The next month, in a program postponed from February for bad weather, the former heads of the FBI and NSA, Robert Mueller and General Keith Alexander, respectively, addressed cybersecurity in the wake of high-profile cyber attacks against insurance companies, retailers, and the U.S. government.

Meanwhile, tickets for The Forum were becoming increasingly difficult to get. Years ago, what is now the Altria Theater often had empty seats for a Forum program. No longer. The last five seasons had sold out well in advance, mostly by renewals. Even congressmen have been known to have a tough time getting in.

Debbie Mangolas, office and ticket sales manager, hears many a tale of woe. "I hear from many people who say, 'I used to have tickets to The Forum but I gave them up. . . . I'd like the same seats again.'" Those seats have long since been filled, of course. Mangolas keeps large, wall-sized charts showing the theater's 3,600 seats—every seat has a name hand written in it. Seats not renewed each season are sold by lottery to new subscribers. "If somebody decides not to renew their subscriptions," she says, "I try to tell them that they should think it over first. They might not get back in—they usually don't."

To expand capacity for the 2012–2013 season, The Forum had created a simulcast room in the capacious downstairs ballroom of the Altria Theater. By the 2015–16 season, the capacity was nearly doubled, to 800 seats, with four large video seats. The room was quickly sold out.

Photograph from a 2013 Richmond Times-Dispatch *profile of The Richmond Forum. Some readers of that piece were surprised to learn that The Forum is run by a staff of only three, overseen by a thirty-member board of directors comprised of community and business leaders from the region. From the left: Debbie Mangolas, office and ticket sales manager since 2010; Dee Raubenstine, director of development and special events since 2000; and Bill Chapman, executive director and producer since 2008.*

THE THIRTIETH ANNIVERSARY SEASON of 2015–16 scheduled several "returns."

Actor Alan Alda, whom the Forum executive council once thought would be starting off the 1987 season, would fulfill their wishes with an appearance . . . twenty-nine seasons later.

And the pairing of Richmonder and professional football star Russell Wilson with renowned professor and author Henry Louis Gates, Jr. represented two returns: Gates' second appearance as a speaker—and Wilson's return to The Forum where, as a fourteen-year-old high school ballplayer, he met baseball star Cal Ripken, Jr., in 2003.

The Forum, as often seemed the case, was coming full circle.

Meanwhile, it was also ever-expanding its reach. Forum programs were being broadcast on public TV and streamed on the Internet. Conversations were being expanded with companion presentations, events, community partnerships, and discussion groups. Through social media, The Forum engaged with subscribers about past and future programs.

"These are the kinds of program extensions and dialogues that we want to continue to grow, so The Forum is more than just a speaker on the stage," Chapman says. "We are continually looking for more ways to bring value to the Richmond community."

Then there is this, for those inclined toward symmetry:

In 1967, *The New York Times* had called The Richmond Public Forum a "BOX-OFFICE SMASH," noting its 4,500-plus-seat sellouts. Over the years, however, The Forum's capacity was steadily reduced as theater renovations cut the number of seats to just over 3,600. However, by the thirtieth anniversary season, coupled with the Simulcast Room and the Student Viewing Room, the Forum's attendance had returned to more than 4,500.

Richmond's forum—back from the ashes not once but twice—was as big as ever.

EXPANDING STUDENT INVOLVEMENT

Shortly after Forum founder Ralph Krueger died in 1993, a memorial fund was established in his honor.

One of Krueger's passions had been to connect The Forum to young people, and the Ralph Krueger Memorial Fund was initially used to make small grants to local schools to help them bring in speakers.

In 2009, the fund was revitalized with the creation of a Student Viewing Room at Forum programs. For the first program, area Boy Scouts and astronomy students were able to attend Neil deGrasse Tyson's Forum presentation—watching him on a closed circuit projection screen—and actually spending time with the "rock star" astrophysicist before he went on stage.

Ever since, 100 students from the area's public and private schools have been in attendance at every Forum program, selected based on the alignment of their study with the evening's speaker or topic.

Speakers spend twenty minutes with the students before the program answering their questions, and most return to chat again during intermission. Most speakers love this time to interact with students, many viewing it as a warm-up before being introduced onto the big stage.

With funding from the Krueger Fund and others, even more students are able to watch the evening's program in the theater itself, with some also being invited to the dinner and receptions.

Student outreach goes beyond program nights.

For several years, The Forum's March speaker, usually an international figure, has been taking a side visit to address 550 student delegates from schools around the Richmond region at the Governor's School Model United Nations at Maggie L. Walker. Former British Prime Minister Gordon Brown and former Federal Reserve Chairman Ben Bernanke did so in 2014 and 2015, respectively. Former Australian Prime Minister Julia Gillard agreed to make the 2016 address, as well.

Rounding out The Forum's outreach to students: Five Richmond Forum Scholars are selected annually to work behind the scenes at each program, about fifty honor students from Trinity Episcopal School serve as pages, and The Forum frequently puts interns to work in the Forum office.

All tallied, today's Forum reaches nearly 1,500 students

Opposite: General Keith Alexander and Robert Mueller visit the Forum Student Room and field questions about cybersecurity issues and careers. Top above: Syeda Haider, a 2013–2014 Richmond Forum Scholar, gets a laugh while introducing the Islam panelists in the Student Room in November 2013. Bottom left: David Blaine wows students and Student Room Manager Jim Bynum before going onstage. Bottom right: The 2014–2015 Richmond Forum Scholars pose after an evening working behind the scenes with Forum speakers and staff. From left to right, they are: Reshini Premaratne and Zoe Nelson, Maggie L. Walker Governor's School; Dylan Lackey, James River High School; Logan Brown, J.R. Tucker High School; and McKenna Brady, James River High School.

MY NIGHT AT THE FORUM: DIANA NYAD

In September 2013, Diana Nyad became the first person confirmed to swim the 110 miles from Cuba to Florida without the aid of a shark cage. She was sixty-four years old. It was her fifth attempt.

She spoke to The Forum in November 2014. She feels strong enough about the evening to share her feelings in detail:

"I've been a public speaker for forty years now, and I find that every audience has its own character, its own personality. But I will say that of all those audiences, all those different stages, my time at The Richmond Forum stands out as a distinctly unique evening. This isn't an auditorium or a hotel ballroom. It's a theater, and a grand, historic, magnificent theater at that. It gave me chills of excitement, to peer out from behind the heavy curtains at the sweep of red velvet chairs, reaching high up into the second balcony. This wasn't your typical corporate event, business people casually checking their phones and email. There was a high-energy buzz of excitement as the crowd found their seats.

"Part of the success of the evening, for me, was to have a chance to attend a dinner with several hundred of the Richmond Forum VIPs and regulars, as well as a session with many of the top students from the area. It was insightful to engage with the community, to understand why they value The Forum, what these evenings do for their culture and their lives.

"I have a fantasy of performing my one-woman theatrical show on Broadway one day. More than any speech I've ever delivered to any crowd, my evening on stage at The Richmond Forum was the closest to Broadway I've been so far. It was a first-class theatrical event. The crowd was educated. They were experienced theater goers. The staff of The Forum were top-notch professionals, making sure I was prepped and had everything I needed.

"I told stories, animated, and fully engaged with all those eyes I saw gleaming at me. And they jumped to their feet in a rousing standing ovation at the end, all of us together sharing the life messages I carried with me swimming all that way from Cuba to Florida: If you just don't give up, if you never ever give up, you will find a way to that other shore you are seeking, no matter the hardships on the way.

"The second half of the evening is equally impactful. The Forum staff has gathered a sampling of audience questions. I loved the chance to click into [the audience members'] curiosity, to kid with them, to come down to a human-to-human exchange with them. I left Richmond the next morning on a natural high. Speaking at The Forum is a noteworthy memory for me: an exceptional gathering of an exceptional group of people for an exceptional event."

MY NIGHT AT THE FORUM: GARRY TRUDEAU

Doonesbury cartoonist Garry Trudeau's January 2015 visit to The Forum was well-timed. Just six weeks earlier, terrorists had attacked the offices of the French satirical publication *Charlie Hebdo,* killing twelve over its anti-Muslim cartoons. Who could better comment on the boundaries of satirical cartoons than the Pulitzer Prize winner?

"Since *Charlie Hebdo* was still being talked about, I just assumed that the audience might be curious about my take on it," Trudeau says.

Trudeau expressed support for the victims but added the magazine had been "punching downward" at a "powerless minority" with "crude, vulgar drawings ... It's not easy figuring out where the red line is for satire. But in my experience, it's worth asking this question: Is anyone, anyone at all, laughing? If not, maybe you crossed it."

The Forum's executive director, Bill Chapman, had met Trudeau in 2009 but it took him three tries to get Trudeau to appear. "I don't really have time to do much speaking," the cartoonist explains. But, The Forum's invitation and materials were impressive—and the set-up was perfect. He especially liked the set design onstage, with large panels from *Doonesbury.*

"I only do a handful of lectures a year, sometimes none," Trudeau says. "But The Richmond Forum was certainly one of the most enjoyable I've ever done. . . . It all starts at the top, so a truly dedicated executive director is critical to the experience. Bill was an experienced, knowledgeable host, guiding me through a seamless experience. He's also very good company, and I had a lovely breakfast with him and his wife the following morning."

OUR NIGHTS AT THE FORUM: ROBERT BALLARD, PLATON, AND MAAJID NAWAZ

Forum programs are developed primarily for the audience, but don't think the speakers don't benefit. Looking back, three who led off different seasons explain what they gained.

ROBERT BALLARD had participated in more than 110 deep-sea explorations but remains best known for his discovery of the famous luxury liner that sank in 1912. When he returned to The Forum in November 2011, after having talked about the *Titanic* in 1999, he knew one topic he didn't want to talk about.

"You hope it isn't all about the *Titanic,*" Ballard says. "People ask about what I want to discover next. I say a UFO—so I don't have to ever talk about the *Titanic* again."

He didn't have to. Ballard talked about the future, his projects and the fast-moving state of technology. He was enthusiastic about "telepresence," or being in another location in a "virtual" sense, able to see and even touch in that location.

Ballard particularly likes coming to Richmond to explain such concepts. "The Richmond Forum, [for] storytelling, it's much more relaxed than other venues. It's dialogue. I excel in that forum-type of provocative setting."

When **PLATON** was announced as the leadoff speaker for the 2012–13 season, a good many no doubt said ... who?

After his program, they knew. "The Richmond Forum was one of the first times someone of that stature had taken a chance to put me on stage," the international photographer says. "I'm not a president, a movie star, an intellectual."

Expectations were low, Platon concedes. "It's always good to be the underdog," he says. "You can always move people much more when they're not expecting it. I'm more alive when the expectations are ZERO."

Platon showed some sixty photographs, including a number that drew either smiles—like those of Bill Clinton and Willie Nelson—or chills—Vladimir Putin and Gaddafi.

He also showed a woman whose soldier husband was killed. She had been shipped his clothes. "She wanted to wear his T-shirt but had not had the courage to open it," he explains. When she did, she burst into tears. "She said, 'I'm crying because I just found out they washed his clothes—and I wanted to smell him again.'"

Few there that evening forgot the moment.

"The Richmond Forum," Platon says, "really allowed me to tell the whole story."

MAAJID NAWAZ sat on one of the more provocative panels in Forum history, the November 2013 grouping of three experts on Islam, each with a different perspective: Ayaan Hirsi Ali, a critic of Islam; Nawaz, a former Islamist who was jailed and now fights extremism, staking out a middle ground; and Feisal Abdul Rauf, an American imam who had proposed an Islamic center near Ground Zero of the September 11 attacks in New York City.

The evening's topic: "Is Islam a religion of violence or peace?" Tensions were high and security was tight. Two speakers had previously received death threats. All Forumgoers went through weapons screenings.

Nonetheless, a calm and rational discussion sprung forth.

"It really struck me as a great success," Nawaz says. Unlike other venues that required a debate, Richmond's allowed a conversation. He noted that audience members had been asked to read a particular book by each of the three. "It was well-organized and they respected their speakers. . . . The audience did their homework, too."

It was not only a success for attendees but for the speakers, Nawaz says. He has continued a dialogue with Hirsi Ali since the event. "All of us," he says, "have arrived at a sort of middle ground." ❟

Top left: Robert Ballard, who had talked in 1999 of discovering the Titanic, *returns to The Forum to discuss telepresence and other technology in November 2011. Top right: Platon captivated The Forum audience in November 2012 with powerful photographs and stories. Bottom: November 2013 Forum panelists Maajid Nawaz, formerly an imprisoned Islamic extremist; Ayaan Hirsi Ali, an outspoken critic of Islam; Imam Feisal Abdul Rauf, a Muslim voice of moderation and tolerance; and moderator John Donvan rise at the conclusion of an enlightening*

CHAPTER 8

"A ROADMAP TO THE FUTURE"

THE ENHANCED VALUE OF A PUBLIC FORUM IN THE 21ST CENTURY

In 1993, as founder Ralph F. Krueger, Jr. was nearing death, he sat down for a never-published interview with a longtime Forum volunteer, Barbara Fitzgerald. Krueger said what he had most lamented about the demise of the second Richmond Public Forum in 1980 was that, for six years, it left the city without something "that made and makes Richmond unique. I'm fond of saying that lots of cities have a symphony, a ballet, good theater, even opera—but no cities have the kind of Forum we have. It brings something special to Richmond—something locals love and the Chamber [of Commerce] can use to bring in businesses."

In time, the new Richmond Forum would be up and running, an extension of the vision shared by Krueger and those who nudged him into a return. That vision would be embraced by the community, who would attend, and by the corporate community, who would attend—and lend financial support. A national reputation would follow, and then an international one among speakers.

So despite Krueger's concerns, The Forum would survive—and thrive. The Forum grew, able to continue to attract top-level speakers, put together important programs, and share the speakers' ideas with ever-larger audiences.

Full houses are the norm now for The Richmond Forum, which is reaching more and more into the community. What will be The Forum's future?

Few people have worked closely with all three leaders of The Richmond Forum during its thirty seasons. Former board member Bart Nasta has been involved since the Forum's inception, first as a fresh-out-of-college Apple computer salesman who tracked ticket sales, then with The Forum's technology itself. Nasta says the three—Ralph Krueger, Ed Rucker, and Bill Chapman—each had a different approach in lining up programs but one thing in common: "They all seem to have an uncanny ability to bring in great speakers."

BUILDING A SEASON BEGINS, as it has since the earliest days, by asking subscribers which speakers and which topics they would most like to hear. Other speaker series may offer a ballot of twenty or thirty speaker names—the Forum itself once offered lists of fifty, but now believes an open-ended approach best reveals what subscribers are thinking. Not surprisingly, the resulting list of names is an unwieldy one, reaching 350 or 400. A self-culling takes place, however. Many of the suggested speakers have no interest whatsoever in public speaking, are contractually tied up at the moment, or are simply known to be weak speakers. A few would break the bank, even The Forum's bank, which, after all, has found enough pennies to bring in world leaders and A-list celebrities. (Those few "ungettables"—the likes of George Clooney, Meryl Streep, and, these days, Oprah Winfrey, for example—aren't motivated to accept speaking engagements and set their price tags accordingly.)

Executive Director Bill Chapman researches the others, traveling to see as many speak as possible, while viewing others online. He gets evaluations from other lecture series, talks to agents and book publishers, and explores interesting combinations of experts who might take on a challenging topic. Then each October, working more than a season out, the board of directors' program committee meets with Chapman. First they consider "headliners" to pursue, then ideas for other programs. The goal is to create a season both dynamic and diverse—diverse in terms of topics, speaker gender, ethnicity, race, and political persuasion—while including a mix of national and international speakers, along with single-speaker and panel formats.

The Forum, as reinvented in 1987, also balances gravitas with entertainment, geopolitics with the arts, civics with sciences, and star-power personalities with little-known experts. Therein, perhaps, lies some of this forum's ongoing popularity and success; earlier forums sometimes seemed mired in seriousness, losing their community following. Today's forum is not afraid to bookend a season with appearances by a former imprisoned Islamic extremist . . . and Steve Martin.

Diversity, however, is hard-won.

Forum subscribers wish there were more women, in particular. "We absolutely need more women," Chapman says. Yet reality sometimes intercedes. Women still hold fewer commanding positions than men in the government and business worlds. Chapman has also found an interesting dynamic: Compared with men, high achieving women often have both more demands on their time and less willingness to give up their weekends, considering them "family time" or otherwise inviolate. Famed photographer Annie Leibovitz, for instance, spent four months considering an invitation before realizing it would be on a Saturday. Full stop: Her weekends belonged to her children. [Historical footnote: Reschedulings aside, only once has a Forum speaker appeared on a day other than Saturday. Bill Clinton would commit only to a Friday. Thus the Saturdays-Only requirement is now: Saturdays-Only . . . unless you're a former president of the United States.]

Politics, too, can be tricky some seasons.

Long gone are the days when The Forum—coincidentally founded by avowed liberal Krueger—had board room discussions about sticking to mainly political conservatives. Yet it can't promise a political balance in any single season. "For instance, we received criticism that our 2012–2013 season was way too liberal," Chapman say. "We had the amazing good fortune that both President Clinton and Steven Spielberg—known to be a Democrat—accepted our invitations in that same season and we weren't about to say to one or the other, 'Sorry, but it turns out that we have too many liberals in the season.'" (The season also included former Democratic Congresswoman Gabby Giffords, though only Clinton among the three specifically talked about politics, and his remarks focused on conciliation rather than partisanship.)

And then there are the realities of success.

Yes, The Forum, in a sense, is sometimes challenged by its own success—or perhaps in at least three senses, more accurately.

First, given The Forum's history of attracting some of the biggest names in the world, Chapman says, "a perception has been created that we can get anybody and, therefore, if we *don't* present a particular person, it must be because we made a decision not to." The Forum may spend months, even years, pursuing a speaker only to see the invitation declined or the booking fall through for any of a hundred reasons—and so the pursuit will begin again the following year and even years after that. The Forum rarely talks about the ones that got away, Chapman says, "so nobody outside of our staff and board knows who we have been actively pursuing, or the work, stress, and nail-biting that takes place in the months leading up to that exciting onstage announcement of the next season's speakers."

Second, not everyone, quite frankly, can play the Forum stage. Many subscribers have seen ten or twenty seasons of the best speakers in the world. "The bar is set very high here," Chapman explains. "Ours is an appreciative but tough house. Speakers can't 'phone it in'; they need to bring their 'A game.'" Moreover, unlike some engagements, the audience on a Forum night is not made up entirely of fans of that night's speaker. Attendees have bought a season's worth of programs, including some they're less excited about than others. "Every speaker needs to win over our audience."

Finally, given the number of big-name speakers who have already come to The Forum, it becomes increasingly challenging to find new names among the major speaker bureaus—and The Forum tries not to repeat speakers without a new approach. "We spend a lot of time these days pursuing amazing people who are not actively on the speaker circuit and figuring out how to reach out to them directly with a compelling invitation," Chapman says. It takes longer. "But in the end, it's critical to continuing to deliver amazing and enlightening evenings for our subscribers. Conversations that we're having with potential speakers right now may not pay off until three seasons from now. It pays to be persistent and patient."

TAKING RISKS CAN BE, well, risky. After an uninspiring performance by one little-known speaker, a presentation so disappointing that sixteen-percent of survey respondents said they left before the Q&A session, Forum Director Chapman reported his assessment back to the board of directors. "It seems to be that if a high-level speaker disappoints, then it reflects on the speaker," he said, according to minutes of that meeting. "If a lesser-known speaker disappoints, it tends to be an indictment of The Forum."

Big names vs. the unexpected? Stars vs. "sleepers"? Which make the best speakers? How big a gamble should one take?

Bart Nasta, involved with The Richmond Forum since its 1987 beginning, says "sometimes the speakers you think will be the best just aren't." Still, Nasta says, he leans toward the stars, for their presentation skills. "I think sometimes the entertainers are universally the best," he says, listing Bill Cosby, Bob Newhart and others. "They're taking, and really doing, their act."

Susan Greenbaum, a singer, as well as a former Forum board member, says not everyone works the stage successfully: "Communication is a skill in itself, of course, and the real excitement for me is when someone I wouldn't have expected to be all that interesting turns out to be engaging and clear, making me much more interested in a topic than I ever thought I would be. Robert Reich, Peter Lynch, and Robert Ballard fit that category for me, as do Reza Aslan and Jon Meacham, who were great together, as Jon is pretty low-key yet hilariously dry, while Reza is a firecracker who is also very funny and clever. The people I expected to be great [usually] were great. Anderson Cooper was much more engaging, honestly, than I'd expected, and a nice guy."

Chapman agrees that the unexpected delight is sometimes the greatest. "When you ask people about their favorite Forum speakers ever," he says, "their answer is usually about the speakers who surprised them the most, the speakers that they knew the least about coming into the evening but who really delivered something special and memorable on stage." Chapman says subscribers trust The Forum to mix in one or two such "sleepers" each season. "It takes the expensive big names to sell the season, but it's very often the less expensive sleepers who deliver the biggest surprises for everybody—Dr. Henry Louis Gates, Jr., Rafe Esquith and Sir Ken Robinson, Platon, and Diana Nyad are great recent examples."

Occasionally, the approach backfires.

"There's nothing worse than an intended sleeper who fails to deliver on our stage," Chapman says. "That's when the trust that we have built can be broken."

One would not have had to tell Ralph Krueger. The Forum founder, having seen nearly a quarter of a century of speakers in two forums, revealed in a late-life interview a few surprises he received. Krueger said a German social psychologist who appeared at The Forum in 1968 was the worst speaker he ever booked. "Erich Fromm was awful. I kept pushing for him and we finally got him and he was just cold—in person and on stage. We were expecting a hands-on kind of person and he could just not have been more distant and withdrawn."

On the other hand, former Minnesota Congressman Walter Judd, in 1966, was the biggest surprise. "He was the most dynamic speaker we've had to date, in my opinion and a nice man to boot," Krueger said. "He was amazing to watch. He gestured with everything he said—grand and appropriate gestures. . . . He was the least well-known of the speakers that year, but got the best audience response."

So who would make up The Forum's "perfect season"? Who would be the "perfect speaker"?

Krueger was asked that question near the end of his life and used what were then Forum categories in answering. "I have lots of those, all different on any given day. Let's see: In the foreign affairs category, Winston Churchill; hard news would be Thomas Jefferson; entertainment, I'd take Bill Cosby again—that was one good show and the audience loved him—science, Joseph Priestly; and business, Lee Iaccoca, but ask me about him in a few years." The same question put to Bill Chapman decades later, asking for a single answer without revealing Krueger's choices, provides a more specific response: "That's a bottomless reservoir of possibilities," Chapman says, "but an evening at The Forum with Abraham Lincoln would be amazing. And I suppose we would have lots of time for Q&A because his speech would be short."

GIVEN THE UNLIKELY prospect of booking Lincoln, what's ahead for The Forum? What will be its charge for the future?

Certain goals are a given: putting together seasons that are compelling, timely and important; reaching a larger and more diverse audience; and continuing the dialogue outside the theater. Beyond that, others are possible in the future: developing satellite Forum programs, providing space for smaller forums to develop, even extending the basic season from its current schedule of five programs.

Ideas abound among Forum leadership and even among devotees who can find very little wrong with The Forum.

Tim Reid, the thoughtful actor/director/producer who has moderated Forum discussions with Quincy Jones and with a *Lincoln* panel featuring Steven Spielberg, Tony Kushner and Doris Kearns Goodwin, says, "I'd like to see it become a bit more diverse." He would like more community forums, necessarily smaller ones, to deal with race and other issues, as well, Reid says. "Maybe we can spin that off into a satellite forum," whether under the aegis of the Forum or just operating with its assistance, he suggests.

Bart Nasta, who says "it really is a forum for the people," would like expanding The Forum's reach, as well. "Are there more opportunities for more shows, smaller venues?" He mentions The Moth, an organization of storytelling events across the nation. "Smaller venues, open mike—get up and talk about your ideas. That gets into a different level of forums."

Former board member Josée Covington wishes the Forum audience included more young people than it does. Given how well run The Forum is, and how provocative its programs are, she also thinks it may be both valuable and possible to consider adding one more large-scale program a year. "Sometimes I say don't mess with a good thing," Covington says. "But wouldn't it be nice to have six programs—one more." Still, given the immense undertaking each program represents, she says, and the competition with arts organizations and other community organizations, perhaps not. "I really think, as successful as it is—should we not leave it alone and be happy?"

THE VALUE OF A FORUM, born of a simpler age, might seem diminished among technological advances. The Depression-era Richmond Public Forum did not compete with TED Talks and YouTube. The antebellum Richmond Lyceum was up against nothing except, occasionally, one of the daily newspapers.

Yet devotees see today's Forum as anything but diminished. Ironically, while Google quickly searches on a smartphone, and while Twitter blasts out 140-character philosophies in a heartbeat, the shared personal experience of The Forum, the fully developed stories and views of its speakers, may be more important than ever.

Richard Sugarman, co-founder of the Richmond-inspired Connecticut Forum, is among those who think so. He says a forum also helps a community be more a community and, very importantly, is a shared experience. "I think people are still very hungry, in fact increasingly hungry, for a life experience; there's nothing like sitting in an audience together." Technology doesn't meet that requirement. "In our DNA is this need to do things together."

There are other values, as well, Sugarman says. "People realize there is more to both topical events and big ideas than we're able to find in traditional media and we're able to find on the Web easily." Moreover, a forum "helps people feel smarter" and actually be smarter. Finally, he says, "I think people really care about celebrity. We care about that."

Josée Covington, a native of Luxembourg, is the co-founder of a Richmond travel agency, and a sponsor of The Richmond Forum since its inception. Not surprisingly, she loves the globe-shrinking powers of The Forum and never misses a program, any program, unless she is out of the country. "The value of a forum is immense," Covington explains. "It is so important to hear and to see what others say and think, [especially] people of other nations." She means their outlook, their impressions, their philosophies imparted during a Forum program. "Everyone comes out of a program, saying, 'Wow, I didn't know that.' . . . That's so important."

Tim Reid agrees. Richmond, he says, is in "the flux of change . . . reluctantly leaving the 20th century." The Forum can be an important facilitator by bringing in outside voices. "You need information," Reid says. "You need a global view." The Forum's approach, relaxed and non-confrontational, allows that sharing. "I think the Forum has a formula, a good formula. . . . There are not many places where people can come together in a quasi-intellectual environment. . . . Other cities should replicate it."

Simple, intelligent conversation, shared by experts with a willing and appreciative audience—that may indeed be one of the best pathways to the future. It may also be one of the best gifts The Forum can share.

Former Virginia Governor Gerald L. Baliles considers that, ultimately, to be the true value of a forum. "The Richmond Forum's focus on challenges of the present is an exemplary investment in how we should prepare for the future—knowledge facilitating understanding that, in turn, permits a more thoughtful search for consensus and direction," Baliles says. "It is a roadmap to the future worthy of emulation by counties, cities, and towns across the country and around the globe."

THERE CAN BE NO ONE VISION as to what The Richmond Forum will be. Challenges and demands change over time. So do opportunities. Ralph Krueger said as much in his report to the board of directors at the close of The Forum's first season, back in 1987. His words ring as true today.

"Some people believe that the president's annual report should be filled with prophecy. I find it difficult to prophesize.

"Next year's Forum and the one that follows for years to come will be what you choose it to be. It will be defined as Pericles defined his army, with 'We Are What We Say We Are.'

"I believe, despite our differences, we are victorious, innovative, committed to excellence, looking for ways to do it better. In short, we are a success. . . .

"Hopefully, in years to come, you will be able to say with some pride, 'I was one of the founders of the new Richmond Forum.'"

LIST OF FORUM SPEAKERS: 1964–2016

The Richmond Public Forum is established by the First Unitarian Church.

1964

Chet Huntley
Mr. President 1964

Gordon D. Hall
From Left to Right

Victor Lasky
Follies of the New Frontier

Norman Cousins
World Report

1965

Harry Golden
Only in America

Dr. William Vogt
Man Against Himself

Dr. Arnold Toynbee
The United Nations and Red China

William F. Buckley, Jr. and **Dr. Arthur Larson**
The National Review

1966

Walter Cronkite
The 20th Century

Justice William O. Douglas
The History of the Supreme Court

Gen. Maxwell D. Taylor
Vietnam Reports

Dr. Walter Judd
Education for Amercia's Role in the World

"SHOULD WE CONQUER SPACE?"

APRIL 8, 1967

Introductions	Mr. Ralph F. Krueger, Jr., President, The Richmond Public Forum
Welcome	Dr. Lloyd E. Line, Jr. Director of Research Texaco Experiment, Inc.
Speaker	Dr. Wernher von Braun, Director, George C. Marshall Space Flight Center

—*Intermission*—

Moderator	Colonel John Powers, President Power House, Inc., Houston, Tex.
Discussion with the Panelists	The Reverend Richard H. Baker III, Rector, St. James Episcopal Church
	Beverly Orndorff, Science Writer, Richmond Times Dispatch
	Dr. John E. Scott, Professor, School of Engineering and Applied Science, University of Virginia
Questions from the audience Supervised by the Screening Panelists	Dr. Walter O. Bradley, Director Division of Natural Sciences, Virginia Union University
	Mrs. Audrey N. Brown, Jr. Housewife
	J. William Kerns, Winner, National Science Foundation Scholarship
	Henry W. Stockmar III, Architect; President, Richmond Astronomical Society

1967

Al Capp
Ask Al Capp

Barry Goldwater
Goldwater Meets the Reporters

Mary S. Calderone
Sex Education & Public Responsibility

Dr. Wernher von Braun (right)
Should We Conquer Space?

THE MOSQUE • SATURDAY EVENING • FEBRUARY 10, 1968 •
THE RICHMOND PUBLIC FORUM

The History of American Comedy

Dick Gregory

1968

Henry Morgan, George Jessel, Dick Gregory and **Roger Price**
The History of American Comedy

Senator Edward Brooke
The World as I See It

Dr. Erich Fromm
On Human Destructiveness

F. Lee Bailey
The Defense Never Rests

1969

Art Buchwald
Have I Ever Lied to You?

Robert Weaver
Dilemmas of Urban America

Dr. Gardner Murphy
Leading ESP Authority

Justice Abe Fortas (right)
with **Lawrence Spivak**

1970

David Brinkley
Here and Now

Dr. Joyce Brothers with **Joe Namath**
Love: 1970

Rep. Gerald R. Ford
The New Federalism

Prof. Edwin O. Reischauer
The Far East

1971

Dr. Samuel Hayakawa
What's Behind Campus Unrest?

David Frost
Man Versus Environment

Dr. Isaac Asimov
A World You Won't Believe

Dr. Margaret Mead
Facing Up to the Future

1972

Harry Reasoner
Freedom and the Law

Ralph Nader (right)
What Can the Consumer Do?

Tran Van Dinh
Red China: Where Next?

Dr. Wernher von Braun
Our Priorities

1973

Paul Tripp
Will Rogers U.S.A.

Barbara Walters
Today and Tomorrow

Rep. Shirley Chisholm
Protest, Order and Justice

Masters and Johnson
Sex: Fact and Fallacy

1974

Art Linkletter

Rep. Sam Ervin
The Constitution

Jules Bergman and **Stewart Udall**
Energy Crisis

Dr. Thomas A. Harris
I'm O.K.—You're O.K.

1975

Ronald Reagan

George Plimpton

Moshe Dayan

John Chancellor

1976

Lowell Thomas

Sam Levenson

Louis Rukeyser

Jimmy Breslin,
Cmdr. Lloyd Bucher,
Victor Marchetti, and
John Henry Faulk

1977

Art Buchwald

Paul Harvey

Frank Mankiewicz, Michael Dann
and **David Halberstam**
25 Years of Television

Archbishop Fulton J. Sheen
The Three Loves

1978

Pearl Bailey

Heywood Hale Broun

Jack Anderson

Henry Kissinger

1979

Howard Jarvis, Jr.

Bob & Ray
(Bob Elliott and **Ray Goulding)**

Arthur Schlesinger, Jr.,
Vincent Bugliosi and
William Manchester

Karen DeCrow and
Phyllis Schlafly

1980

Ralph Nader and
Dr. Norman Rasmussen
Debating Nuclear Power

Ann Landers

Jack Kilpatrick and
Shana Alexander

Bob Woodward

1981–1986

The Forum goes dark.

THE
RICHMOND
FORUM
Post Office Box 14687
Richmond, Va. 23221

Short-lived logo of the new Forum.

1986

The Richmond Forum is established as an independent non-profit organization.

1987

Ted Koppel
The News and the News Makers

Hodding Carter, Paul Duke
and **Larry Speakes**
Iran: Yesterday and Today

Diane Sawyer with
Brent Scowcroft

Charles Kuralt

1988

Oprah Winfrey

Marvin Kalb, Jeane Kirkpatrick
and **Vladimir Pozner**
The Super Powers

George Will
Public Affairs, Public Policy and American Society

Art Buchwald
I Think I Don't Remember

IF ANYONE CAN TELL YOU HOW AMERICAN POLITICS GOT SO CRAZY, GEORGE WILL.

The best thing about the Richmond Forum is the chance to meet, question and personally interact with some of the brightest authorities and best-known celebrities in the world. People like George Will, columnist for *Newsweek* and political commentator on *World News Tonight* and *This Week in Washington.* Don't miss your chance on March 11 to hear George answer your questions and maybe ask Richmond a few of his own. It's another exciting evening at the Forum, this time brought to you by Colonial Savings & Loan. Tickets just $15 at the Mosque (call 780-4213) and most Standard Drug Stores. Showtime 8 p.m. And while you're calling, be sure to line up tickets for the final show of the 1988 Forum Season as well: It's the Triumphant Return of Art Buchwald, Friday, April 29, sponsored by C & P Telephone Co., with additional funding by Crestar Bank.

The Richmond FORUM

BUT IF YOU'RE NOT AT THE MOSQUE ON FRIDAY, MARCH 11, GEORGE WON'T.

Logo used from 1988 - 2008

1989

Sam Donaldson

Henry Kissinger and **John Chancellor** (above)

William F. Buckley, Jr. and **Charles Rangel**
Should Drugs be Legalized?

Dr. Carl Sagan

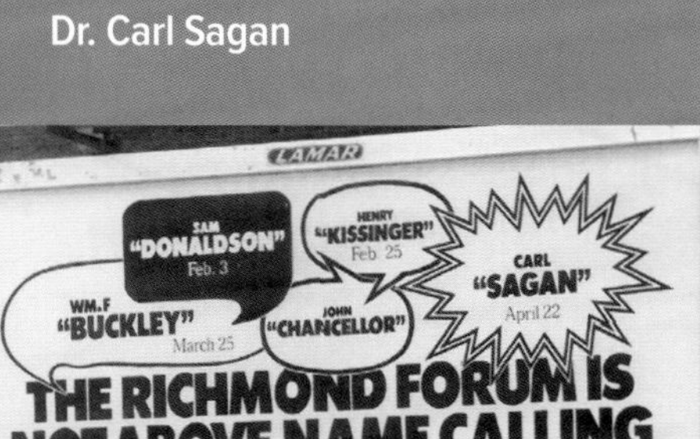

1990

Paul Duke, Howard Fineman, and **Charles McDowell**

Frank Carlucci, Bettina Gregory, George McGovern, William Proxmire, and **William Rusher**
Perspectives: From Right to Left

Mike Wallace
The Press: Credible or Incredible?

Alistair Cooke
A Brief History of American Humor

The Forum goes from four programs each season to five.

1990–91

Chancellor Helmut Schmidt

Adm. William Crowe, Gen. Alexander Haig, Robert McFarlane and **Edwin Newman**
Crisis in the Persian Gulf

H. Ross Perot

Art Buchwald and **Andy Rooney**

James Burke, Dr. Frank Drake and **James Lovell**
Space and Beyond

1991–92

Barbara Walters

PM Margaret Thatcher

Larry King with **General Norman Schwarzkopf**

Patricia Cornwell, Dr. Victor McKusick and **Dr. Marc Micozzi**
DNA: From Catching Criminals to Constructing Dinosaurs

Mark Russell

1992–93

Terry Anderson

Hiroki Kato and **T. Boone Pickens**
Japanese-American Trade Debate

Dr. Joyce Brothers
Why Our Mates Do the Things They Do

Bill Cosby

Mikhail Gorbachev with **Cokie Roberts**

1993–94

Lamar Alexander, Marvin Cetron and **Sen. Warren Rudman** with **Chris Wallace**
America in the Year 2000

Louis Rukeyser with **Frank Cappiello** and **Michael Holland**
Investment Trends in the 1990s

President George H. W. Bush
The World as I See It

Dr. Elisabeth Kubler-Ross
Life, Death and Transition

Bob Newhart

The Forum moves to the Robins Center at the University of Richmond for two seasons as the Mosque undergoes renovation.

1994–95

Gen. Colin Powell
The American Military and a Changing World Order

Walter Cronkite
American Foreign Policy in the 1990s

Dave Barry

Tom Clancy
High-Tech Espionage and the Armaments of the Future

Jack Kemp and **George Mitchell**
Economic Policy and the Future of Business in America

1995–96

PM Brian Mulroney and **Ambassador Carla Hills**
Open Markets and World Trade

Neil Armstrong, Eugene Cernan, Dick Rutan with **David Hartman**
Space and Flight: The First and Last Men on the Moon

Calvin Trillin

Charles Kuralt
America Behind the Headlines

David Gergen, Pierre Salinger, Sheila Tate, Bob Woodward with **Ed Bradley**
The Presidency, the Press and the People

1996–97

Dick Cavett and **Carl Reiner**

Paul Volcker

Doris Kearns Goodwin and **David McCullough**
To Preserve and Protect: The Story of the American Presidency

Andrew Lloyd Webber with **David Frost**

Marcia Clark, Philip K. Howard, Dr. Rodney Smolla and **Kym Worthy** with **Prof. Arthur Miller**
The Legal System in America

1997–98

Bill Moyers
Genesis and the New Millennium

Wynton Marsalis
Jazz in America

PM Shimon Peres
Peace and Perspectives on the Middle East

Mary Tyler Moore

Peter Lynch
Fundamentals of Investing

1998–99

PM John Major
The European Economic Union and the Global Economy

Robert Bennett and **Dr. William Bennett** with **Tim Russert**
Values in America

Harry S. Dent and **Lou Dobbs**
The Economy of the New Millennium

Lily Tomlin

Dr. Robert Ballard and **Jean-Michel Cousteau**
Discovering Undersea Worlds

The Forum returns to the renovated and rechristened Landmark Theater.

1999–2000

Julie Andrews

Todd Brewster and **Peter Jennings**
The Century

Ray Brady, Michael Connors and **John Krubski**
Technology and the New Marketplace

Archbishop Desmund Tutu (below)
The Search for Spiritual Values in Today's World

James Carville and **Newt Gingrich**
Campaign 2000 Issues and the Contract with America

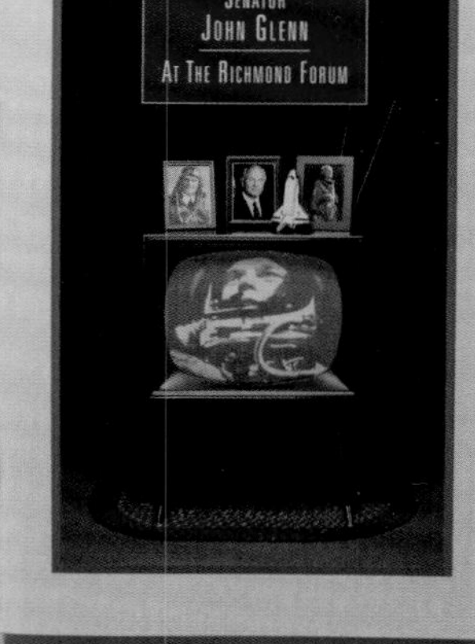

2000–01

Sen. John Glenn

Tom Brokaw

PM Benjamin Netanyahu (below)

Frank McCourt
A Salute to Ireland

Dr. William Kelso
The Rediscovery of Jamestown

2001–02

Hal Holbrook
Mark Twain Tonight!

Rabbi Marc Gellman and **Msgr. Thomas Hartman**

Dick Clark
Music: The Soundtrack of our Lives

Doris Kearns Goodwin and **David McCullough**
The Art of Writing Presidential Biography

Madeleine K. Albright, James A. Baker III with **Gwen Ifill**
World Affairs and U.S. Foreign Policy in the 21st Century

2002–03

Ken Burns
The Lewis & Clark Expedition and the Opening of the American West

Rudolph W. Giuliani

PM Benazir Bhutto and **Queen Noor** with **Gwen Ifill**

Louis Freeh
Intelligence, Justice and National Security

Sen. Fred Thompson

2003–04

Cal Ripken, Jr.

Robert Shiller and **Jeremy Siegel**
"The New Financial Order" vs. "Stocks for the Long Run"

Candice Bergen (above)
Photographs and Stories

PM Mary Robinson
Achieving Human Rights

Thomas L. Friedman

2004–05

Gen. Tommy Franks

Michael Beschloss and **Walter Isaacson**
Key Presidential Elections and Decisions That Have Influenced the Course of American History

Tim Russert
A View From Washington

Fareed Zakaria

Frank Gehry

2005–06

Robert Redford

Sherry Lansing

Gen. Colin Powell

Tom Wolfe

Rick Wagoner

2006–07

Burt Rutan

Macolm Gladwell and **Alvin Toffler**

B. B. King

Jim Lehrer

Dr. Jared Diamond

2007–08

President Vicente Fox

Carly Fiorina

Michael Douglas

Dr. Henry Louis Gates, Jr.

David Brooks
Current Events and the 2008 Presidential Election

New Forum logo introduced.

2008–09

PM Tony Blair (below)

Reza Aslan and **Jon Meacham**
Faith and Politics

Smokey Robinson with **Daphne Maxwell Reid**

Terry Bradshaw and **Howie Long** with **Ben Hamlin**

Marion Nestle and **Michael Pollan**
In Search of Real Food

2009–10

Dr. Neil deGrasse Tyson

Greg Mortenson
One Person Can Change the World

Steve Forbes
How Capitalism Will Save Us

Condoleezza Rice
The U.S. and the World

David Plouffe
Democracy Meets Technology

2010–11

President Ellen Johnson Sirleaf
Africa and its Place in the World

Laura Bush

Anderson Cooper
A 360-Degree Look at World Events

Dr. George Church
The Personal Genomics Revolution

David Blaine
Pushing the Limits of Human Endurance

2011–12

Dr. Robert Ballard
The Last Great Frontier

Robert Gates

Quincy Jones with **Tim Reid**

Charles Krauthammer and Robert Reich with **John Donvan**
The American Social Contract

Sir Ken Robinson and **Rafe Esquith**
Revolutionizing Education

2012–13

Platon
International Portraits of Power

Steven Spielberg, Doris Kearns Goodwin, and **Tony Kushner** with **Tim Reid**
Bringing History to Life on Film

President Bill Clinton
Embracing our Common Humanity

Capt. Mark Kelly with **Gabrielle Giffords**
American Spirit

Dr. Jane Goodall
Making a Difference

2013–14

Ayaan Hirsi Ali, Maajid Nawaz and **Imam Feisal Abdul Rauf** with **John Donvan**
Islam: A Religion of Violence or Peace?

Dan Buettner
The Science of Happiness

President George W. Bush
Inside the Oval Office

PM Gordon Brown
2025: Shaping a New Future

Steve Martin and **Martin Short** (above)
A Very Stupid Conversation

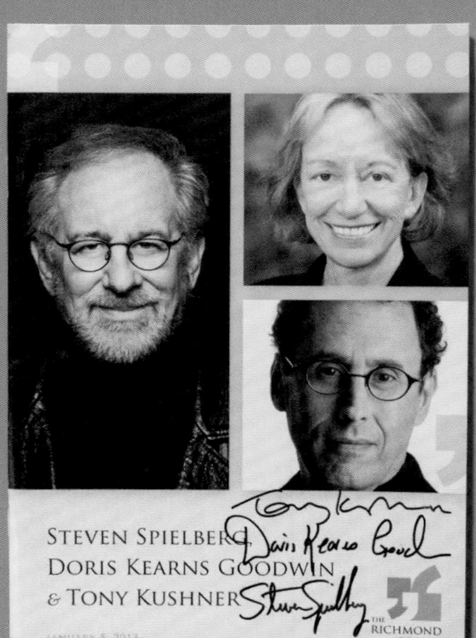

OVAL OFFICE
FUNNY
2025
ISLAM
THE RICHMOND FORUM
WELCOME TO THE 2013-2014 SEASON.

2014–15

Diana Nyad
An Extreme Dream

Garry Trudeau
What a Long, Strange Strip it's Been

Ben Bernanke (left)

Dr. Daniel J. Levitin and **Rosanne Cash**
Your Brain on Music

Gen. Keith Alexander and **Robert Mueller** with **John Donvan**
Protecting America in the 21st Century

2015–16

Michael Sandel
The Hard Questions of Democracy

Alan Alda
Things I Overheard While Talking to Myself

James Balog
Eyewitness to a Changing World

PM Julia Gillard
A Commanding Woman's View

Russell Wilson and **Dr. Henry Louis Gates, Jr.**
The Roots of a Champion

And now, part one comes to its conclusion

Before leaving...this intrusioh

As I ~~humbly express to~~ say to all of you.

Thanks from the forum for ~~all that~~ what people do.

For ~~attending meetings~~ solving problems. Helping do it.

Every day seeing through it.

For calling speakers. Panelists, too.

For writing letters we thank you.

For those who sold so willingly

For thougands given corporately

For handling all the legal stuff

Our thanks will never be enough.

For running totals on the computer.

For being a loyal forum rooter.

For writing books to help us sell.

For keeping minutes very well.

For advertising so ~~y could~~ people know

~~Clever folks~~ the forums back you sold the show.

For lighting, staging, even sound.

When it worked the best around.

For dinners planned. For a nifty trolley.

For helpful ushers, programs jolly.

For T ed, Paul Duke, Sawyer too.

HoddingnCarter our best to you.

For Larry Speakes and Old Iran

For General Scocroft quite a man

For Charles Kuralt you lightened our load

Glad you found Richmond on the road

To all the folks who didn't picket.

To each of you who bought a ticket

I could go on...don't want to bore e m.

Thank you/...for the Richmond Forum

See you in fifteen minutes

ACKNOWLEDGMENTS

A book is almost always a collaborative effort, despite the appearance of only the author's name on the cover. That is especially the case with this book, and acknowledgments must start with the staff of The Richmond Forum: Executive Director Bill Chapman, Director of Development and Special Events Dee A. Raubenstine, and Office and Ticket Sales Manager Deborah S. Mangolas. Bill was nothing less than the originator of the idea of the book, its guiding light, a wonderful collaborator, and half of the design team—not to mention gracious when I blew right through a couple deadlines. He and Dee were tireless researchers and sounding boards, as well. Debbie nearly wore out the office copying machine on my behalf, and was always a cheerful face. To say the three were indispensable is a literal truth: Not only did they make this book infinitely better, but it could not have existed without them. Appreciation also goes to Kevin Flores, who partnered with Bill on this beautiful design, and Natalie Kohlhepp, the Forum intern who photographed many items within these pages.

The files of The Forum, the Richmond Public Library, the Library of Virginia, Dementi Studio, and the *Richmond Times-Dispatch* and *The Richmond News Leader* were particularly useful, containing thousands of pages of documents, newspaper clippings and photographs that helped form the bones of the story. Nicole Kappatos, Andrea Bedson, and Heather Moon at the *Times-Dispatch* were especially helpful. Useful as well were the personal files and photographs of perhaps half a dozen people associated with The Forum. So, too, were Barbara Fitzgerald's unpublished transcript of an interview with The Forum's principal founder, and especially the book-enriching personal treasures of the founder's daughter, Anne Krueger, who entrusted them to FedEx and The Forum. I thank those persons for their generosity.

Opposite: At the final program of the 1987 season of the newly launched Forum, founder Ralph Krueger pulled this thank-you poem from his pocket and read it from the Mosque stage.

I found no one person who held a perspective on The Forum's full history but, collectively, dozens helped piece it together with their stories. I am indebted to these interviewees, most of whom worked with or for The Forum at one time or another: Gerald L. Baliles, Michael Bland, Tim Butturini, Josée Covington, Barb Fitzgerald, Jerry Fleshman, Susan Greenbaum, Mark Hourigan, Elinor Kuhn, Jack Maxwell, Jacques Moore, Doug Nabhan, Bart Nasta, Bill Nelson, Jeff O'Flaherty, Margaret Pace, Judy Pahren, Phillip G. Perkins, Mark Pounders, Susan B. Rekowski, Grahame Rees, Tim Reid, Harry Rhoads, Doyle Robinson, Richard Sugarman, Linda Warren, and Lorna Wyckoff, and, of course, Bill Chapman, Dee Raubenstine, and Debbie Marigolas. Likewise, I am indebted to these Forum speakers who shared their experiences of coming to the stage in Richmond: Robert Ballard, David Blaine, Maajid Nawaz, Diana Nyad, Platon, and Garry Trudeau. Finally, among the many attendees sharing memorable stories were Jim Albertson, Bonnie Atwood, April Cain, Susan Cruse, Howard Fabry, Robert and Barbara Mann, Lindsey Moran, Robert Salsitz, Jennifer Shoaf Swann, and Susan Tucker. Whatever information, insight, and perspective are found in this book are through the efforts of all these people, as well as of others not named, and I thank them all. Any errors of fact or interpretation are my own.

My appreciation extends to Hew Stith, as well as Bill, Dee, and Debbie, along with my wife Vicki, and our adult children—Lindsay McAllister Zarse, Ryan McAllister, and Dr. Jamie McAllister Deitrick—who assisted in proofreading, a thankless but crucial job.

Finally, I thank Ralph Krueger and all those who built, loved, and supported The Forum over the years. Too many of them, both those who worked and volunteered behind the scenes and those who appeared on the Forum stage, have now passed on. Their lasting impact is here . . . between the lines of every page of this story.

IMAGE CREDITS

The author and The Richmond Forum express appreciation to the following photographers, individuals, and publications for use of their news stories, photographs, and artifacts. All items shown in this book but not listed below are from the files of The Richmond Forum. Unless otherwise indicated below, all paper items appearing in this book were photographed by Natalie Kohlhepp.

p. ii: Photo by Natalie Kohlhepp. **p. ix:** Photo by Bill Chapman. **p. xi:** Photo by Dementi Studio.**p. xii:** Photos by Angelo Minor, Action Photo. **p. xiv:** Adobe Stock. **p. 3:** *Richmond Dispatch.* **p. 6:** *Richmond Times-Dispatch* and courtesy of Richmond Public Library. **p. 8:** FDR photo by Elias Goldensky. **p. 9:** *Richmond Times-Dispatch.* **p. 11:** Program booklets courtesy of Richmond Public Library. **p. 13:** Photo: *Richmond Times-Dispatch.* **p. 16:** Clipping: *The Richmond News Leader.* **p. 19:** Top clipping: *The New York Times.* Lower right clipping: *Richmond Times-Dispatch.* **pp. 20–21:** Ford photo: *Richmond Times-Dispatch.* **pp. 22–23:** Photo courtesy of Anne Krueger. **p. 24:** Nader photo by Thomas J. O'Halloran. **p. 25:** Kissinger photo by Marion S. Trikosko. **p. 26:** Clippings: *Richmond Times-Dispatch.* **p. 27:** Photo by Dementi Studio. **p. 28:** Photo by Taylor Dabney for *New Age.* **p. 29:** Clipping courtesy of Anne Krueger. **p. 30:** Photo courtesy of Anne Krueger. **p. 31:** Official photo. **p. 34:** Photo by Dementi Studio. **p. 36:** Forum ad courtesy of Barbara Fitzgerald. Photo by Dementi Studio. **p. 37:** Top and bottom left photos by Dementi Studio. **p. 38:** Photo by Dementi Studio. **pp. 39–45:** Forum ads courtesy of Barbara Fitzgerald. Photos by Dementi Studio. **p. 46:** *New Age.* Cover photo by Taylor Dabney. **pp. 48–49:** Photos by Dementi Studio. Clipping: *USA Today.* **pp. 50–53:** Photos by Dementi Studio. Gorbachev invitation courtesy of Susan Rekowski. **p. 54:** *Richmond Times-Dispatch.* **p. 55:** Illustration by Bill Nelson. **pp. 56–57:** Illustrations by Bill Nelson. Photo by Dementi Studio. Signed program books courtesy of Susan Rekowski. **p. 58:** Photo by Dementi Studio. **pp. 60–61:** Photos by Dementi Studio. **p. 62:** Bush photo and stick pin courtesy of Jenna Shoaf Swann. Photograph of stick pin by Natalie Kohlhepp. **p. 63:** Photo: *Richmond Times-Dispatch.* **p. 64:** Publicity photo. **pp. 65–67:** Photos by Angelo Minor, Action Photo. **p. 68:** Photos by Angelo Minor, Action Photo. Ticket stub courtesy of Susan Rekowski. **p. 69–70:** Photos by Angelo Minor, Action Photo. **p. 72:** Top photo by Angelo Minor, Action Photo. Bottom photo: NASA. **p. 73:** Top and bottom photos by Angelo Minor, Action Photo. Balloon photo by Natalie Kohlhepp. **p. 74:** Photos by Angelo Minor, Action Photo. **p. 75:** Top photo by Angelo Minor, Action Photo and courtesy of Doug Nabhan. Bottom photo by Robert Marland. **p. 76:** Top photo: *Richmond Times-Dispatch.* Bottom photo by Angelo Minor, Action Photo. **p. 78:** Tutu photo by Angelo Minor, Action Photo. **p. 80:** Table card photo by Natalie Kohlhepp. Bottom photo by Angelo Minor, Action Photo. **p. 81:** Top photo by Angelo Minor, Action Photo. Ticket stub courtesy of Susan Rekowski. **p. 82:** Photos by Angelo Minor, Action Photo. **p. 83:** Publicity photo. **pp. 84–86:** Photos by Angelo Minor, Action Photo. **pp. 88–89:** Photos by Angelo Minor, Action Photo. **p. 90:** Photo by Angelo Minor, Action Photo. **pp. 92–97:** Photos by Angelo Minor, Action Photo. **p. 98:** Sirleaf photo by Angelo Minor, Action Photo. **pp. 98–99:** Photo of question sheets by Natalie Kohlhepp. **p. 100:** Photo by Angelo Minor, Action Photo. **p. 101:** Photo by P. Kevin Morley. **p. 102:** *Richmond Free Press.* **p. 103:** Photo by Angelo Minor, Action Photo. Thank-you note courtesy of Mark Hourigan. **p. 104:** Top photo by Bill Chapman. Bottom photo by Angelo Minor, Action Photo. **p. 105:** Top left and bottom photos by Angelo Minor, Action Photo. Glass photo by Natalie Kohlhepp. **p. 106:** Photo by Angelo Minor, Action Photo. **p. 108:** Top and bottom left photos by Angelo Minor, Action Photo. Knife photo by Bill Chapman. **p. 109:** Photo by Angelo Minor, Action Photo. **p. 110:** Photo: *Richmond Times-Dispatch.* **pp. 112–115:** Photos by Angelo Minor, Action Photo. **pp. 116–118:** Photos by P. Kevin Morley. **p. 119:** Top photo by P. Kevin Morley. Medallions photographed by Natalie Kohlhepp. **p. 120:** Photos by P. Kevin Morley. **p. 121:** Photo by Angelo Minor, Action Photo. **p. 123:** Photo: *Richmond Times-Dispatch.* **p. 124:** Photo by P. Kevin Morley. **p. 125:** Top and bottom right photos by P. Kevin Morley. Bottom left photo by Angelo Minor, Action Photo. **pp. 126–127:** Photos by P. Kevin Morley. **p. 129:** Top photos by Angelo Minor, Action Photo. Photo of M. Obama (on video screen in top right photo) by Platon. Bottom photo by P. Kevin Morley. **p. 130:** Photo by P. Kevin Morley. **p. 138:** Von Braun photo: NASA. **p. 139:** Fortas photo: U.S. Supreme Court. Nader photo by Thomas J. O'Halloran. **p. 140:** Theater photo by Dementi Studio. Forum ad courtesy of Barbara Fitzgerald. **p. 141:** Kissinger and Bush photos by Dementi Studio. **p. 142:** Netanyahu and Tutu photos by Angelo Minor, Action Photo. **p. 143:** Bergen photo: publicity still. Blair photo by Angelo Minor, Action Photo. **p. 144:** Martin/Short and Bernanke photos by P. Kevin Morley.

Dust jacket front cover: Reagan photo courtesy of Anne Krueger. Winfrey, Koppel, and Kissinger photos by Dementi Studio. Rice, Brokaw, Blair, Goodall, King, Spielberg, and Clinton photos by Angelo Minor, Action Photo. Cronkite photo: publicity still. **Dust jacket back cover:** Photo by Angelo Minor, Action Photo. Bush photo (on video screen) by Platon. **Dust jacket inside back flap:** Author photo by Matt Stanton.